HUNTER-GATHERER
SUBSISTENCE AND SETTLEMENT
A Predictive Model

STUDIES IN ARCHEOLOGY

Consulting Editor: Stuart Struever

Department of Anthropology
Northwestern University
Evanston, Illinois

HUNTER–GATHERER
SUBSISTENCE AND SETTLEMENT
A Predictive Model

MICHAEL A. JOCHIM
Department of Anthropology
University of California
Santa Barbara, California

ACADEMIC PRESS New York   San Francisco   London
A Subsidiary of Harcourt Brace Jovanovich, Publishers

Passages from Richard E. Lee and Irven De Vore, editors, *Man
the Hunter* (Chicago: Aldine Publishing Company); copyright
© 1968 by Wenner–Gren Foundation of Anthropological
Research, Inc., are reprinted by permission.

ACADEMIC PRESS, INC.
111 Fifth Avenue, New York, New York 10003

United Kingdom Edition published by
ACADEMIC PRESS, INC. (LONDON) LTD.
24/28 Oval Road, London NW1

Library of Congress Cataloging in Publication Data

Jochim, Michael A
      Hunter-gatherer subsistence and settlement.

      (Studies in archeology series)
      Bibliography: p.
      1.   Economics, Prehistoric–Mathematical models.
2.   Economics, Prehistoric–Data processing.   3.   Econom-
ics, Primitive–Mathematical models.   4.   Economics,
Primitive–Data processing.   I.   Title.
GN799.E4J62   330'.9'01   75-40609
ISBN 0–12–385450–4

PRINTED IN THE UNITED STATES OF AMERICA

Contents

Part Two ARCHEOLOGICAL APPLICATION

List of Illustrations

List of Tables

Introduction

The object of this study is to construct a model of the economic behavior of hunters and gatherers. This model is based on explicit generalizations derived from numerous ethnographic studies, and represents an attempt to assemble and codify observed cross-cultural regularities in economic goals and behavior. Many assumptions about such peoples appear in the anthropological literature; this model seeks to examine the validity of these assumptions and to gather those most generalized into a coherent system. The purpose of the model is the generation of a set of predictions about the nature of a hunting and gathering economy in a particular environment. The model's value is threefold: (1) it operationalizes our expectations about how hunter—gatherers would use a given environment; (2) it allows us to compare these expectations to actual patterns of utilization; and (3) it generates predictions about a great variety of activities and their products, thereby allowing its application to the archeological record containing various classes of remains.

Most archeological investigations of prehistoric hunter—gatherer economies have been either very general or very specific. Some have examined variations in lithic and faunal assemblages over large areas in an attempt to determine patterns of association or covariation among them. For example, Mellars (1970) attempted to correlate single animal species or faunal communities with known industries or facies in the West European Middle Paleolithic. Freeman (1973) analyzed evolutionary trends in resource use in the Upper Paleolithic of Cantabrian Spain. More specific approaches have focused on small areas or single sites, and have involved an examination of sites for evidence of economic activities and seasonality. The work of Bouchud (1954) with the Middle and Upper Paleolithic of France is a well-known example of such an approach, although Binford (1973) has challenged the accuracy of seasonality based on skeletal aging techniques. Often this approach is accompanied by an attempt to fit together sites that differ in these respects into a yearly cycle, as Brinch-Petersen (1973) has done for the Danish Mesolithic. In many cases, however, there exist seasonal gaps in the archeological evidence which are filled by loose analogy with living hunter—gatherers.

A different approach is taken by Clark (1972). Given the winter occupation at the British Mesolithic site of Star Carr, with its emphasis on red deer as prey, and assuming that the population would follow its main winter prey to its summer haunts, he concludes that summer sites should be located on the uplands nearby. It is questionable, however, whether the red deer would have been of equally great importance year-round; Butzer (1971) has suggested that the Star Carr population may have emphasized fishing in the summer, rather than the hunting of red deer. Thus, the question of the determinants of resource use becomes significant, especially as they may effect a changing seasonal pattern of exploitation. The economic strategy of one season cannot necessarily be generalized over the rest of the year. In addition to the problems of applying analogies or extending seasonal strategies, this general approach requires faunal preservation with unambiguous clues of seasonality in tooth and antler development or age structure.

In areas where sites preserving faunal material are rare, a classification of sites by lithics is often the approach, but here the difficulties are much greater. Any statement about the economy or nature of activities at a site would require a functional classification of tools, which only recently is receiving attention, primarily through use-wear analysis. In addition, there is the problem of the nature of changes in industries through time—whether these are functional, stylistic, or both—which is especially important when dealing with mixed occupations. Further difficulties derive from the bias introduced by surface-collected material as compared with excavations, from the uncertainty of the importance of the non-"tool" aspect of the lithics, from the lack of information about the non-lithic aspect of the industry, and finally, from lack of knowledge about the determinants of lithic deposition.

An approach that does not place reliance upon clear-cut artifactual evidence (as normally conceived) is the model developed by Thomas (1972, 1973) for the North American Great Basin. Starting with the ethnographic representation of

Shoshonean subsistence patterns as presented by Steward, Thomas operationalizes these patterns in a computer model to produce predictive statements about the location and type of lithic deposition that would result. He is then able to test the hypothesis that past economic strategies resembled those of recent times by comparing the archeological remains with his predictions. Such an approach, because it generates a variety of implications about classes of data which intuitively seem to provide little information, would be especially useful in areas containing ambiguous archeological material. Unfortunately, for many regions and time periods, comparable ethnographic groups are not available to provide a model of subsistence behavior. For such cases, therefore, the approach presented here, which is capable of generating such a model, should be most useful. By making a number of explicit assumptions of how hunter—gatherers interact with their environment, based on regularities among observed ethnographic groups, a coherent system of subsistence behavior may be formulated in a reconstructed prehistoric environment. Such a system may then be used to generate implications for comparison with the archeological record.

Acknowledgments

For their help and encouragement, I would like to thank Robert E. Whallon, Jr., Richard I. Ford, Christopher S. Peebles, and William R. Farrand, all of the University of Michigan.

Much of this work took form during a year spent in Tübingen, West Germany, and for their courtesy and assistance I wish to thank Professor Hansjürgen Müller-Beck and Dr. Wolfgang Taute, both of the Institut für Urgeschichte of the University of Tübingen. Finally, I would like to express my gratitude to the German Academic Exchange Service (DAAD) for making the year in Tübingen possible.

PART ONE

THE MODEL

CHAPTER ONE

General Assumptions and Organizational Principles

Consideration of prehistoric economies should be grounded in the theories of economic anthropology, since the problems encountered in studying present-day "primitive" economies may indicate which cross-cultural regularities might be assumed to have operated in the past as well. One of the major debates in the literature of economic anthropology has concerned the applicability of "formal" economic theory outside of western market societies. Polanyi (1959) defines formal economics as referring to a definite situation of choice among the different uses of means, induced by a scarcity of these means, but denies the general applicability of this concept: Not only may scarcity of means not be the inducement for choices, but choice may not even be necessary in gaining a livelihood. Dalton (1961) agrees: "It is not economizing calculation induced by 'scarcity' which is universal, but rather the need for structured provision of material goods [p. 20]."

Considerable disagreement with this position exists in the literature (Burling 1962; Cook 1966; Herskovits 1952; LeClair 1962). After stressing the importance of both material and nonmaterial wants, LeClair (1962) points out: "What also becomes apparent is that all needs—wants are mutually competitive, in that

3

there is at least one category of means which is common to all. That category is human energy—what the economist refers to as 'labor' [p. 1184]." Herskovits (1952) agrees with a universal need for choice in allocating resources among alternative ends, and further states that, "on the whole, the individual tends to maximize his satisfactions in terms of the choices he makes [p. 18]." Burling agrees to the significance of the principle of maximization as a rule guiding the necessary choices in economic behavior, but emphasizes (as does Herskovits) the variability of possible satisfactions to be maximized.

The need for choices, as espoused by general economic theory, will serve as the primary assumption underlying the model developed here. Choices of usable resources, decisions as to their proportional use and time of utilization, and the demographic and spatial arrangements chosen in order to accomplish the exploitation, all allot human time and energy and are visualized as structuring the subsistence and settlement patterns of a human group. Even granting the proposition that relatively small amounts of energy may be expended by hunters and gatherers in the food quest (Lee 1968; Sahlins 1968), the allotment of these expenditures depends on choices among competing or mutually exclusive activities; the "scarcity" pertains to time and energy devoted (by choice) to subsistence.

A second important assumption concerns the nature of these choices, whether they are the result of long-range planning and consideration of goals or are more immediate and opportunistic. An assumption of definitely organized economic activities and settlement will be made here. An opportunistic element to take advantage of local temporal and spatial deviations from the general pattern of resource availability is certainly present in all hunting and gathering societies, but this is to be seen as random "noise" against a background of patterned activities.

The observation of present hunter–gatherers indicates that such organization of extraction activities is a widespread principle of adaptation:

> Too often the nomadic movement of such people has been regarded as merely aimless random wanderings; ... they form a regular and orderly cycle carried out systematically and with a rhythm ... in step with the seasonal changes themselves [Thomson 1939: 209].

> Waswanipi then have a very substantial knowledge of the environment in which they live, and this knowledge makes plausible their claims for the reliability, efficiency and affluence of their subsistence system; their expertise also suggests that it is possible to choose when to use resources [Feit 1973: 120].

With the focus of this model construction on the role of choices and decisions, a consideration of general decision-making theory is appropriate to the understanding of the assumptions and procedures involved. The major assumption underlying all theories of choice is that of the rational decision-maker:

> We call an individual rational if he takes into account the possible consequences of each of the courses of action open to him; if he is aware of a certain preference order among the consequences and accordingly chooses the course of action which, in his estimation, is likely to lead to the most preferred consequence [Rapoport 1960: 107–108].

This assumption is contained in economic theory as well, and as Herskovits (1952) states: "The principle of maximizing satisfactions by the conscious exercise of choice between means is valid because we find that this does occur in all societies. The cross-cultural perspective, however, gives us pause when defining 'rationality' [p. 24]." The primary determinant of the variability of what is "rational" would seem to be the structure of the preference order. This, in turn, depends on the culturally defined goals and value systems and will be considered later. Conditionally, then, this assumption of rationality will be included in the model.

Following this assumption, there are four important concepts in decision theory: the state of knowledge of the decision-maker, the criteria for the decision, the form of the solution, and the procedures involved. The state of knowledge can be characterized as one of:

Certainty: If each action is known to lead invariably to a specific outcome.

Risk: If each action is known to lead to one of a set of possible specific outcomes, each occurring with a known probability.

Uncertainty: If each action has as its consequence a set of specific outcomes, but where the probabilities of these are completely unknown (Luce and Raiffa 1957).

Among hunter–gatherers the state of "partial uncertainty" would seem to operate, since the exact probabilities of the consequences of various economic choices are not known, but at best are estimated from previous experiences and new scouting information. This process of estimation corresponds to the generation of a subjective probability distribution over the states of nature, thus reducing the decision problem to one of "partial uncertainty."

The problem of decision-making under uncertainty has been approached by the technique of game theory, as a one-person game against nature (Luce and Raiffa 1957). This concept of a neutral opponent, rather than a rationally antagonistic one, actually reduces the problem from a "game" to a "gamble," which is much simpler. As Rapoport (1960) states: "The only rational act in a gamble is the calculation of odds [p. 111]." As we shall see, however, economic decisions first require the reconciliation of competing objectives, in order to arrive at the preference order. The context of economic decisions, in any event, shall be viewed as one of partial uncertainty, in which the estimation of a probability distribution for the consequences is a primary concern.

Given the framework of a "game against nature" or a "gamble," there are numerous criteria possible for guiding the decision-making process (Dillon and Heady 1960). Among these are

Wald criterion: This focuses on the minimum yield or payoff for each of the defined states of nature for each alternative act or strategy chosen, and picks the strategy with the highest minimum payoff; this is a very conservative criterion, and assumes a hostile nature.

Savage criterion: This seeks to minimize regret; that is, it advocates choosing that strategy whose worst performance has the least discrepancy from the potential best in that state of nature, so that the regret for any choice is minimized; this is also conservative and assumes a hostile nature.

Hurwicz criterion: This requires an estimate of the level of pessimism of the decision-maker, and modifies the Wald criterion accordingly; equivalent to the Wald criterion if the decision-maker is completely pessimistic; rarely applicable because of the difficulty in estimating the level of pessimism.

LaPlace criterion: Advocates taking the strategy with the highest average payoff over all states of nature; this position can be disastrous in the short-run, and would not be expected to guide decisions upon which the survival of a group depends.

Simon satisficer criterion: This seeks, not to maximize, but to satisfy some predetermined aspiration level; this is descriptive, attempting to explain how people do act, rather than normative, or attempting to determine how they should act.

An example from Dillon and Heady (1960) shows how these different criteria can prescribe different decisions. Given a game matrix in which the numbers in the cells represent the yields or payoffs to the player, S1—S4 are the states of nature, and A1—A4 are the strategies available to the player:

	S1	S2	S3	S4
A1	25	35	0	15
A2	15	20	5	10
A3	0	60	0	0
A4	1·5	45	0	0

The strategies advocated by the various criteria are:

Wald: A2
Savage: A4
Hurwicz: A2 or A3, depending on the level of pessimism
LaPlace: A1
Simon: A2 with any aspiration level greater than zero

Thus the choice of criteria is very important to the decisionmaking process. The Simon satisficer principle will be used here as the guiding criterion for several reasons. First, because it represents an attempt to be descriptive rather than normative, it may reflect real-world decision processes more faithfully. Second, some hunter–gatherer decisions involve the procurement of nonedible material items such as hides, antler, and bone; the usual high mobility of these groups, however, militates against the maximization of material acquisitions. Third, the presence of conflicting goals or objectives guiding the decisions would dictate the acceptance of submaximal levels of attainment, which might lead to the development of submaximal levels of aspiration.

A determination of the form of solution is equally important. A basic dichotomy exists in theories of choice between pure and mixed strategies. As the terms imply, a pure strategy represents a specific one among those available, while a mixed strategy is a combination of several of the options in certain proportions. In general, games in which pure strategies are considered best according to the various criteria are rare, and mixed strategies, when possible, are usually prescribed. The practice of mixed strategies in economic decisions would take the form of: simultaneous performance of more than one activity, simultaneous exploitation of more than one location or region, and sequential changes of activities and locations utilized. Since such practices are seen among all hunter–gatherers, the assumption of mixed-strategy solutions will be used in the construction of this model.

An important goal guiding economic behavior of hunter–gatherers appears to be the minimization of effort—or at least the maintenance of its expenditure within a predefined range. After observing the small amount of time spent on exploitation among the !Kung and Hadza, Marshall (1968) asks: "Why do they not gather more at a time? [p. 94]." The answer seems to lie principally in the generalization formed by Paine (1973): "I posit a principle of least effort by hunters in regard to their hunting [p. 303]." This generalization follows the "law of minimum effort" so useful in geographic studies of settlement location (Haggett 1965; Garner 1967), of industrial location (Hamilton 1967), and of consumer behavior (Huff 1961). It will be assumed here that considerations of effort limitation underlie all economic choices.

The procedures involved in decision-making are nicely summarized by Saaty (1972): "Decision-making involves the identification of values, objectives, priorities, means, resources, and constraints.... Decision rules are then introduced and methods (qualitative or quantitative) are developed to apply these rules [p. 1061]." The specific problem area must be delimited first, of course, and then the procedures of identification and rule application will include the specification of those values, means, etc. that are relevant to the problem. In economic problems, these procedures of identification and specification require the consideration of a large number of resources, alternative activities and locations, constraints, and objectives, all with complex interrelationships. An approach to this complexity requires some organizational principles—a structure for the approach. The systems approach presents a structure that is particularly well-suited to the modeling of decision problems. As presented by Churchman, the basic considerations in systems analysis are almost identical to those of decision-making:

1. The total system objectives and, more specifically, the performance measures of the whole system.
2. The system's environment: the fixed constraints.
3. The resources of the system.
4. The components of the system, their activities, goals, and measures of performance.
5. The management of the system (Churchman 1968: 29–30).

A system itself may be defined as "a set of parts coordinated to accomplish a set of goals [Churchman 1968: 29]."

Here, then, is a structure for approaching the decision-making processes: The subsistence and settlement behavior of a group of hunter—gatherers will be viewed as the result of a set of decisions which resolve specific interrelated problems, the consideration of which is best accomplished through a systems approach. Identification of the problems will determine the boundaries of the system, and the objectives guiding the solution of the problems will provide the goals of the system.

Before the identification process can proceed, however, one more matter must be considered: the general issue of causative priorities, that is, the major criteria for judging "relevancy" to the problems of subsistence and settlement. It is clear that the conditioning factors of economic behavior among hunter—gatherers are multiple, so that no deterministic approach can be justified. Just as clearly, these factors can be of a vastly different character, deriving from the natural or social environments, and can be seen as having historical, ideological, or physically adaptive origins. Moreover, those factors important in structuring the behavior of one group may be of little significance to another. In order to construct a general model of hunter—gatherer economic behavior, generalizations derived from ethnographic studies of present-day groups will be used to determine the emphasis and approach taken here.

> The activities and population distribution of people who are hunters, trappers, and fishermen are in large part determined by faunal population cycles and migration, by

limits and changes in ... technology, and by variations in ... the types of fauna economically important [Slobodin 1973: 141].

Ecological considerations are of the utmost importance in determining the social and economic structure of Cree communities. Ecological considerations are tied to local plant–animal resource communities ... [Fisher 1973: 131].

In these statements, the most important factors conditioning the economic behavior of hunter–gatherers are seen to involve their relationships with elements in the natural environment, and a consideration of these relationships in a systemic framework constitutes an ecological approach:

One of our aims is to discover the place of the human population within the ecosystem in which it exists. In the analysis of the ecosystem relations of a particular local population, our starting point would probably be the material exchanges (with other plants and animals) in which the local population is directly involved [Rappaport 1969: 175].

The position taken here, then, will be that of human ecology, in which "the culture, or part of the culture, of a human population is regarded as part of the distinctive means by which the population maintains itself in the ecosystem [Rappaport 1969: 185]."

This approach focuses on the structuring of the relationship of a group to its natural environment, with primary consideration given to characteristics of the natural environment. Priority may be given to an examination of the exploitive activities and their implications for settlement patterns and demographic arrangements, because these are the areas of clearest articulation of man and his environment. The ecological approach thus provides a focus of inquiry, a general framework of logical priority. Consideration of important nonenvironmental factors is not ignored, but must be included within an ecosystem model which derives its primary structure from the relationships of man and the natural environment. It must be remembered, however, that the exploited natural environment is culturally defined, so that the "cognized" environment may differ from that seen by the ecologist. Specifically, the definition of exploitable and desirable resources depends, to a large extent, upon technology and value systems, and this process of definition must be examined.

In addition to providing a focus and priority structure, the ecological approach has other advantages. It allows the investigation to partake of general ecological theory and its concepts of adaptation, stability, diversity, and trophic level, which can help illuminate the function and structure of relationships in a human ecosystem. Furthermore, it allows a comparison of human and animal behavior: "Culture is commensurable, in so far as ecological relations are concerned, with the behavior of populations of non-human animals [Rappaport 1969: 181]." Thus one can refer to regularities of behavior patterns in an attempt to determine principles of adaptive relationships between a population and its resources.

In summary, the general assumptions and organizational principles to be used in this model may be listed as follows:

Assumptions
1. Economic behavior is the result of conscious choices.
2. These choices are deliberative rather than opportunistic.
3. The deliberation is rational, based on preferences among consequences.
4. The probabilities of the outcomes of choices are uncertain and must be estimated.
5. The choices seek to satisfy predetermined aspiration levels, not to maximize any specific measures.
6. The choices will allow or prefer mixed-strategy solutions.
7. A desire to limit effort underlies all economic decisions.

Organizational principles
1. The problems requiring solutions or choices can be conveniently formulated as systems.
2. The problems can best be approached in the context of human ecology.

CHAPTER TWO

Approach Structure

Given this view of a subsistence—settlement system as the patterning of behavior as a result of solutions to problems, the identification of these problems is the next consideration. The focus of this investigation is the arrangement of economic activities in time and space, which directs attention to the following problems faced by an exploiting population:

1. *Which* resources should be used?
2. *How much* of each resource should be used?
3. *When* should each resource be used?
4. *Where* should the resources be procured?
5. *How many* people can and should procure the resources?

These, in turn, may be combined into three major problem areas:

1. Resource use schedule.
2. Site placement.
3. Demographic arrangement.

Each of these problems may be considered in a systematic framework, as a subsystem in the overall network of economic relationships.

The sequence of their consideration here rests on an assumption of general causative priority: that the determination of resource use tends to precede and condition the site placements and demographic arrangements of a hunter–gatherer group. The operation of influences in the reverse direction, as well as that of factors independent of resource use, is not to be ignored, but to receive secondary consideration. Reasons for taking this position on causal sequence derive from ethnographic generalizations, specific ethnographic examples, and from studies of animal behavior.

Helm (1969b) states:

> If I wanted to diagram the situation as I see it, I would draw arrows from both exploitative and community pattern toward settlement pattern: the latter appears to be more of a dependent variable [p. 152].

and elsewhere:

> In hunting-and-gathering societies, the directives underlying settlement patterns (as opposed to community patterns) are based on the exploitative pattern [Helm 1969a: 213].

In Murdock's (1969) investigation of the correlation between exploitative and settlement patterns the causal priority is given to the former, in that he seeks to "weigh the relative influence of each [subsistence activity] on the forms which settlement assumes [Murdock 1969: 144]." Similarly, Steward advocates an investigation into "the extent to which the behavior patterns entailed in exploiting the environment affect other aspects of culture," implying primary importance of the subsistence activities (Steward 1959: 41).

In numerous specific ethnographic studies as well, the nature of resources and subsistence activities is considered to be the primary factor conditioning both site placement and demographic arrangements. Steward (1969) remarks that "subsistence upon shellfish required that the Alacaluf and Western Yahgan remain fragmented in family units except rarely when a whale was stranded on the beach [p. 188]." Knight (1965) states that a replacement of caribou by moose in burned-over forests of Labrador was the main cause of important changes in Montagnais–Naskapi demographic arrangements and regions exploited. Among the Central Eskimo, Damas (1969) observes

> It seems evident, then, that the occurrence of large winter aggregations has a strongly deterministic base in the method of sealing that was generally the sole reliable means of livelihood at that season. ... Fragmentation during much of the remainder of the year's cycle bears relation in a general way to the mode of hunting and the dispersal of game [pp. 283–284].

And Campbell concludes that "the major Tuluaqmiut encampments were mainly predicated upon the habits of the caribou [Campbell 1968: 15]."

Finally, in an archeological context, Flannery stresses the "functional association between band size and resource" in prehistoric Mesoamerica (Flannery 1971: 358).

Furthermore, studies of nonhuman animal behavior indicate the importance of resource distribution and patterns of exploitation on the demographic arrangements of the exploiting populations. Horn's study of blackbirds reveals the dependence of the spacing of colonies on the food source distribution (Horn 1968). Kummer generalizes that animal dispersal is usually motivated by the scattered distribution of resources (Kummer 1971). Numerous studies of chimpanzee behavior indicate a general dichotomous pattern of demographic behavior that depends on the nature of the environment (forest or savanna—woodland) and the concomitant differing distribution of resources (Itani and Suzili 1967; Izawa 1970; Nishida 1968; Sugiyama 1968, 1969; Suzuki 1969).

Thus the three subsystems of resource use, site placement, and demographic arrangement will be structured so as to give greater independence and causative priority to the resource use schedule, and the initial consideration will be given this subsystem.

Resource use schedule

Site placement ⇌ Demographic arrangement

CHAPTER THREE

Subsystem I: Resource Use Schedule

Goals

The consideration of resource use scheduling as the primary subsystem will follow the procedures outlined by Churchman (1968) as important for the analysis of any system:

1. Identification of goals, components.
2. Identification of means, resources.
3. Identification of the environment.
4. Identification of measures of performance.
5. Identification of management considerations.

The goals of this system are the objectives guiding resource procurement by hunter—gatherers. The source of these goals must be the ethnographic record; the values of western society must be screened out as much as possible. Those objectives which seem widespread, if not universal, among present hunter—gatherers are the only ones suitable for inclusion into this general model. Since the goals in resource procurement are rarely stated, reliance will be placed on reasonable inferences drawn by the ethnographer when possible, and on other information in the reports which seems to imply specific goals.

The primary function of economic activities is the provision of the necessary sustenance for the population. This is a biological fact, not a cultural value, although the structuring of the provision is governed by many other culturally defined objectives. The minimum number of calories necessary for the biological viability of the population provides a minimum aspiration level. The lack of large surplus accumulation and of large-scale redistribution systems in most hunter–gatherer societies, and the presence of conflicting demands on time and energy indicate that the actual aspiration level is not far above this minimum, and that maximization of caloric intake is not an objective operating among hunter–gatherer populations. Sahlins' description of the "affluent society" of hunter–gatherers is based on an assumption of limited material aspirations (Sahlins 1968: 85). The primary objective of economic activities will be seen as the satisfaction of caloric needs of the population. Since not only calories but also nonfood manufacturing materials may be considered necessary for human viability, satisfaction of these needs must be included as well.

To satisfy these food and nonfood needs of the population, a certain security level of income must be maintained, which involves a consideration of risk-minimization. The entire structure of the economy for many groups is shaped partly by this consideration. As Paine (1973) stresses, "the ecologic importance to hunters of having several prey-species should be noticed [p. 304];" stability of an ecosystem increases with the number of links in the food web. This principle seems to be recognized by hunter–gatherers:

> The Waswanipi hunting cycle is a model for integrating various harvesting activities so that each is used at the appropriate time, and so that at least two resources can be used at each period [Feit 1973: 120].

> The variation in numbers of animals of each species killed is extreme; sufficient supplies for subsistence [of the Ojibwa] are obtained only by exploiting all known resources in order to counteract temporary shortages of one or another [Dunning 1959: 31].

> During the dry season the [!Kung] diet becomes much more electric.... It is this broad base that provides an essential margin of safety during the end of the dry season when the mongongo nut forests are difficult to reach [Lee 1968: 35].

The importance of different resources and activities is also partly determined by consideration of risk minimization. In discussing the importance of gathering in !Kung economy, Lee (1968) arrives at a relevant distinction: "In short, hunting is a high-risk, low-return subsistence activity, while gathering is a low-risk, high-return subsistence activity [p. 40]." He then draws a generalization: "Wherever two or more kinds of natural foods are available, one would predict that the population exploiting them would emphasize the more reliable source [p. 41]." Among the Cree, too, reliability is an important consideration: "Waswanipi hunters use the animal resources available to them on a sustained yield basis while maximizing the efficiency and security of their subsistence activities insofar as this is compatible with maximum sustainable yields [Feit 1973: 124]." And Dunning attributes the importance of fishing among the Ojibwa to the fact that it is "the most reliable source of food [Dunning 1959]."

Security is important also in locating sites. Among the Indians of the Great Slave Lake area, "even when traveling, the camp is generally pitched at a good spot so that the catch of fish may insure a food supply in event of failure of the chase [Mason 1946: 18]." Similarly among the Tlingit, the large villages were located on the banks of large rivers, in conformity with their certain fish supply (Oberg, 1973). And among the G/Wi: "Despite the attractions of good water and the large game population, the dune woodlands are not permanently inhabited by Bushmen. The range and amounts of plants edible by man are evidently not sufficient to furnish a reliable food supply in all seasons [Silberbauer 1972:277]." Finally, reliability appears to be a value guiding the awarding of respect: Among the Wanindiljaugwa, "consistently good hunters are well-known and respected as such [Worsley 1961: 172]." And, "Cree who are considered outstanding hunters are those who do not experience ups and downs; numerically they may not have the most kills in any one year, but they consistently have the greatest success [Feit 1973: 117]."

As suggested earlier, the limiting of effort forms a second important goal guiding economic behavior of hunter–gatherers. Lee (1968) cites a primary goal structuring the subsistence activities of the !Kung as "the desire to live well with adequate leisure time [p. 41]." Economic behavior of the Pitjandjara of Australia changes seasonally so as to maintain "easy living" (Tindale 1972). And the general subsistence strategy chosen by the G/Wi Bushmen is regarded as the result of considerations of energy expenditures and wastage (Silberbauer 1972).

Ease of exploitation is an important criterion guiding specific food selection by many groups as well:

> In choosing from among a number of available species [the G/Wi's] criteria of preference are, in order of importance, the thirst and hunger-allaying properties of the plant food, the ease with which it may be exploited, and lastly, its flavor [Silberbauer 1972: 283].

> [The !Kung] tend to eat only the most attractive foods available at a given season and bypass the less desirable ones in terms of taste and/or ease of collection [Lee 1972: 343].

> For each animal species the Waswanipi harvest, they attempt ... to utilize it at times when chances of success are highest and the efficiency of capture is maximized [Feit 1973: 120].

> Moose and sheep are equated by Kutchin hunters in difficulty of pursuit [while] caribou are considered easy to approach [Slobodin 1973: 142].

> With the exception of two ungulates, the arctic ground squirrel was the most important food mammal [among the Tuluaqmiut]. Adult arctic ground squirrels typically weigh only two or three pounds, but they are usually fat, are easily captured, and are abundant north of the forest [Campbell 1968: 13].

The exclusion of certain resources seems to depend, at least in part, on their difficulty of exploitation:

> Mountain goats occurred, but were rarely hunted [by the Flathead] because of the abundance of game easier to get and considered more valuable [Teit 1930: 298].

> Ostrich nests are commonly robbed [by the G/Wi]. The average annual take is three eggs per household, which is surprisingly small considering the popularity and the nutritive value of ostrich eggs and the fact that these birds lay in October when food is scarcest. The explanation probably lies in the sparse distribution of nests [and] the difficulty of making an extensive search in October, when travel is full of hardships [Silberbauer 1972: 284].

Not only food selection, but the timing of exploitation of most resources depends, to a great extent, upon considerations of reducing effort or cost:

> The [Dogrib] Indians say that this time of year is good for moose hunting, as they are easily approached [Helm 1972: 67].

> November and December are the best trapping months [for the Dogrib]: it is not too cold or dark for men to travel easily, and the fur animals also are "traveling" (that is, more in evidence and easier to take) [Helm 1972: 71].

> Waswanipi hunters then have a detailed knowledge of moose behavior and so can hunt moose specifically when the animals are concentrated in a few locations which can be easily searched [Feit 1973: 120].

And among the Tlingit, the structure of the calendar is partly determined by a change in subsistence costs:

> The Tlingit year begins with the July moon. This is the month when the great schools of salmon first appear in the rivers, when the period of abundant and easily obtained food supply begins [Oberg 1973: 65].

Finally, the consideration of effort in terms of distance traveled is clearly operating in the following two situations:

> [Among the Hadza] if two animals are killed on the same day, the more distant one may be abandoned [Woodburn 1968: 53].

> [For Pitjandjara women] a walk greater than three miles is sufficient to induce grumblings and cause scolding of their husbands [Tindale 1972: 245].

This widespread evidence supports the assumption that the reduction of effort to a predefined range is an important objective operating in hunting-and-gather-

ing societies. A significant determinant of this level of effort expenditure is the
need for some degree of population aggregation, which is costly. This is a general
requirement of social and biological viability, as Williams states:

> The maintenance of a social structure among animals, including man, requires that individuals
> not be distributed over the landscape in simple correspondance to the distribution of food
> resources. In other words, the concomitant of social organization is a nonhomogeneous
> distribution of the population with respect to resources [Williams 1974: 8].

That such aggregation must, at least for part of the year, be suprafamilial, has
been demonstrated (Wobst 1974). The fact that the average local band of hunter—
gatherers is composed of 25 people, an occurrence so common that 25 has been
called a "magic number," indicates the generality of suprafamilial aggregations
(Lee and DeVore 1968: 245). It is also clear that this forms an objective separate
from technological necessities:

> While social factors may have influenced the size and location of summer and winter
> groupings, they must have been preeminent in the autumn aggregations; that is, after a
> period of fragmentation the desire to expand social contacts must have been the over-
> whelming motive for aggregation, since there was certainly no economic advantage at a
> period when economic activity was almost at a standstill [Damas 1972: 24].

The stated purposes and apparent functions of these aggregations are manifold
and varied: provision of mates, exchange of foodstuffs, cooperative exploitation,
trade in nonfood items, performance of ritual and curing, sharing of information.
Most significant at this point, however, is the generality of the desire for some
periods of aggregation. The important consideration here is the influence of this
objective on the effort expenditures of a population.

   Thus there are two major goals guiding resource-use decisions which may
be considered as necessary, based on generalization of observed regularities
among hunter—gatherers:

1. The attainment of a secure level of food and manufacturing needs.
2. The maintenance of energy expenditure within a predefined range,
   determined partly by the need for population aggregation.

Some additional goals are widespread, but seem to qualify more as desires
than needs. One of these is the procurement of good-tasting foods. The importance of taste as a consideration in food selection is indicated in the quotations
given above for the !Kung and G/Wi Bushmen (p. 17). The difficulty in dealing
with the question of taste, however, derives from its relative nature: The sense
of taste is relative both to cultural groups and to individuals. One generalization
does seem valid: Fat is a positive component of taste. Among the Attawapiskat
Cree, beaver meat is "regarded as tasting best in early winter, when fat is most

abundant," and rabbit meat is little prized "probably largely because of its lack of fat [Honigmann 1961: 160]." Other groups of hunter–gatherers also value fat highly:

> The general size, fatness, condition of skin and pelage, and "grade" of meat are the physical conditions of caribou that determine their desirability for Nunamiut [Gubser 1965: 299].

> [Among the Copper Eskimo] it appears that caribou were not widely hunted during their spring migration—the usual reason given for not hunting them is that during May herds migrated and the meat was lean and the skin perforated by warbles during that period [Damas 1972: 13].

> Bear are greatly desired as food [by the Mistassini], especially because of the large amount of fat they yield. They are taken at every opportunity, but are eagerly sought during the fall when they are fattest.... Beaver rival bear as an item relished in the diet because of their high fat content.... Hare are another source of food, although of limited importance, except in years of abundance. In effect, they are starvation food, since they possess very little fat [Rogers 1972: 11–112].

The above citations all derive from populations in cold climates, and the importance of dietary fat among such people has long been recognized: "The diet of the Mistassini is high in fat content and is designed to combat the cold and to provide the necessary calories needed for hard work [Rogers 1972: 117]." The high value placed on fat is not, however, confined to cold climates:

> The Pitjandjara consider the best meats to be kangaroo and euro, making little distinction between them. They are selective with such animals. When killed they immediately feel the body for evidence of the presence of caul fat. If the animal is "njuka," or fatless, it is usually left, unless they are themselves starving [Tindale 1972: 248].

> The underground species [springhare, porcupine, antbear, and warthog] are highly desired because they are very fat, and animal fat is one of the elements most scarce in the Bushmen diet [Lee 1972: 344].

> Fat, like honey, is greatly sought after [by the Wanindiljaugwa]. In recounting a hunting-success, one is always asked, "Was it fat?" [Worsley 1961: 170].

Another goal guiding economic decisions, and related to the concept of taste, is the desire for variety in the diet. Apart from its risk-reducing influence, a heterogeneous resource base is valued for preventing monotony of the diet. Among the Wanindiljaugwa of Australia, "quantity, variety, and to a lesser extent, quality of food are still the major concerns in the settlements [Worsley 1961: 175]." And generalizing from the ethnographic record, Worsley states: "It is often assumed that among the simpler peoples the importance attached to an economic product is a simple function of the utilitarian significance of that item in the diet.... It is the rare thing, not the staple, which is often prized most highly [Worsley 1961: 165]." The welcome of a seasonal change of diet has been noticed among several groups. In describing the activities for the month of March, Oberg notes: "The Tlingit fisherman feels both the monotony of a dried fish diet and the restrictions of the village.... Everyone feels the urge of spring and excitement rules the village [Oberg 1973: 65—66]." And finally, summarizing the basis of !Kung subsistence, Lee generalizes: "It would be theoretically possible for the Bushmen to survive entirely on vegetable foods, but life would be boring indeed without the excitement of meat feasts [Lee 1968: 41]."

Also significant in shaping economic behavior is the desire for prestige. The definition of prestige is culturally bound and may differ among groups, but its universal importance seems clear. Among California Indians, a primary concern was the heightening of prestige (Baumhoff 1963). Among the Ojibwa, high status accrued to the successful hunter (Dunning 1959). Only the men of the Fort Nelson Slave hunt large game, and success in this type of hunting confers the greatest prestige (Honigmann 1946). In the California northwest, "from the Yurok and Tolowa northward there was the ultimate goal of prestige [Suttles 1968: 64]." And the intimate connection between prestige and subsistence has been examined by Suttles (1960), who hypothesizes: "For a population to have survived in a given environment for any length of time, its subsistence activities and prestige-gaining activities are likely to form a single integrated system [p. 296]."

A final consideration important in structuring subsistence activities is the differentiation of sex roles. The factors leading to this differentiation will not be discussed here; the fact that such a division of labor appears to be universal is the important concern: "It seems to be certain that the differentiation of the activity field according to sex is a universal phenomenon among modern food gatherers [Watanabe 1968: 75]." This separation of activities is reinforced by a differentiation of prestige allotment: "Women played as great a role as men in food production [among the Ainu]; nevertheless, their status was lower. The basic reason for this was that exploitation of resources required symbolic control, and its means and rights were exclusively in the hands of the men [Watanabe 1968: 457]." The importance of this reinforced sex role differentiation, independent of any immediate conflict of mutually exclusive activities, is indicated by Honigmann's (1961) explanation of male inactivity during early summer among the Attawapiskat Cree: "There are few traditionally male pursuits that can be done in summer—fur trapping is over, geese are gone, and large game is lacking; fishing with nets is traditionally women's work and thus is continued to be done by them [p. 57]." Thus there are four additional goals guiding economic behavior, which are here classified as "desires" rather than "needs" because they often seem to have secondary priority. That is, in times of economic stress, such as drought or harsh winters, these objectives frequently go unmet. Dietary variety, the tastiest and most prestigious foods, and even the traditions of sex role differentiation all may be sacrificed to the necessities of meeting the primary objectives.

In summary, these secondary goals are as follows:

3. Desire for good-tasting foods.
4. Desire for variety.
5. Desire for prestige.
6. Desire to maintain differentiation of sex roles.

Resources

If this is a decision-making system, then the resources of the system are the means utilized in the decision-making process. Among the Cree, decisions depend "on integrating information from a variety of sources—signs of the animals, weather conditions, the behavior of the animals, dreams and visions, and the hunter's past success [Feit 1973 : 117]." And Laughlin (1968) generalizes about hunting decisions: "The point here is simply that the enormous range and complexities of animal behavior; the influence of situation factors . . . must all be read into the decision-making machinery of the hunter [p. 309]." Hence the decisions depend largely on the evaluation of signs regarding resource behavior and climatic patterns, and a detailed knowledge of resource behavior is an impressive trait of hunter–gatherers:

> The aborigine's knowledge of the characteristics of these species is considerable. . . . Since his interest in these species is derived from their importance as food, he is not quite so concerned about the less relevant characteristics of the plants and animals, those features which are of no concern from the point of view of foodgetting [Worsley 1961: 158–159].

> By necessity, Tuluaqmiut hunters possessed extensive knowledge of nature in general. However, by choice as well as necessity, they were specialists in zoology [Campbell 1968:9].

Among the hunters themselves, exploitive success and its concomitant respect are seen to derive from such knowledge: "Umialit ['rich men'] were considered very intelligent men who carefully observed the habits of all the animals and the conditions affecting them: climatic, topographic, other animals, and the presence of man [Gubser 1965: 181]." The overwhelming importance of this knowledge in structuring economic decisions is stressed by Feit: "Waswanipi then have a very substantial knowledge of the environment in which they live and this knowledge makes plausible their claims for the reliability, efficiency, and affluence of their subsistence system; their expertise also suggests that it is possible to choose when to use resources [Feit 1973: 120]." Based on these observations, the resource use schedule will be viewed as the adaptation of predatory human behavior primarily to resource behavior in order to meet the predetermined goals of the system.

The various aspects of resource behavior which are relevant to these goals must be identified; based on ethnographic reports, the resource attributes most often taken into consideration by hunter—gatherers are:

1. Weight (w)
2. Density (d)
3. Aggregation size (a)
4. Mobility (m)
5. Fat content (f)
6. Nonfood yields (n)

Justification for the choice of these attributes must derive from the demonstration, first, that they are, in fact, considered by hunter—gatherers, and second, that they relate directly to the goals in the decision-making process.

Among the Tuluaqmiut, the factors of weight, density, aggregation size, skin condition, and fat content receive great emphasis as food selection criteria for all classes of resources:

> Of the resident species [of birds], only 5 are suitable as food; the others are not inedible, but are uncommon, small, or solitary [Campbell 1968: 10].

> Swans, geese, and ducks are relatively large and fat, and if abundantly available would provide a valuable source of food [Campbell 1968: 11].

> Some are small, nearly all are solitary, none occurs abundantly ... with the result that carnivores have never represented more than a small fraction of the total diet [Campbell 1968: 12].

> The larger the caribou, the more it is desired except when the consideration of skin, rut, or fatness is paramount [Gubser 1965: 299].

In addition to being considered in combination, these attributes can, at times, each be of primary importance:

> Adult males are preferred [as prey] but only because they are generally larger [Woodburn 1968a: 53].

> If rabbits are abundant, both early and late summer may see these animals figure more prominently in the diet than they did in the study year 1947—8 [Honigmann 1961: 43].

> In the second half of summer an unidentified species of hairless caterpillar ... is enthusiastically sought; a good swarm brings a band hastening across country [Silberbauer 1972: 284].

> The period of real usefulness [of caribou] began in August when back fat had begun to form and the new fur provided excellent inner garments [Damas 1969: 274].

The importance of mobility as a factor in food selection is stressed in the Waswanipi accounts of the best moose-hunting times. Feit summarizes:

> Waswanipi hunters then have a detailed knowledge of moose behavior and so can hunt moose specifically when the animals concentrated in few locations which can be easily searched, when the moose are immobile, or less mobile than the hunter [Feit 1973: 120].

Thus the attributes chosen are definitely taken into consideration by hunter—gatherers when making their economic decisions. Furthermore, these attributes relate directly to the objectives guiding these decisions. In satisfying nutritional needs, the major consideration is the food provided by the resource, and this involves the weight and general abundance or density of each resource. The meeting of manufacturing needs involves consideration of the nonfood yields (hide, fur, antlers). The security of these yields depends on those factors which determine the probability of localizing and capturing the resource, primarily its general density and mobility. Population aggregation is permitted at low cost by spatially concentrated high-yield resources, and thus is affected by unit yield (weight and nonfood yield), the potential number of units per capture (aggregation size) and the potential distance necessary to travel per capture (mobility).

Among the secondary objectives, taste is related to fat content rather universally; other factors such as bitterness are involved but cannot be easily approached here. Variety is a concept that does not involve any of the resource attributes directly, but rather concerns resource proportions and therefore is logically deferred. Prestige is culturally defined, but often seems to be attached to luxury items, high-risk resources, the tastiest foods, and to the largest items (which can be more easily and widely shared). Thus prestige would involve weight, fat content, the nonfood yields, and the density and mobility. Finally, the differentiation of sex roles frequently is accomplished through a dichotomization of resources exploited according to their cost and prestige values, and therefore would be related to all of the resource attributes considered here.

Environment

The environment of a system consists of those factors affecting its performance but relatively free of influence from the system itself. In this case, relevant environmental factors consist of climatological, geographic and seasonal conditions of the specific area involved which cause variation in the important resource attributes. Historical factors determine which plant and animal species are present. The range and distribution of temperature, precipitation, elevation, and soils affect the general abundance and distribution of the flora and fauna. And, perhaps most important, the seasonal patterning in the environmental conditions induces a patterned variation in many of the resource attributes. The structure of the growing season affects the development and availability of plant species; the weight and fat content of animal species change with the availability of their food resources. Behavioral patterns related to food and reproduction cause variation in group size and mobility. The condition of skins and antlers is affected by climatic and behavioral factors. The complexity of causal factors will not be investigated here; the consequent patterned variation of resource attributes will be generalized from ethological studies and taken as given. Nor will the more random changes in these attributes, caused by smaller-scale environmental events such as storms and fires, be taken into account, although their existence is certainly significant, especially in regard to considerations of risk.

Measures of Performance

In order to assess the relevance of variations in resource attributes to the goals guiding the decision-making process, it is necessary to construct measures of performance for each goal. That is, an expression which rates each resource in terms of its pertinent attributes must be formulated for each goal. One of the major problems in this procedure is the assessment of the relative importance of each attribute—for example, is density more or less important than mobility to the consideration of risk, and how much so? In the absence of any empirical information on this point, the assumption must be made here that those attributes deemed pertinent are of equal significance. The major function of the measures of performance will be to structure the attributes in the proper relationship to the goals, thereby allowing a relative evaluation of the various resources.

1. *Secure food and nonfood income:* A resource is of greater significance to meeting this objective the greater its weight and nonfood yield, and its risk decreases as the density increases and as its mobility decreases. Thus a resource may be rated by:

$$wnd/m$$

2. *Population aggregation at minimum cost:* A resource is less expensive as a basis for population aggregation the greater its unit yield (weight, nonfood yield) and its aggregation size, and the less its mobility, and may be rated:

$$wna/m$$

3. *Taste:* A resource is tastier the greater its fat content:

$$f$$

4. *Variety:* This objective does not relate directly to resource attributes, but rather imposes a condition to be considered after the resource evaluation.

5. *Prestige:* A resource is more prestigious the greater its weight, fat content, nonfood yield, and mobility, and the lower its density:

$$wnfm/d$$

6. *Sex Role Differentiation:* This objective also requires a consideration after the initial resource evaluation, specifically an examination of the cost and prestige score distributions.

Management Considerations

There are four principle management considerations in the structuring of the decisions regarding resource use: the method of converting resource scores into proportional use for each goal; the relative importance and relationship of the goals; the method of combining and reconciling the goals; and the type of solution acceptable.

For each goal, resources receive a score according to the measures formulated. The construction of a list of all the resources considered, along with their scores, would then allow the calculation of the sum of these scores for each goal. The simplest procedure then will be used to determine resource use according to that goal: It will be defined as the proportional score of each resource.

For each goal:

$$\text{resource use \%} = \frac{\text{resource score}}{\text{sum of scores}} \times 100$$

In the presentation and discussion of the goals, the observation was made that the first two of these (secure provision of food and of nonfood needs, and support of population with minimum cost) were of constantly greater significance, while the others more often went unsatisfied, especially in times of economic hardship. Based on this observation, these first two goals will be used to determine a basic solution of resource use. Once this determination is made, however, the consideration of the other goals will be used to provide necessary modifications of this solution. Interaction with the other subsystems of site placement and demographic arrangement will also provide modifications of the basic solution.

Given that the basic solution will derive from the first two goals, the method of determining this solution must be formulated; that is, the combination and reconciliation of these goals must be accomplished. Again, in the absence of empirical evidence to the contrary, the simplest method will be used. The basic solution for each resource will be:

For two goals:

$$\text{total resource use \%} = \frac{\text{sum of 2 resource use \%'s}}{2}$$

Finally, this method of determining resource use presupposes a mixed-strategy solution, a supposition which can be defended by some of the goal considerations themselves. A pure strategy would be the specialization and concentration on one resource alone. Militating against such overconcentration are: considerations of risk-reduction, which advise spreading the risk, even away from a single low-risk item; the desire for prestige, whose definition requires the contrasting presence of low-prestige items; the structuring of sex role differentiation, requiring at least a dual economic focus; and lastly, the desire for variety.

The method of calculating resource use presented here depends essentially on the compromising of two different views of resources: in terms of their security (wnd/m) and their aggregate yields (wna/m). Incorporated into both views is the attribute of resource mobility (m). This attribute, however, actually has two different components. One relates to the absolute mobility, or average distance travelled per unit time. The other refers to the regularity of spatial behavior, to the ability of man to predict the location of the resource. Thus, migrating caribou may show high absolute mobility but be relatively "localizable" if hunters can predict interception points.

This dichotomous nature of resource mobility reflects a dichotomy stressed in several ecological studies of general food selection among animals (MacArthur 1972; MacArthur and Pianka 1966; Emlen 1966). In these discussions, the general feeding strategy, the dietary composition, and the relative proportions of different foodstuffs all have been related to resource attributes affecting: (1) the search for, and (2) the pursuit and capture of the resource. Animals can be divided into "searchers" (such as foliage-gleaning birds) and "pursuers" (lions) according to their allotment of time in the food quest. These different food quest techniques result in differences in dietary structure: Searchers tend to be generalists, while pursuers tend to be specialists.

Returning to a consideration of resource mobility, it may be seen that the component of "localizability" relates directly to the search time; if the location of a resource can be predicted, then the necessary search time is minimized. On the other hand, the absolute mobility of a resource influences the pursuit time necessary for its capture. Thus, both search and pursuit times will increase with an increased resource mobility, but with different components of this mobility. In addition, other resource attributes affect the search and pursuit of the resource. Overall resource density has an important effect on search time, but little on pursuit time; as density decreases, necessary search time increases. Aggregation size of the resource has greater relevance to pursuit time, since it determines the yield per pursuit; as aggregation size decreases, the effective pursuit time per kilogram captured increases. Animal weight (including nonfood yields) is relevant to both search and pursuit times, since these are calculated according to kilogram of capture; as weight decreases, the search and pursuit times per kilogram captured increase.

From the above discussion of the relationships of search and pursuit times to resource attributes, the following proportional formulations may be determined:

$$\text{search time} \propto \frac{m}{wnd}$$

$$\text{pursuit time} \propto \frac{m}{wna}$$

These formulations are the inverse of the formulas derived earlier for resource evaluation according to security and yield: A food that is rated high with regard to security (high wnd/m) would tend to have a low search time per unit weight; a food rated high in terms of yields allowing population aggregation (high wna/m) would have a low pursuit time per unit weight. Thus, the dichotomy stressed in general ecological studies is maintained in the method of resource evaluation developed here. A compromise of the two major goals of food selection tends to effect a compromise of the desires to minimize the search and pursuit times as well.

Example

In order to demonstrate this method of determining resource use, an example can be constructed using four hypothetical resources:

- A. A plant species (*"Acorn"*).
- B. A small animal species (*"Bunny"*).
- C. A species of fish (*"Carp"*).
- D. A large herbivore (*"Deer"*).

Each will be assigned values for the relevant attributes: weight in kilograms, fat content in grams per kilogram, density as individuals per square kilometer, aggregation size as individuals per group. Two of the attributes are more difficult to quantify: nonfood yield and mobility. Since, in the measures of the goals, nonfood yield always occurs along with weight, the approach used here will be to view nonfood yield as a factor increasing the effective weight by some proportion. That is, if an animal has antlers in good condition, its weight will be increased by perhaps 10%, and thus n will equal 1.1; if a resource has no utilizable nonfood products, n is equal to 1.0. The proportion of increase used here is arbitrary and derives from an inferred relative importance of nonfood yield.

Mobility could ostensibly be expressed in terms of kilometers traveled per unit time, or square kilometers of dispersal per unit time, but unfortunately such information is difficult to obtain for the various resources. Some information on home ranges of different animal species is available, but a comparison of those of terrestrial species to a similar concept for riverine resources is problematic. In addition, when home ranges of males and females partially overlap, the determination of an expression combining the two is difficult. Furthermore, information detailed enough to express the seasonal changes in home range is not obtainable for many species. Finally, the concept of mobility as used here is understood to be partially "site-specific" rather than "individual-specific." That is, the mobility of a resource is important as it affects the possibility of locating the resource, as well as to the extent that it affects the effort of pursuing the resource. The figures used for mobility here, then, must also reflect this "localizability" as well as possible using whatever pertinent information is available. Most important is that the relative order of magnitude correctly reflects the differences among the resources.

The values assigned to each of the four species is shown in Table 1.

Given these values, the scores for the resources for each goal can be calculated as follows:

	A	B	C	D	Sum
Secure income	1000	300	600	22	1922
Low-cost aggregation	100	3	20	220	343

And the proportional use according to each goal is:

	A	B	C	D
Secure income	.52	.16	.31	.01
Low-cost aggregation	.29	.01	.06	.64
Sum	.81	.17	.37	.65

Finally, the proportional use according to the combined goals is:

	A	B	C	D
Proportional use	.41	.09	.19	.33

TABLE 1

Sample Resource Attributes

	Resource			
Attribute	A	B	C	D
Weight	.001	3	1	200
Density	1000	100	30	1
Aggregation	100	1	1	10
Mobility	.001	1	.05	10
Nonfood	1	1	1	1.1
Fat content	3	5	7	10.

Following this initial example, some variations may be introduced to indicate the types of changes in resource use thereby produced:

Subarctic area with low plant potential:
Changes: for resource A, $d = 100$, $a = 10$

	A	B	C	D
New proportional use:	.07	.15	.34	.44

Area with large fish run:
Changes: for resource C, $a = 10$, $m = .02$

	A	B	C	D
New proportional use:	.24	.06	.56	.14

Area with low plant potential and large fish run:
Changes: combination of changes for resources A and C above

	A	B	C	D
New proportional use:	.03	.08	.73	.16

Area with low plant potential and large gregarious migratory herbivore:
Changes: for resource A, as above; for resource D, $a = 30$, $m = 2.0$

	A	B	C	D
New proportional use:	.05	.13	.28	.54

Through these rather simple examples, the procedure for determining resource proportions is demonstrated, and the effect of different resource configurations on the predicted utilization becomes evident. The problem of scheduling the *timing* of utilization is approached by the same considerations, but in a series of time units chosen so as to take into account the variation in resource attributes during the year. Intervals of one month seem the most suitable, because information on animal behavior in these terms is available and because the month appears to be a unit significant in hunter–gatherer time reckoning. For each interval, the value according to the goal measures can be calculated for a resource; from this distribution of scores, the monthly distribution of its utilization can be determined.

Modifications

Consideration must be given to several factors not directly related to resource behavior which have the potential for significantly modifying the basic resource use solution as just presented. Many of these factors are technological in nature, and thus their importance depends on the group in question. The first of these is the practice of storage techniques, which accomplish a temporal distribution of income. This practice can have three important implications for resource utilization: *(1)* During the period in which storage activities are practiced, emphasis may be placed on the procurement of more "storable" resources, and thus attributes not considered here may assume primary importance; *(2)* during this same period, material aspirations may increase greatly as a result of aiming procurement at future needs, thus emphasizing considerations of yield at the expense of prestige, variety, or sex role differentiation; *(3)* during the period of consumption of the stored resources, both of the primary goals may be satisfied, and the secondary goals of variety, taste, prestige, and sex role differentiation may assume greater significance.

A second type of modifying factor derives from imposed limitations on procurement. Conditions such as heavy snow cover, steep or rocky terrain, flooded ground, or the breaking up of ice can interfere with human mobility and thus cause a drastic increase in the cost of procuring the more mobile resources. In addition, the spatial distribution of two prescribed resources may be totally disparate, so that a "spatial tension" may be said to exist between the procurement of the two. This, too, would increase the exploitation cost of one or the other and would affect their proportional utilization. Related to this is what may be called "technological tension"—that is, the increase in cost required by maintaining different exploitation technologies simultaneously, whether in terms of material equipment or appropriate task group size. This tension may lead to the emphasis of one technology at a time, similar to the development of specific "searching images" by nonhuman predators. Thus, there may be some threshhold of importance, above which an activity will tend to occupy all the time and energy of the population.

A third class of modifications consists of aids to procurement which tend to decrease the cost of exploitation. Devices such as snowshoes, skis, and canoes greatly increase human mobility in relation to that of the resources. Traps, weirs, and fences not only allow an extension of procurement activities, but also tend to increase the efficiency of capture. This class of modifications thus can counteract the cost-increasing factors discussed earlier. Finally, the set of goal considerations which led to the formulation of a mixed rather than a pure strategy (variety, prestige, risk, and sex roles) can also affect the specific proportional use of resources. For example, should a basic solution prescribe a period of utilization solely of low-prestige items, or a period of concentration upon one resource, these considerations may alter these prescriptions somewhat, at the expense of the primary objectives, such as cost reduction.

Application to an Ethnographic Group

The previous examples indicate that the method of determining resource use responds in an appropriate manner to changes in resource configurations. It still must be demonstrated that it is capable of approximating the resource use patterns of an actual group. The Round Lake Ojibwa will be used here because they are one of the few groups in the ethnographic record for which detailed subsistence information is given (Rogers 1962). This is a group of some 256 hunter—fisher—trappers living in northern Ontario, a region of coniferous forests broken by many lakes and streams. The major animal species in this area are moose, beaver, hare, otter, mink, marten, muskrat, ermine, and squirrel. Caribou are no longer abundant, and are restricted to one small part of the region. Carnivores are present but are of rather low density. Grouse are permanent residents and waterfowl are seasonal. The most abundant fish are perch, pike, whitefish, lake trout, sucker, and sturgeon.

In order to determine and compare the overall proportional utilization, the resources considered here will be: moose, beaver, small game, and fish; together, these account for 90% of the wild food diet during the year. The object of this comparison will be to approximate the relative importance of these in the total diet, and their pattern of utilization during the year. The first step in this pro-cedure is the determination of values for the resource attributes pertinent to the primary economic goals: weight, density, mobility, aggregation size, and non-food yields. Some of these values can be taken from biological and ethological literature; others will have to be derived.

Moose range in weight according to age and sex; as an average value, 700 pounds or 318 kilograms will be used (Peterson 1955). Beaver also show a range of values; 44 pounds or 20 kilograms seems to represent an average weight (Warren 1927). For both small game and fish, approximate averages of the weights of the different species included will be used: for small game, 1.6 kilo-grams, and for fish, 1.0 kilogram (Eddy and Surber 1947; Jackson 1961; Spector 1956; White 1953). Since moose provide usable skins, antlers, and long bones, and beaver supply pelts and large teeth, the value of their nonfood yields will be 1.1 for each. Small game are valued for their pelts, and so will receive a value of 1.05. And fish, having little in the way of useful by-products, will be given a value of 1.0. The average aggregation size may also be estimated from the litera-ture. Moose are solitary or found in small groups. In one study, their mean monthly aggregation size was 1.6, although, from further data presented, the average often seems to be somewhat larger (Bergerud and Manuel 1969). A value of 1.8 will be used here. Beaver lodges house between two and eight animals (Warren 1927), and an average aggregation size of 5 will be used here. The small game species are, for the most part, solitary or present in small family groups; a value of 2 will be used. The values for the fish range widely, depending on species and time of year; for much of the year, they are solitary, although during spawning, the effective group size can be quite large. Because of the short duration of the spawning season, values of 2 to 3 seem to approximate the order of magnitude of a yearly average, and a value of 2.5 will be used here.

Moose densities in eastern North America have been estimated at one moose per 5 square miles (Peterson 1955) and one per 6 square miles (Pimlot 1961), but Rogers estimates one per 10 square miles (or .04 per square kilometer) in the Round Lake region. This last estimate will be used here, because it was made for the specific area in question, and because the moose has recently penetrated this region, displacing caribou. In order to determine a density figure for small game, densities of each species were estimated from the available literature (Jackson 1961; Kendeigh 1961; Southern 1964) as shown in Table 2.

Using these figures and the average weight for each, the biomass of each animal was calculated. Finally, the sum of these biomasses was divided by the average weight of all the species, giving a density for these "average small game species" of 136 per square kilometer. For estimating fish density, figures of "average annual production in pounds per average square mile of territory," as given by Rostlund were used. For the region of northern Ontario, production ranges between 100 and 200 pounds (Rostlund 1952:303). Since the Round Lake region has a large water area, the higher figure of 200 pounds per square mile, or 35.5 kilograms per square kilometer, seems appropriate. Given an average individual weight of 1.0 kilogram, this figure of 35.5 also represents the density.

Estimates of beaver density were not obtainable and so must be derived. For the Waswanipi Cree, who inhabit a region very close to that of the Round Lake Ojibwa, Feit states that "beaver are twice as productive as moose [Feit 1973: 121]." This ratio of productivity can be used to derive a measure of beaver density. Productivity can be expressed by weight time density:

For moose:

$$wd = 318 \times .04 = 12.7$$

Thus, for beaver:

$$wd = 2 \times 12.7 = 25.4$$

and if $w = 20$, then $d = 1.3$ beaver per square kilometer.

TABLE 2

Small Game Densities

Animal	Individuals per km²
Hare	100.0
Squirrel	150.0
Muskrat	50.0
Ermine	7.5
Marten	.25
Mink	.25
Otter	.013

Statements from Feit can also be used to determine the ratio of mobility values for the four resource groups. As formulated earlier, the score of a resource with respect to cost is: wna/m: That is, the higher this score, the less expensive, or the more efficient, is the procurement of the resource. According to Feit, the ratio of efficiency for the exploitation of the four resource groups is as follows (Feit 1973: 121):

Moose : Beaver : Fish : Small Game
100 : 20 : 10 : 3

From these figures, the ratio of mobility values can be derived. Beaver will be assigned an arbitrary mobility of 1.0. Feit's ratios concern only food yields, and so consideration of nonfood products must be left out of the formula, which now becomes: wa/m. From this formula, beaver efficiency is:

$$(20 \times 5)/1 = 100$$

From the ratios given by Feit, it follows that the other efficiency measures are:

Moose   500
Fish   50
Small game   15

And from these, the following relative mobility values can be obtained:

Moose   1.15
Fish   .05
Small game   .20

Thus, the attributes of the four resource groups are summarized in Table 3.
From these, the scores according to the two goal considerations may be calculated:

	Moose	Beaver	Fish	Small game
Secure income	10.8	28.6	887.5	1142.4
Low-cost aggregation	547.5	110.0	50.0	16.8

TABLE 3

Round Lake Resource Attributes

Attribute	Moose	Beaver	Fish	Small game
Weight	318.0	20.0	1.0	1.6
Density	.04	1.3	35.5	136.0
Aggregation	1.8	5.0	2.5	2.0
Mobility	1.15	1.0	.05	.2
Nonfood	1.1	1.1	1.0	1.05

And the proportion of the total score for each goal shown by each resource is as follows:

	Moose	Beaver	Fish	Small game
Secure income	.01	.01	.43	.55
Low-cost aggregation	.76	.15	.07	.02
Sum	.77	.16	.50	.57

And the average of these proportional scores is:

Moose	Beaver	Fish	Small game
.39	.08	.25	.29

Finally, since the resources considered account for only 90% of the wild food diet, the preceding values should be multiplied by .9 to yield values for comparison. These predicted values, and the actual values of proportional utilization as given by Rogers are presented in Table 4.

The predicted relative proportions of each resource group are very similar to the actual proportional dietary importance among the Round Lake Ojibwa. The fact that beaver are more important than predicted may relate to their high market value—an attribute not considered here. The discrepancies are relatively minor, considering the wide possible deviation from the average values for attributes used here.

Perhaps a more important comparison would be between predicted and actual *seasonal patterns* of utilization of each resource group. In order to predict this pattern, the seasonal variation of the resource attributes must be determined. Most animals show patterned weight changes according to seasonal changes of diet and behavior. The most important events shaping such changes are: birth, causing weight loss for females; rut, which results in significant weight loss for males; and a usual winter–summer dichotomous distribution of food availability (Wandeler and Huber 1969). The magnitude of these changes can range widely—from 20% of the minimum yearly weight for roe deer to 80% for chamois—and seems to depend to a great extent upon the severity and timing of the rut and on winter food availability. For moose, rut occurs in September and October, and is rather subdued, similar to that of roe deer (Grzimek 1970). For males, then, the highest weight is attained just before rut, and is approximately 20% higher than its minimum weight. For females, the

TABLE 4

Predicted and Actual Round Lake Resource Proportions

Proportion	Moose	Beaver	Fish	Small game
Predicted	.35	.07	.23	.26
Actual	.31	.15	.26	.18

minimum weight occurs just after birth in May and June, the maximum just before. For beaver, the major weight changes relate to the seasonal diet availability: Toward the end of winter, stored food tends to run low and beaver weight reaches a low point; the highest weight occurs in late fall before the beaver retires to the lodge. The magnitude of these changes is also rather low.

For the various fish species, the weight changes can be quite large. Weight is highest just before spawning, and lowest in late winter (Rostlund 1952). Of the species available to the Round Lake Ojibwa, whitefish and lake trout spawn in September and October; most of the rest spawn in June and July.

Changes in aggregation size also depend on food availability and reproductive behavior. Among the moose of Wyoming, the largest aggregations occur in late winter (2.8 average) and during rut (Denniston 1956). In eastern North America the tendency to aggregate is not so pronounced (Pimlot 1961), and average sizes for late winter groups range up to 2.3. In Newfoundland, the homogeneity of moose distribution is best in summer, and single animals are most common. Thus, a sharp contrast exists between late winter and mid-summer, and a secondary concentration tendency occurs during rut. Beaver group size is rather constant and will be treated as such. A lodge usually houses two adults plus the young of 1 or 2 years. During birth, the male often leaves for a short time, but returns soon after the older offspring have left (Warren 1927). The fish species are normally solitary except during spawning, when the tendency to gather in shallows and at stream mouths results in an effective concentration. Few of the species form true schools, but many of the spring spawners tend to remain in the shallows during the summer.

The mobility patterns of animals also show distinct seasonal changes related to food distribution and reproduction. In western North America, with great altitudinal differences, pronounced low-altitude late winter yarding of moose occurs. In the east, the yarding is not generally so distinct, but significant changes in local density have been demonstrated in Newfoundland (Bergerud and Manuel 1969). Moreover, the emphasis of reduced moose mobility in late winter is evident in numerous ethnographic studies. On the other hand, maximum dispersal and mobility are shown by moose in midsummer. Beaver mobility shows a distinct dichotomous pattern: During the winter months, the animals are well localized (albeit rather difficult to obtain) in their lodges in icebound rivers and lakes; during the warm months, they are relatively much more mobile, although usually within a 400-meter radius of the lodge (Kleiber and Nievergelt 1973). The fish species are least mobile just before and during spawning and, to a lesser extent, during the warm summer months (for the spring spawners); in late fall, winter, and early spring, most fish are deep and, if not mobile, then certainly relatively more difficult to locate.

Since the Round Lake area contains a variety of habitats, and in this respect is very similar to its surrounding regions, no significant seasonal changes in general resource densities are expected; therefore, these will be treated as constant. Similarly, the nonfood yields will be viewed as constants, since the seasonal changes in the condition of skins and antlers are not in phase, and the values of bones and teeth are constant. The pattern of the changing attributes for the three resources can therefore be approximated by Table 5.

The constant values are:

Moose:	$d = .04,$	$n = 1.1$
Beaver:	$d = 1.3,$	$n = 1.1, a = 5$
Fish:	$d = 35.5,$	$n = 1.0$

From these values, the pattern of scores for each of the two goals can be determined.

Moose score	J	F	M	A	M	J	J	A	S	O	N	D
wnd/m	23	23	20	10	8	7	7	7	15	14	16	16
wna/m	1350	1350	1106	460	276	160	165	239	726	704	664	782

And the fraction of the goal total in each month is:

Moose	J	F	M	A	M	J	J	A	S	O	N	D
wnd/m	.14	.14	.12	.06	.05	.04	.04	.04	.09	.08	.10	.10
wna/m	.17	.17	.14	.06	.03	.02	.02	.03	.09	.09	.08	.10

The average of these two fractions for each month, and thus the proportional distribution of the moose contribution to the diet is:

	J	F	M	A	M	J	J	A	S	O	N	D
Moose	.16	.16	.13	.06	.04	.03	.03	.04	.09	.09	.09	.10

TABLE 5

Round Lake Resource Attributes by Month

Resource attribute	Month											
	J	F	M	A	M	J	J	A	S	O	N	D
Moose w	320	320	320	330	340	290	300	310	330	320	320	320
a	2.3	2.3	2.2	1.9	1.4	1.0	1.0	1.4	2.0	2.0	1.7	2.0
m	.6	.6	.7	1.5	1.9	2.0	2.0	2.0	1.0	1.0	.9	.9
Beaver w	19	18	18	19	19	20	21	22	22	22	21	20
m	.2	.2	.2	.2	1.0	1.8	1.8	1.8	1.8	1.8	1.0	.2
Fish w	.6	.6	.7	.8	1.0	1.5	1.4	1.4	1.4	1.0	.9	.7
a	1.0	1.0	1.0	1.0	2.0	6.0	5.0	5.0	3.0	2.0	1.0	1.0
m	.07	.07	.07	.05	.04	.01	.01	.01	.03	.04	.06	.06

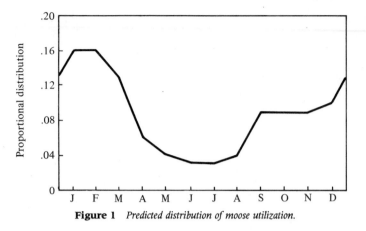

Figure 1 *Predicted distribution of moose utilization.*

The predicted distribution of moose utilization is shown in Figure 1.

A similar process may be used to describe the pattern of utilization of the beaver population:

Beaver	J	F	M	A	M	J	J	A	S	O	N	D
wnd/m	135	130	130	135	27	16	17	17	17	17	30	145
wna/m	525	495	495	525	105	61	64	67	67	67	116	550
%wnd/m	.17	.16	.16	.17	.03	.02	.02	.02	.02	.02	.04	.18
%wna/m	.17	.16	.16	.17	.03	.02	.02	.02	.02	.02	.04	.18
Average	.17	.16	.16	.17	.03	.02	.02	.02	.02	.02	.04	.18

The predicted distribution of beaver utilization is shown in Figure 2.

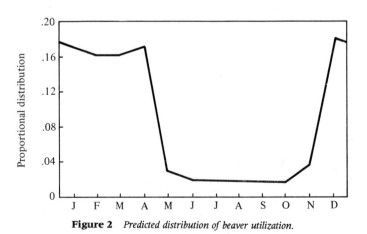

Figure 2 *Predicted distribution of beaver utilization.*

And for fish:

Fish	J	F	M	A	M	J	J	A	S	O	N	D
wnd/m	300	300	357	560	900	5300	5000	5000	1667	900	533	417
wna/m	9	9	10	16	50	900	700	700	133	50	15	12
%wnd/m	.01	.01	.02	.03	.04	.25	.24	.24	.08	.04	.03	.02
%wna/m	—	—	—	.01	.02	.35	.27	.27	.05	.02	.01	—
Average	.01	.01	.01	.02	.03	.30	.26	.26	.07	.03	.02	.01

The predicted distribution of fish utilization is shown in Figure 3.

No mention has been made yet of small game. Among most hunter–gatherers, this class of resources is procured throughout most of the year; the major determinant of its importance is its general abundance. In many cases, the timing of its utilization does not seem to be related to any specific attributes of this class of resources. This may be due, in part, to the fact that seasonal changes in the attributes of small game are less pronounced and are of less direct significance to their desirability or to the success of trapping. Most often, the timing of the utilization of small game seems to be tied to the schedules of other resources. That is, small game importance seems to increase as the importance of other, competing procurement activities decreases. If this is so, it implies a hierarchical approach to scheduling decisions: only some resources are evaluated first, and once these are scheduled, others are considered and used to fill in the temporal "gaps." Lee (1968) seems to imply such a hierarchical position among the !Kung: "In short, the Bushmen of the Dobe area eat as much vegetable food as they need, and as much meat as they can get [p. 41]. Feit (1973), too, discusses a hierarchical approach to resource procurement among the Cree: "The Waswanipi then use the most efficiently harvestable resources, namely moose and beaver, first, and then they shift to other less efficiently harvestable but more productive

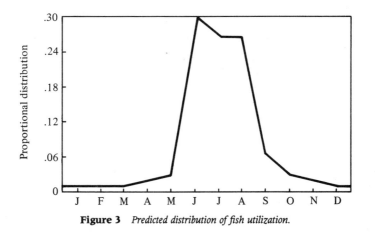

Figure 3 *Predicted distribution of fish utilization.*

TABLE 6

Predicted Proportional Resource Contribution to Total Yearly Diet of the Round Lake Ojibwa

Resource	Month											
	J	F	M	A	M	J	J	A	S	O	N	D
Moose	.056	.056	.046	.021	.014	.011	.011	.014	.032	.032	.032	.035
Beaver	.012	.011	.011	.012	.002	.001	.001	.001	.001	.001	.003	.013
Fish	.002	.002	.002	.005	.007	.069	.060	.060	.016	.007	.005	.002
Sum	.070	.069	.059	.038	.023	.081	.072	.075	.049	.040	.040	.050

resources [p. 124]." Feit sees the principle structuring this hierarchy as efficiency, with the less efficient foods being the second-choice ones. This principle does not explain the Bushman case, however, since the second-choice vegetable foods are shown by Lee to be more efficiently harvested [Lee 1968: 40]. If, on the other hand, prestige were seen as the structuring principle, then both cases could be explained. Both vegetable foods for the Bushmen, and small game for the Cree, are considered mundane—small, common, and low-risk—and are accorded little prestige. The term "rabbit starvation," which is common among northern groups, indicates the second-choice nature of this particular small game species.

Small game here will be accorded this second-place status: Its use will be seen as inversely related to the utilization of the other classes of resources. In order to do this, the relative utilization of these other resources must be totaled for each month. Since moose was predicted to represent 35% of the diet, this should be multiplied by the fractions of importance distributed by month, to give the monthly contribution of moose to the total yearly diet. Similar procedures can be done for beaver and fish, and the results are presented in Table 6.

Since the four resource groups together form 90% of the total diet, then the monthly distribution of this is .90/12 = .075. Small game, then, will be seen to fill in the total for each month to this level, and thus a monthly distribution of small game utilization can be determined, and is given in Table 7.

TABLE 7

Predicted Proportional Contribution of Small Game to Total Yearly Diet of the Round Lake Ojibwa

Resource	Month											
	J	F	M	A	M	J	J	A	S	O	N	D
Small game	.005	.006	.016	.037	.052	—	.003	—	.026	.035	.035	.025

TABLE 8

Predicted Distribution of Small Game Utilization of the Round Lake Ojibwa

	Month											
Resource	J	F	M	A	M	J	J	A	S	O	N	D
Small game	.02	.03	.07	.15	.22	—	.01	—	.11	.15	.15	.10

From these figures, the proportional distribution of utilization of small game can be determined, and is presented in Table 8.

From the figures for the contribution to the total yearly diet, the relative monthly importance of each resource can be calculated, with other resources assumed to provide a standard of 10% each month. These figures are given in Table 9.

The predicted distribution of small game utilization is shown in Figure 4.

This assumption of a constant 10% contribution by other resources is made for simplicity, primarily because these other resources were not examined for their attribute behavior. Figures for the general abundance of waterfowl and caribou were not available; for this reason, their relative contribution could not be evaluated. It is true, however, that these resources both will have bimodal curves of utilization: the waterfowl in spring and fall when they are present in great numbers and are spatially concentrated, and caribou in fall and late winter, the periods of rut and yarding. Given these bimodalities, their contribution will not be of constant importance, and the utilization of the other resources will be affected accordingly.

These predicted patterns of utilization can be compared to those actually shown by the Round Lake Ojibwa. Rogers presents information that allows for the determination of the pounds of food contributed by each resource group each month (Rogers 1962), which is summarized in Table 10.

It is apparent that the monthly procurement of these foods is not constant, as was assumed in estimating small game proportions. Two major factors

TABLE 9

Predicted Resource Contributions to Monthly Diets of the Round Lake Ojibwa

	Month											
Resource	J	F	M	A	M	J	J	A	S	O	N	D
Moose	.67	.67	.55	.25	.17	.13	.13	.17	.38	.38	.38	.42
Beaver	.14	.13	.13	.14	.02	.01	.01	.01	.01	.01	.04	.16
Fish	.02	.02	.02	.06	.08	.82	.72	.72	.19	.08	.06	.02
Small game	.06	.07	.19	.44	.62	—	.04	—	.31	.42	.42	.30
Other	.10	.10	.10	.10	.10	.10	.10	.10	.10	.10	.10	.10

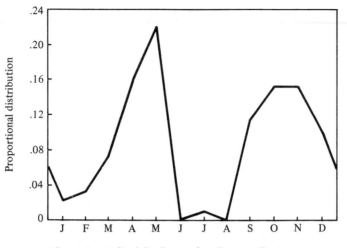

Figure 4 *Predicted distribution of small game utilization.*

appear to cause this monthly variation: storage practices, which allow irregular procurement to provide a constant level of dietary intake; and the use of "store foods" in the diet, which are not considered here, and which may contribute varying amounts to monthly diets (especially in the summer months, when the people are gathered around the post). It is hoped, however, that the pattern of wild food procurement, relative to one another, is not seriously disrupted by these factors, and that a comparison between predicted and actual utilization may still indicate broad similarities.

From this data on actual procurement levels, the percentage contributed each month by each resource group can be calculated, and is given in Table 11.

The general patterns of utilization are very similar: Graphs of the predicted

TABLE 10

Actual Amount of Food Taken Each Month by the Round Lake Ojibwa[a]

Resource						Month						
	J	F	M	A	M	J	J	A	S	O	N	D
Moose	720	720	720	160	160	80	80	80	200	200	280	280
Beaver	96	58	77	116	693	—	—	—	—	—	173	539
Fish	94	156	31	62	156	624	499	375	562	468	125	—
Small game	194	187	188	69	764	15	15	15	75	75	238	291
Other	98	98	98	149	149	17	17	17	105	105	12	12
Sum	1202	1219	1114	556	1922	736	611	487	942	848	828	1122

[a]In tens of pounds.

TABLE 11

Round Lake Actual Procurement: Monthly Proportions

Resource	Month											
	J	F	M	A	M	J	J	A	S	O	N	D
Moose	.60	.59	.65	.29	.08	.11	.13	.16	.21	.23	.31	.23
Beaver	.08	.05	.07	.21	.36	—	—	—	—	—	.19	.45
Fish	.08	.13	.03	.11	.08	.85	.82	.77	.59	.54	.14	—
Small game	.16	.15	.17	.12	.40	.02	.02	.03	.08	.09	.26	.24
Other	.08	.08	.09	.27	.08	.02	.03	.04	.12	.13	.09	.07

and actual schedules make this clear (Figures 5 and 6). Some of the discrepancies have already been mentioned: The contribution of beaver is generally greater than predicted, and this may be partly due to the high market value of its fur; actual fish utilization is also greater than predicted, and may relate to the congregation of the group around the post in summer, where land resources may have been scared off; and the contribution of other resources is not constant, but shows peaks in spring and fall, paralleling the abundance peaks of migratory waterfowl. Two other discrepancies, however, are only now evident: the great actual importance of beaver in spring, and the higher than expected contribution of fishing in fall. The discrepancy regarding the importance of fall fishing probably derives from an underestimation of the significance of

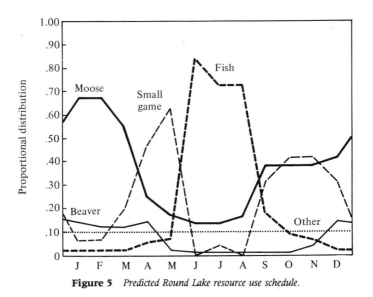

Figure 5 *Predicted Round Lake resource use schedule.*

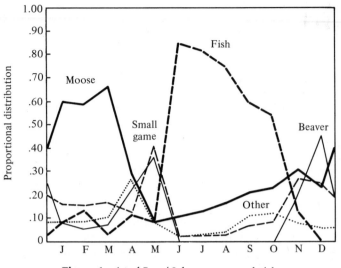

Figure 6   *Actual Round Lake resource use schedule.*

the fall-spawning whitefish and lake trout, which together apparently form a greater part of the fish resource than predicted. The fact that ethnographic reports from this region emphasize these species supports this conclusion. The spring importance of beaver apparently coincides with their emergence from the lodges. Although this emergence results in an increase in absolute mobility, as estimated, the beaver at this time are rather sluggish, so their capture is relatively easy, especially when compared to extracting them from an icebound lodge in winter. The concept of "mobility" or "localizability" should intuitively include these considerations, but does not easily handle them quantitatively.

This examination of the Round Lake Ojibwa should make clear that the methods derived here can perform very well in approximating the behavior of a real group. Despite some discrepancies, it is possible to estimate the proportions of resource utilization and the changing patterns of their exploitation. The success of this example should allow a greater confidence in applying the methods to prehistoric groups.

Derivation of Economic Seasons

It was argued previously that resource use decisions tend to be relatively independent and tend to structure the spatial and demographic arrangements of a population of hunter–gatherers. The view taken here is that the procurement schedule assumes a sequence of configurations, each with a different combination and emphasis of resources, and that each configuration may require or permit a different location and group size. The time interval used in determining the schedule has been the month, even though several months show very similar proportions of resource utilization. Broadly, these clusters of similar months parallel the climatic seasons, but since resources respond differently to climatic factors, and since the timing of mating and reproductive events varies among resources, the actual configurations of relative importance may differ from the seasons themselves. These different configurations of resource utilizations will be called "economic seasons," and are viewed as the units of spatial and demographic responses of the population.

In order to determine these economic seasons, the patterns of resource utilization must be examined for sharp changes, for discontinuities which might prompt a distinct alteration of activities by the population. A change of dominant resource from one month to the next is perhaps the most obvious such alteration, but abrupt changes in the importance of other resources may also be significant. If one examines the curves of predicted resource utilization by the Round Lake Ojibwa, the different seasons may be delineated. The months of January through March are all very similar, with moose the dominant resource. April, however, is abruptly different, and similar to May, with small game being dominant, and fish of increased importance. The months of June through August, then, seem to form another unit, with fish the dominant resource. Another abrupt change occurs in September, with moose and small game of increasing importance, and fish declining in significance. The months of September through December form a continuum with no abrupt changes: Moose and beaver increase steadily in importance, while fish decreases and small game continues to be significant. From these predicted values, these months could be treated as one season, or divided into two seasons between October and November, to indicate the changing values of fish and beaver.

Thus, four or five seasons of activities can be derived from the predicted schedules of utilization. These can be compared to the actual pattern shown by the Round Lake Ojibwa. Rogers states that the Indians now recognize four seasons similar to ours, but nevertheless he finds it convenient to divide the year into five seasons when discussing their economic activities: late winter (January–March), spring (April–May), summer (June–early September), fall (late September–early October), and early winter (late October–December). The first three seasons parallel those predicted. The fall season is sharply delineated by the importance of waterfowl and of whitefish, factors either not considered or underestimated here. Finally, in early winter, small game and moose assume great importance. Thus, as far as these predictions were carried, they did quite well in estimating the economic seasons.

CHAPTER FOUR

Subsystem II: Settlement Location

Goals

As discussed in the preceding chapter, the location of settlements among hunter—gatherers will also be viewed as the result of a set of decisions. The decisions concern the spatial arrangement of the population in order to meet a number of goals. The duration and location of settlements are certainly influenced by many considerations, but the primary factors seem to be related to subsistence. As Murdock (1969) says, "It has long been recognized that the form, size and fixity of human settlement bear a definite relationship to the modes of exploiting the natural environment to provide subsistence [p. 129]." A specific study of moves made by households among the Birhor reveals the importance of economics as a motivating factor: "When a move will occur is, in most instances, decided by immediate economic factors. Most of these are subsumed under the two items (7) seasonal moves and (8) intraseasonal moves to improve hunting. . . . These two factors then account for 91% of the total [Williams 1974: 74]." Different economic activities, focused on specific resources, can directly affect the settlement pattern of the exploiting population: "Beaver . . . is continuous

47

(throughout the hunting season) and imposes some degree of sedentariness on the hunger; hunting of the other animals mentioned is, by contrast, discontinuous, and involves to some extent, adopting temporarily the nomadic characteristics of the prey [Tanner 1973: 109]." Not only the behavior, but the general spatial arrangement of economic resources can significantly influence human settlement patterns: "One of the fundamental factors relevant to the high stability of residence among the Ainu may have been the distribution of the ecological zones within narrow river valleys they inhabited [Watanabe 1968: 72]." Even among members of the same cultural group, settlement patterns can vary according to local economic factors: "We find [Tlingit] villages on the banks of these rivers from which the people moved only in May to make fish oil out of the eulachon which crowded the mouths of the rivers. . . . In regions where salmon were scarce, the Indians became expert seal hunters, and we find a threefold division of settlement [Oberg 1973: 57]."

Given the importance of economic factors in determining human settlement patterns, the structure of these patterns is logically derived from the economic seasons. According to Ricklefs, (1973) all organisms "must synchronize their activity to temporal patterns in the environment [p. 167]," and such patterns are clearly perceived hunter–gatherers: "The Labrador Eskimo, like their congeners in other sections, divide the year into seasons corresponding to the appearance of game or other natural conditions [Hawkes 1916: 28]." The impact of such seasons on spatial behavior is evident among many groups. For the Nootka:

> The distances between the salmon streams, herring grounds and the outer coast were so great that they could not have been effectively exploited by a completely sedentary group. Use of all the seasonal resources involved seasonal changes of residence [Drucker 1951: 59].

> The annual productive cycle ... involved not only a highly organized pattern of seasonal migration, but also a complex social system that ensured a constant readjustment between population and available food resources [Ruddell 1973: 264].

Similar clear seasonal patterns of movement have been reported for many other groups (for example, Balikci 1968; Rogers 1962, 1963; Lee 1969; Teit 1930).

Thus, the seasonal variations of economic resources seem to comprise an important set of considerations guiding settlement decisions; the goals of the resource use decisions would then play a role in these settlement choices as well, Since these goals, however, have already been utilized in the derivation of the specific proportional resource uses, settlement decisions must relate to the structuring of the procurement of the resources in these proportions. The great importance of effort conservation among hunter–gatherers has already been discussed; the spatial correlate of this principle is distance minimization. Hence, the primary goal guiding settlement decisions will be viewed as the minimization of the travel distance necessary to procure resources in the pre-determined proportions. The emphasis on proximity to resources is evident in Lee's (1969) summarization of Bushman foraging strategy: "At a given moment, the members of a camp prefer to collect and eat the most desirable foods that are the least distance from standing water [p. 81]."

In addition to this economic goal of proximity to resources, two other objectives seem to underlie settlement decisions of hunter—gatherers. One common objective of site placement is the provision of shelter. Among the Mistassini: "Since protection from the weather is not so important in the fall and spring, camp is often established within a mile of a place where nets can be set. In winter, protection from the wind is desired, often necessitating a camp location several miles from the nets [Rogers 1963: 46]." Similarly among the Nunamiut: "When a family decided to build [a caribou skin tent] they selected a site that provided water, willows for firewood, and protection from the wind [Gubser 1956: 69]." And on the Northwest Coast: "A few Nootkan groups lived throughout the year on the exposed coast, but the majority of the population tended to concentrate in the protected sounds [Ruddell 1973: 256]." In warm climates, too, a concern with protection from the elements appears to condition settlement location:

> Part of the country consists of open grass plains but the Hadza never build camps there. Camps are invariably sited among trees or rocks and, by preference, both [Woodburn 1968: 50].

> [For Pitjandjara campsites] granite boulders are favored for their warmth when the sun has been on them, and they give coolness in their shade [Tindale 1972: 244].

Together with protection from the elements is a concern for texture and dryness of the ground surface. Among the Pitjandjara, "warm sandy ground is the first choice; rough rocks and clay are avoided [Tindale 1972: 244]." The Mbuti locate their camps on a slight slope for water runoff in case of rain (Turnbull 1965).

Another objective operating in site location is the concern for a view, both for game animals and for other human populations:

> A camping area with one elevated place from which there is a general view of the surrounding country is considered desirable [by the Pitjandjara] even though the young men who live near it are subject to wind changes ... they watch euros and other game or observe and interpret the smoke fires they see on the horizon [Tindale 1972: 243].

The Ngatatjara also situate their camps so that they are removed from, and have a view of the water source, in order to "allow game to approach the water without being disturbed, thus allowing the men to hunt from blinds [Gould 1968: 118]."

The primary goals which operate in settlement placement among hunter–gatherers, then, may be summarized as follows:

1. Proximity of economic resources.
2. Shelter and protection from the elements.
3. View for observation of game and strangers.

Resources

The resources of this site location subsystem are the factors considered in making the decisions of when and where to move settlements. Since these decisions concern the arrangement of human populations in space, then the important considerations involve the spatial distribution of the factors relevant to the objectives of the decisions. Pertinent to the economic goals are the various food and nonfood resources themselves. The importance of the spatial distribution of general food resources is clear:

> A Nunamiut band was a shifting aggregation of households that located itself in a region which offered good opportunities for exploiting the caribou and other elements of the environment [Gubser 1956:165].

> The attractiveness of a locality is measured [by the Wanindiljaugwa], not by the pleasantness of the view, but by its food-producing potentialities, although aesthetic appreciation is by no means absent [Worsley 1961:174].

An important consideration in locational analysis is the uneven distribution of resources and their effect on settlement distributions (Haggett 1965). Beginning with an idealized regular lattice of settlements, all analyses recognize that, "when resources are localized, the different requirements will exert varying pulls on the location of the settlement, and the lattice will be correspondingly distorted [Haggett 1965]." In his discussion of settlements in Northern Foxe Basin, Crowe (1969) examines the "pull" of each resource, and the resulting location of sites aimed at their exploitation. For example: "Because of the mobility of the caribou and (until recently) their wide distribution, this resource did not 'pull' settlement away from the coastal core [p. 6]." The "pull" of food resources seems to be sufficient to account for the location of settlements among many groups:

> The importance of caribou and Dall sheep [to the Tuluaqmiut] explains why so many settlements of this type were situated well up toward the heads of creeks or elsewhere high in the mountains, where the sheep dwell the year around and where a few scattered caribou live in the summer [Campbell 1968: 17].

> The Kwakiutl lived seasonally in permanent villages, moving during the spring, summer, and fall among several village sites located for their fishing possibilities [Weinberg 1973:230].

Specific relocations can be caused by the "pull" of a resource concentration in another area: "By the time salmon reached the headwaters of the Idaho streams, the run was very weak, but strong enough to cause an annual Flathead migration [Turney-High 1937: 125]." Moves can also be due to the exhaustion of local food resources, such that the local "pull" is no longer effective:

> It is seldom possible for a [G/Wi] band to remain at one campsite for longer than four weeks. After such a long period of exploitation, plant food supplies dwindle and it is probable that game animals eventually learn to avoid the area [Silberbauer 1972: 302].

> The Bushmen typically occupy a camp for a period of weeks or months and eat their way out of it [Lee 1969: 81].

The distribution of nonfood resources can be equally, or even more important to settlement decisions. Among these resources, water and fuel are consistently of greatest significance. In arid environments, the location of water sources can be critical:

> Because of these soil factors, the distribution of water sources, in space and through time, is by far the most important ecological determinant of Bushmen subsistence. The availability of plant foods is of secondary importance, and the numbers and distribution of game animals are only of minor importance [Lee 1969: 78].

> The Hadza consider that about three or four miles is the maximum distance over which water can reasonably be carried and camps are normally sited within a mile of a water source [Woodburn 1968: 50].

In cool, temperate regions as well, water sources are significant in settlement locations. Among the Ainu, sites were usually chosen close to drinking water, and fishing and hunting grounds (Watanabe 1964).

The distribution of fuel sources is, as might be expected, of vital importance in cold climates, but fuel location seems to be equally important in warm regions as well. The factors that determine choice of campsites by the Pitjandjara include a supply of firewood: "A rough measure of the importance of native water is given by the radius of the ring of woodless country around it [Tindale 1972: 244]."

The noneconomic objectives of shelter and a view necessitate consideration of other elements of the environment. The evaluation of topography, soils, vegetation, precipitation and temperature, and the presence of rock outcrops, caves, and shelters all become directly relevant here in the decision-making process (in addition to their indirect importance through their influence on the economic resources).

Environment

This system's environment consists of those factors influencing the means that are used to make the decisions regarding site location. In this case, the specific regional patterning imposed on the various resources is involved. The immediate spatial distribution of soils, elevation, vegetation, temperature, precipitation, wind direction, and rock forms define the opportunities and constraints. The seasonal changes of temperature, precipitation, and wind direction determine the altering configurations of relevant criteria. This spatio-temporal patterning must be examined in conjunction with the resource use schedule in order to define the site characteristics important in each season.

Measures of Performance

Measures of performance in this decision-making subsystem must permit the evaluation of site locations—that is, they must relate the different locational attributes to the various objectives. If a particular factor is uniformly distributed in space, then it should exert no "pull" on settlement location. If the distribution is uneven, or in clusters, the "pull" of that resource derives from the center of distribution of each cluster. The distance from a site location to this center, then, provides a measure for determining proximity to the resource. Measures for the other goals are not easily quantified, but the various attributes may be evaluated as to their relationship to these goals. Uneven distributions of temperature and precipitation will result in regions relatively warmer and drier in winter and cooler in summer, which would be more favorable and protected in northern latitudes; climatic patterns of tropical and subtropical areas would demand different constellations of these factors. The lower the elevation and the denser the vegetation, the greater is the shelter from wind and precipitation. Rock outcrops, rock shelters, and caves provide great protection from the elements. Sand and other loose substrates provide drier camping sites; more compact and smaller-grained substrates, on the other hand, tend to be smoother and to provide a flatter and more comfortable camping site. Southern-facing slopes tend to be warmer and drier in northern latitudes. Availability of a view is favored by higher elevations in relation to surrounding areas, and by more open vegetation. Measures for the goals of protection and view would derive from a consideration of these various factors of the specific landscape.

Management Considerations

The most important consideration is the structuring of the spatial satisfaction of the objectives. In an ideal situation, where the centers of distribution of all resources coincide and co-occur with conditions of adequate shelter and a view, then there is no problem: The settlement is located at this central point. But in all real situations, the spatial distributions of resources do not coincide, and the distance to each center cannot be minimized. In this case, some method of reconciling the various "pulls" must be found. In modeling settlement solutions, two approaches to determining the method of reconciliation might be used: generalization from studies of actual hunter–gatherer site placement, and utilization of a predictive analogue model of possible general relevance. Both approaches will be discussed here, one to furnish the underlying principles and structure, the other to demonstrate one technique for realizing these principles.

As discussed previously, a hierarchical approach to resources apparently operates in hunter–gatherer scheduling decisions. This structure seems to characterize many different aspects of human decisions and activities. The importance of hierarchical organization is emphasized in most models of settlement location: Among the assumptions underlying virtually all such models, Garner (1967) includes the following:

> The organization of human activity is essentially hierarchical in character, both in spatial and non-spatial aspects;
>
> Human occupance is focal in character; the areal structure of the occupance of the earth's surface is composed of a number of hierarchically nested orders of spatial functional organization, and in this way, movement-minimization, accessibility, agglomerations and hierarchies are linked together to form a system of human organization in space [pp. 304–305].

An examination of ethnographic studies reveals several hierarchical principles apparently structuring spatial behavior. One such principle is that resources vary in their importance to site location according to their level of security. The greater the security of a resource, the greater is its "pull" on settlement:

> [Among the Tlingit] the mainland rivers were supplied with fish practically the year around. In conformity with this certain food supply we find large villages on the banks of these rivers [Oberg 1973: 57].
>
> When the Wanindiljaugwa gathered as a tribe for the annual religious ritual ... they frequently selected a spot where there was an abundance of burrawongs ... to maintain a large community for several weeks [Worsley 1961: 164].
>
> One fish species, the lake trout, was very important, and it had much to do with the locations of major Tuluaqmiut settlements.... In those uncommon bad years when the game failed, the few trout lakes became crucially important to band survival. And even in usual or typical years ... there were short periods when game was scarce, and ... lake trout were accordingly sought after [Campbell 1968: 10].

Conversely, one might view the major structuring principle as deriving from the prestige value of the resource. Since prestige value seems to depend, to a great extent, on factors of high-risk, then the most prestigeous resources tend to be those of lowest security. Thus, in many cases, the higher the prestige of a resource, the lower is its "pull" on settlement. This formulation applies to *specific* site location; whenever possible sites are situated so as to provide access to general regions of high-prestige resource distribution, but the specific site chosen seems to depend more on the low-prestige, high-security resources. An implication of this generalization is that people would be willing to travel farther from camp to procure high-prestige resources. This implication agrees with the widespread division of activity fields around a settlement, with most gathering and much small game trapping done close to camp, while big game hunting extends far beyond (Watanabe 1968: 75). The value of a resource, whether measured in dollars or prestige, seems to be important in determining any industrial location: "Industries will tend to be located nearer the sources of their materials and fuel ... the lower the value ... of the raw materials [Hamilton 1967: 374]." Nonfood resources can be placed in this security–prestige hierarchy too, with firewood and water being of low prestige and thus situated close to camp sites.

One problem with this formulation of the opposition between security and prestige is revealed in the following: "If a number of caribou are killed far from base camp, the [Mistassini] men bury them in the snow and return to camp. Base camp is then moved to within a few miles of the kill [Rogers 1963: 40]." The caribou are a high-risk, high-prestige resource which, after the kill, have become a very secure item, and thus a move to their vicinity is understandable in terms of reducing distance to secure resources. But strictly speaking, the prestige of caribou has not decreased because their security has suddenly increased.

Perhaps a better structuring principle for human spatial behavior might be seen in the mobility of resources: A resource is more important in determining site location the lower its mobility. Thus, relatively immobile resources, which tend to be more reliable, would determine site location nearby, while highly mobile resources, which are often of high prestige, would be less important in the specific location of a settlement. A killed caribou, then, would be immobile, and thus draw settlement to it, while retaining high prestige by virtue of its size, scarcity, and fat content. One advantage to viewing resource mobility as the major structuring principle is that a relationship is established directly between the movement in space of a resource and the spatial behavior of the exploiting population.

This hierarchy of importance of resources to settlement decisions seems to structure a hierarchical spatial organization around a site, which can be conveniently viewed in three levels or zones. These zones tend to correspond to the immediate site location, the nearby "female" activity field, and the farther "male" field (Watanabe 1968: 75), or, to modify an existing term (Jarman 1972), "mini-," "micro-," and "macro-catchments." Provision of shelter, a view, fuel, and water seem to determine the immediate site location. That firewood and water tend to exert equal "pull" is indicated by diagrams of camps of the Pitjandjara (Tindale 1972: 242). When the water source and firewood are about a mile apart, camps are located in between, a half-mile from each. When the two resources are 2 miles apart, camps again occur in between, approximately 1 mile from each. These resources, and the factors determining shelter and a view, are not mobile, and define the specific site location. The next concentric zone seems to be determined by, and to be exploited for, resources of low mobility (and relatively high security). This is the zone usually exploited by women for vegetable foods and small game, and for the G/Wi is usually within a radius of 5 miles of camp (Silberbauer 1972: 287). The farthest zone is defined by and provides the resources of greatest mobility, that is, big game. This is the "male activity field" of Watanabe, which for the G/Wi usually extends to a radius of 15 miles (Silberbauer 1972: 290). The actual size and shape of these zones will depend on topography, density and seasonal use proportions of the various resources in the specific area. This seasonal proportion in the diet is important in determining broad regions suitable for exploitation, but the most important resource is not always the closest; the actual location depends on the relative mobilities. As cited before, for example, Tuluaqmiut camps are often situated close to trout lakes, even though fish are of little importance. Even in spring and fall, when caribou are of overwhelming importance, camps are made on large lakes (Campbell 1968: 16).

Thus, settlement location and spatial behavior of hunter–gatherers tends to show the "hierarchically nested orders of spatial functional organization" discussed by Garner (and cited previously, p. 53), and this organization is apparently structured by a hierarchical evaluation of resources according to their mobility. In the hypothetical case that two resources have the same mobility, then it might be assumed that other factors affecting security, cost, or prestige would be important: Sites would be closer to more abundant resources and to less clustered items (so that longer trips would be to the more clumped resources and provide a larger yield per trip). The effect of weight of a resource seems to work in both directions: The higher the weight, the greater the security measure—but also the greater the prestige. The higher the weight, the higher the yield per trip—but also the higher the cost of transporting this yield.

This set of generalizations may be compared to a model commonly used in settlement analyses. As Clarke (1972) states:

> Thus Zipf's principle that the volume of activity over distance declines as a function of the distance from the reference site provides a frame for archeological catchment area analysis and the Chinese Box territorial models. Even gravity models may be employed to simulate interaction between activities within sites or between sites within systems. . . . These and many other theories and measures are fundamentally relevant to the spatial information enshrined in archeological observations [p. 49].

The gravity model is an attractive device for interrelating distance, mass, and interaction and would seem especially appropriate for the analysis of differential "pulls" of various resources on a settlement. One problem with this model, however, is that it tends to be "unidentified." According to Harvey (1969):

> We may postulate a model and find that the model gives excellent results, but that it is impossible to find any firm theoretical interpretation. . . . The rank–size rule, for example, appears to have no firm theoretical interpretation, and the gravity model is, to a lesser degree, in this category. In each case several theories have been developed to explain these regularities, but the model itself does not indicate in any way what the nature of that theory should be [p. 159].

A gravity model of site location will be presented here, and its performance will be evaluated according to the principles derived from ethnographic generalization. This presentation has the purpose of demonstrating one technique of handling site location and resource "pulls" quantitatively. Its importance will be to estimate the magnitude of the differential importance of various resources, and the technique will be considered suitable to the degree that it approaches the actual principles of settlement behavior already discussed.

One formulation of the gravity model is:

$$I = \frac{M_1 M_2}{R^2},$$

where M_1 and M_2 are the mass or population of two bodies or camps; R is the distance between the two bodies or camps; and I is some measure of interaction between the two. In this application, the aim is to analyze interaction between a human population and various resources. The interaction with a resource is proportional to the dietary importance of that resource, and so:

$$I = kp,$$

where p is the dietary proportion of a resource and k is a constant. One of the interacting masses is the human population at a settlement, and this remains constant in the formulations for different resources. Thus:

$$M_1 = K \text{ (constant)}.$$

The mass of a resource cluster equals the weight of an individual times the number of individuals per cluster, or:

$$M_2 = wna.$$

The gravity model may then be reformulated:

$$kp = \frac{Kwna}{R^2},$$

and rearranged to solve for distance:

$$R^2 = \frac{Kwna}{kp}.$$

Since the interest here is on the relative magnitudes of the distances to resources, the constants can be ignored, to give:

$$R^2 = \frac{wna}{p}.$$

This model can now be applied to the hypothetical four-resource example discussed earlier. As will be recalled, the resources were:

A. A plant species.
B. A small game species.
C. A fish species.
D. A large herbivore.

From the values assigned to the attributes of these resources, the relative distances of a settlement to these resources can be determined as follows:

	A	B	C	D
wna	0.1	3.0	1.0	2200
p	40	9	19	32
R	.05	.58	.23	8.30

Thus, a site location closest to the immobile, secure plant food is defined, with fish and small game being situated farther away, and the big game species much farther away. It must be emphasized that these relative distances depend solely on dietary importance and cluster size. They do not take into account the actual spatial distribution of the resource clusters. The greater the degree of overlap, the smaller should be the differences among these distances. The smaller the overlap, the greater the differences, and the larger the concentric zones about a site. A limit on the size of these zones is set by the limits of human mobility, and if the satisfaction of the resource use schedule cannot be accomplished within these limits, then alternative solutions exist: multiple, sequential base camps during a season, and satellite extraction camps.

TABLE 12

Relative Distances to Sample Resources According to Gravity Model

Sample area	Resource			
	A	B	C	D
Area of low plant potential	.04	.45	.17	7.00
Area of large fish run	.07	.70	.42	12.50
Area of low plant potential and large fish run	.06	.61	.37	11.80
Area of low plant potential and herd migration	.04	.48	.19	11.00

The distances prescribed for the four-resource example as it was modified can also be determined, and are given in Table 12. Thus, despite varying importance to the diet, the orders of magnitude of these distances remain the same for the four resources.

The behavior of this gravity model can also be investigated by devising examples in which two resources have identical attributes except for one, in order to evaluate the effect of a particular attribute on the predicted relative distance. The calculation of these examples is presented as follows:

1. If two resources are identical except that resource 1 is more mobile than resource 2: $m_1 > m_2$, then from the method derived in the resource use subsystem, the proportional use of resource 1 is less than that of resource 2: $p_1 < p_2$. Since

$$R^2 = wna/p, \quad \text{and} \quad (wna)_1 = (wna)_2 = K,$$

then

$$(R_1)^2 = K/p_1 \quad \text{and} \quad (R_2)^2 = K/p_2.$$

Since $p_1 < p_2$, it follows that $(R_1)^2 > (R_2)^2$ and $R_1 > R_2$. Thus, a location *closer to the less mobile resource* is predicted.

2. If two resources are identical except that resource 1 has a greater density: $d_1 > d_2$, then it follows that $p_1 > p_2$, and since

$$(R_1)^2 = K/p_1 \quad \text{and} \quad (R_2)^2 = K/p_2$$

then

$$(R_1)^2 < (R_2)^2 \quad \text{and} \quad R_1 < R_2.$$

Thus, a location *closer to the denser resource* is predicted.

3. If two resources are identical except that resource 1 has a cluster size twice that of resource 2: $a_1 = 2a_2$, then in the calculation of dietary percentages:

$$\left(\frac{wnd}{m}\right)_1 = \left(\frac{wnd}{m}\right)_2$$

and the predicted proportions based on security are

$$50\%(1) \quad \text{and} \quad 50\%(2).$$

Since

$$\left(\frac{wna}{m}\right)_1 = \left(\frac{wna}{m}\right)_2$$

the predicted proportions based on low-cost yield are

$$67\%(1) \quad \text{and} \quad 33\%(2).$$

Thus, the predicted overall proportional utilization is:

$$(50 + 67)/2 = 59\%(1) \quad \text{and} \quad 41\%(2).$$

If

$$R^2 = wna/p, \quad \text{and} \quad (wna)_1 = 2(wna)_2,$$

then let

$$(wna)_2 = K \quad \text{and} \quad (wna)_1 = 2K$$

Then

$$(R_1)^2 = 2K/59 = 0.034K,$$

and

$$(R_2)^2 = K/41 = 0.024K.$$

Thus

$$(R_1)^2 > (R_2)^2 \quad \text{and} \quad R_1 > R_2.$$

Hence, a location *closer to the less clustered resource* is predicted.

4. If two resources are identical except that resource 1 weighs twice as much as resource 2: $w_1 = 2w_2$, then $p_1 = 67\%$ and $p_2 = 33\%$. Since

$$(wna)_1 = 2(wna)_2,$$

let

$$(wna)_2 = K \quad \text{and} \quad (wna)_1 = 2K.$$

Then

$$(R_1)^2 = 2K/67 = 0.03K,$$

and

$$(R_2)^2 = K/33 = 0.03\,K.$$

Thus

$$(R_1)^2 = (R_2)^2 \qquad \text{and} \qquad R_1 = R_2.$$

Hence, *weight alone seems to have no effect* on site location.

Thus, this gravity model predicts relative distances to resources, and with all other attributes equal, predicts site locations closer to:

1. Less mobile resources.
2. More dense resources.
3. Less clustered resources.

The response to mobility of a resource agrees with the structuring principle derived from ethnographic studies. The responses to resource density and cluster size agree with the assumptions about the effects of security, cost, and prestige if mobility were a constant. This gravity model, therefore, performs in agreement with the principles of settlement behavior already discussed, and may be considered one method suitable for estimating the "pull" of various resources on settlement.

In addition to the method of reconciling different goals and analyzing resource "pulls," there is another important management consideration in this subsystem. The problem of *where* to locate settlements has received most attention; the *duration* of settlements still must be discussed. Some motivations for moving camps have already been mentioned: response to a resource "pull" in another area, and exhaustion of local resources. The timing of some changes of resource "pulls" should be quite evident from the predetermined resource schedule: The change of seasons is often marked by the appearance of a nut crop, a fish run, migratory waterfowl, or by the migration of a herd of big game. Other changes are not so dramatic, but equally important in their effect on settlements. Elevational differences often determine a gradual shifting of resource foci through the differential ripening of plant foods and gradual altitudinal shifts of animals. The possibility of resource exhaustion depends on the various resource densities, the limits on human mobility, the population of the settlement, and the efficiency of harvesting activities. Hinderances to human mobility, such as deep snow or steep slopes, and aids to mobility, such as canoes and snowshoes, help to define the territory exploitable from the settlement. The harvesting efficiency depends largely on technology, that is, on devices which increase the size of a catch (nets, weirs, fences), or which extend the reach of the exploiter (traps, snares). The population of a settlement determines the dietary total, and thus the necessary caloric contributions from each resource.

Within the framework of these generalizations, there is a wide range of configurations that the actual settlement system can assume, and this range is reflected in the several classifications of settlement systems that have been published (Chang 1962; Beardsley 1956; Butzer 1971). All these classifications differentiate on the basis of a limited set of criteria: territoriality, degree of sedentarism, and degree of reoccupation of sites. Reoccupation would seem to be conditioned by the number of locations available suiting the cost–yield configuration of that season, including resource location and the existence of natural shelters. Sedentarism may be viewed as desirable (from the point of view of minimum effort for site relocation), but subject to the seasonal resource "pulls." Short-term satellite extraction camps are one attempt to widen the catchment of a location, which would help increase sedentarism by a segment of the population. But the cost of satellite camps must be weighed against the possible savings of moving the base camp. As used here, "base camp" will refer to a location (a site or series of sites with generally similar locational traits in relation to resource distribution) occupied for at least one season by all of the consuming population. A "satellite extraction camp" would be a location occupied by a segment of the consuming population (a producing population) usually for part of a season.

An example may help in the investigation of resource potential. Turning back to the Round Lake Ojibwa, during the 3-month late winter season, moose were predicted to provide 63% of the diet. Harvesting efficiency for moose hunting has been estimated at 10% for the Round Lake (Rogers 1962), and measured as 27% for the Waswanipi Cree (Feit 1973: 123). Individual caloric needs may be approximated at roughly 2000 kilocalories per day (Lee 1969: 89), or 180,000 kilocalories for a period of 3 months. The population of this winter camp averages 10 to 15 people. Thus, caloric needs of the camp population for the 3 months range from 1,800,000 to 2,700,000 kilocalories, or an average of 2,250,000 kilocalories. Of this average, 63% is 1,417,500 kilocalories, to be provided by moose. Moose supply approximately 2000 kilocalories per edible kilogram (McCance and Widdowson 1947:89), and provide about 50% of their body weight in edible material (White 1953: 396), and would therefore yield about 320,000 kilocalories per animal. Thus, the number of moose needed to provide 63% of the late winter diet is 1,417,000 divided by 320,000, or approximately 5 moose. At 10% harvesting efficiency, a catchment containing 50 moose is necessary; with an overall moose density of .04 per square kilometer, an area of 1250 square kilometers is needed. This would require a radius of exploitation of about 20 kilometers. At a harvesting efficiency of 27%, a catchment with a radius of about 12.3 kilometers is necessary. The average of these two figures is a radius of approximately 16 kilometers.

According to Rogers (1962), there are 18 winter trapping territories of the Round Lake Ojibwa, "based in part on the old areas of habitual use by particular families [p. C22]." These territories range in size from 77 to 554 square miles, and have an average area of 278 square miles, or 712 square kilometers. If this average area is represented by a circular catchment around a winter camp, it would have a radius of about 15 kilometers, which is in close agreement with that predicted from resource potential.

Discussion

The actual form of a settlement pattern must be adapted to the resource distributions of the specific area inhabited, and this general model can only elucidate the broad structural principles. It does seem possible, however, to make some general statements about environmental regularities which are important to many groups. In many arid regions, for example, the distribution of water shows a pattern of alternating spatial expansion and contraction, and the distribution of food resources tends to follow this same pattern. Consequently, the distribution of human settlements tends to follow this pattern of shifting resource "pull." Among the Pitjandjara:

> [In May and June] water supplies usually have been well replenished by summer rains, and it is the time for dispersal of the several different hordes.... Rain time is good time— everywhere is a camp.... The green herbage has attracted kangaroos, euros, and many small mammals, and in later days rabbits, so that the rewards of hunting are increased.
>
> With the ... gradual drying up of all but the most reliable waters, people turn back toward their summer refuges on the main waters. ... Many of the larger game animals and birds... are increasingly compelled to seek water, and so many fall ready victims to hunters lying in ambush near water [Tindale 1972: 234–238].

In temperate and subarctic regions, on the other hand, a regular pattern of resource shifts often follows the seasonal needs for shelter, common to both game animals and humans. In hilly or mountainous areas, for example, winter tends to drive animals down into protected valleys, and humans seeking both shelter and game will be drawn to the lowlands as well. Among the Flathead Indians, summers were spent fishing in large lakes and hunting in the mountains, while in winter the people returned to the main river valley where snowfall was lighter and the climate milder (Teit 1930). Not only topography, but also vegetational distribution—the contrast between open country and forest— can impose a pattern related to shelter. Among the Attawapiskat Cree, many families spend summers in the coastal marshes or open tundra, but in winter, they move inland to the sheltered forest (Honigmann 1961). The Dogrib often enter the Barrens in summer to hunt caribou, while winters are spent in the forest (Mason 1946). Tuluaqmiut winter camps were established "in sheltered canyons and coves, either just within the forest boundary, or in mountain valleys in the tundra zone," while summer settlements "were situated well up toward the heads of creeks or elsewhere high in the mountains, where the sheep dwell the year around and where a few scattered caribou live in the summer [Campbell 1968: 16—17]."

In addition to these shared patterns of food and nonfood resource distribution, there seem to be some general regularities in the distributions of secure and prestigious resources in different seasons. In winter, the distribution of large game tends to overlap that of plants, fish, and small game. At other times, however, the distributions of these two classes of resources may be distinctly separate. In regions where mountains occur near the coast or near large lowland lakes, big game species will usually occur in the high elevations in summer, while the more secure resources will exert a greater pull from the coast or lakeshore. Similarly, in early spring, large game commonly moves to higher elevations before the development of plant foods (or the accessibility of fish) at these heights is sufficient to pull the base camp. Another disparity in the distribution of these two resource classes can occur at the border between different vegetational zones. For the Flathead, for example, the valley forests and slopes offered much plant food, small game, and deer in some seasons, while the nearby plains were the home of bison herds which could not be exploited from the valley camps. In all these examples, a common response by hunter—gatherers is to place the base camp near the secure resources and to widen its catchment by establishing satellite extraction camps near the more mobile, high-prestige resource. The Flathead sent out hunting parties to the plains, while some of the population remained in the valley; Ainu men established hunting huts at high elevations away from the main river for bear and deer.

CHAPTER FIVE

Subsystem III: Demographic Arrangements

Goals

The focus of the decisions considered in this chapter is the arrangement of the human population in space. As Trigger (1973) states:

> An important aspect of adaptation is the distribution of population. . . . Two aspects of the distribution of population require explanation: the overall population of an area, i.e. the population density, and the actual pattern of settlement [pp. 35–36].

One of the major conclusions of human ecological studies is that population density and distribution are not automatically determined by factors of the natural environment, but rather that they represent adjustments to these factors by means of choices. The goals guiding these choices, therefore, must be examined. As in the other systems discussed, a concern for limiting effort is assumed to be important.

A primary goal of this system must be the provision of food for all members of the population. The determinants of human population density have been widely discussed. Food resource potential has been stressed, for example, in Birdsell's study relating Aboriginal population to rainfall (and its effect of food availability) (Birdsell 1953). Similarly, Baumhoff has investigated aboriginal California population densities in relation to their food resources (Baumhoff 1963). And Hayden has formulated models of hunter—gatherer population control tied to general food resource levels (Hayden 1972). The problem of calculating food availability, or carrying capacity, has been studied by Casteel, who then investigated the relationship of population density to this calculated potential (Casteel 1972). An important contrast, however, exists between the absolute carrying capacity and the capacity as culturally defined. Several authors stress the importance of cultural decisions regarding resource use to the population density attained (Damas 1969; Deevey 1968; Wobst 1974). Not only does population density appear to be maintained at a level well below that supportable by general food resources, but it also seems to be affected by other factors as well. Douglas emphasizes the importance of prestige resources to population size (Douglas 1966). The cultural definition of carrying capacity depends to a great extent on the various objectives discussed in the resource use decisions, and thus the population density should be related, not to the total biomass of foodstuffs available, but to the availability of foodstuffs in the predetermined proportions.

Given the proportions of foodstuffs to be obtained, their procurement with minimum effort significantly affects the arrangement of the population in space—not only the location, as previously discussed, but also the size of the co-residing group. First of all, through its effect on general population density, the provision of food influences group size. For a given group size, the lower the possible overall density, the larger the area which must provide support for this group. Since physical limits to mobility, together with the objective of minimizing effort, imposes limits on the size of the area exploited, this in turn defines the limit of coresident group size. Food procurement directly affects group size as well. The greater the degree of spatial concentration of resources, the greater the yield of a single site catchment as defined by distance-minimization considerations, and therefore, the larger can be the coresiding group. Conversely, the more dispersed the resources, the smaller the catchment yield, and thus the smaller the group supportable.

This relationship between the distribution of resources and group size of the exploiting population seems to be effective among many nonhuman animals:

> Dispersal is usually motivated by the scattered distribution of resources.... Most striking is the flexibility of spacing behavior observed within the same species, depending on specific situations [Kummer 1971: 221].

> Horn's study of blackbirds reveals that if the food supply is evenly distributed in a stable pattern, it is advantageous for pairs to establish territories over which they have more or

less exclusive control; if the food supply is both concentrated and shifting in location, it is of advantage for pairs to cluster together in a central location [Wilson 1971: 194—195].

Within and between species of nonhuman primates, group size shows a definite relationship to resource distribution. In the Budongo Forest, the size of chimpanzee foraging parties increases as their food supply shows larger concentrations by area (Sugiyama 1968). In a savanna—woodland environment, chimpanzees tend to concentrate when the food supply is concentrated and to disperse when food becomes scarce (Izawa 1970; Suzuki 1969). Within the forest, the food supply of herbivorous gorillas tends to be evenly distributed, while that of the frugivorous chimpanzees is more localized and concentrated; gorillas show rather small group sizes, while chimpanzees tend to show a wider range of dispersal and concentration (Nishida 1968).

Carnivores also often have a group size responsive to resource distribution:

> When large herds migrate out of the area, the pride disperses and the lionesses feed mainly on small game. When the herds return, or when the lions hunt buffalo, the members rejoin [Schaller 1972a: 42].

> As migratory herds retreat to the woodlands, [hyena] clans on the plains tend to break up. ... Hyenas from several clans may associate without animosity around a prey concentration, to dissociate again when food becomes scarce [Schaller 1972b: 39].

Changes in group size among many hunter—gatherers also show a definite relationship to the spatial pattern and abundance of resources. Among the Central Eskimo:

> The aggregation of people into large winter groupings can be argued as being strongly related to the expediencies of mauliqtug sealing. ... Fragmentation during much of the remainder of the year's cycle bears relation in a general way to the mode of hunting and the dispersal of game [Damas 1972: 283—284].

While among the Hadza:

> At the peak of the dry season, when water is scarce and when the berries ... ripen in huge quantities near to these few sources of water, the majority of the inhabitants in each of these areas may be found concentrated in a few large camps. ... In Tli'ika and especially in Han!abi, these two popular berries are less numerous and less concentrated than in Mangola and Sipunga and the people there usually remain more dispersed at the height of the dry season [Woodburn 1968: 104].

Further examples are numerous, and the following may be cited:

> [Ngatatjara] camp size is directly dependent on the abundance of local water and food resources. The aborigines tend to disperse over the countryside with individual extended

families settling near reliable water sources in drought areas, while in areas of heavy local rains larger groups tend to come together [Gould 1968: 119].

By late May, the ice is gone, fish rise in the streams, bears emerge, and migratory birds arrive from the south. In the past this period of abundance was cause for a communal gathering of numerous smaller groups [of Montagnais] on the shores of Lake Michikamau [Fitzhugh 1972: 195].

When the [Wanindiljaugwa] aborigines in former times gathered as a tribe for the annual religious ritual ... they frequently selected a spot where there was an abundance of bur-rawongs, so that the nut might be made up into bread and thus serve to maintain a large community for several weeks [Worsley 1961: 164].

In the fall and spring of the year, all Nunamiut households join together to form bands in anticipation of the seasonal migration of the caribou [Gubser 1965: 61].

The size of human groups thus seems to be strongly related to the abundance and spatial patterning of the resources to be procured. The procurement of resources in the predetermined proportions, while maximizing security, also affects decisions about group size: The larger the coresiding group, the greater the number of possible food procurers, and thus the higher the chance that *some* food will be brought into camp. Also, the larger the cooperating group of exploiters, the larger the game that could be procured (such as elephants), thus widening the potential resource base, and the greater the harvest possible of a particularly abundant resource, which might be stored for later, less secure seasons. Finally, the larger the group, the less danger there is of losing resources to predators or competing populations. These advantages of larger groups depend on the practice of sharing among the coresiding group members. The prevalence of sharing among hunter—gatherers has been well documented. An interesting observation on sharing is that, in the Siberian—Central Asian area, "food-sharing increases to the north and decreases to the south [Eggan 1968: 85]." This differential frequency of sharing may be related to the decreasing security of subsistence with latitude, paralleling the decreasing abundance and variety of food resources (Lee 1968: 42). As Leacock (1973) stresses: "The stringency of life in the north woods enforces so immediate an interdependence that sharing is a more total, "spontaneous," or "unstructured" affair than the regulated reciprocity generally obtaining in more settled societies [p. 94]." Thus, it is logical that decisions about group sizes by populations concerned with economic security should consider the advantages of group aggregation, which would tend to increase the shared resource yield.

In addition, noneconomic factors significantly influence decisions about group size. A major objective guiding these decisions must be the insurance of reproductive viability. For a population to survive, it must maintain a level of interaction such that individuals can mate and reproduce. Wobst has examined this problem extensively (Wobst 1974), and while his specific findings will be considered later, his general conclusion was that, given some assumptions about demographic structure and mating behavior, a minimum size for the mating network of hunter–gatherers can be estimated. If the individuals of such a network are uniformly distributed as individuals in space, then the cost of interacting, in terms of distance traveled, is a maximum. Conversely, if all members of a network coreside, the cost is minimized. Thus, population aggregation for low-cost reproductive viability is an important objective in decisions about group size.

Another goal that must be considered in relation to these decisions is the desire for social interaction. The importance of this desire is stressed by Damas (1969) in his discussion of the Central Eskimo. For the large groupings in winter, "Social motives for aggregation are also apparent. The winter assemblages provided opportunity for reaffirming social ties that had not been realized during much of the preceding phases of the year's cycle [p. 284]." And in discussing the fall sewing aggregations:

> Economic activities were virtually at a standstill . . . and cannot be thought of as providing crucial factors in bringing about the aggregations. . . . Rather, it is easier to imagine that the attraction of extending contacts . . . was the chief motive for joining into larger groups at that period [p. 285].

Social interaction is also important to the Mistassini:

> Except for caribou hunts, where cooperation is essential for a successful hunt, the main purpose of association is for companionship and for the education of the younger members. . . . In summary, the band is of limited significance in the lives of the Mistassini except for the social interactions it allows during the summer and the opportunity to secure marriage partners [Rogers 1972: 123].

The G/Wi, too, demonstrate social motives for aggregations:

> The band temporarily migrates as one community to the territory of an allied band. This synoecious emigration is made during seasons of plenty when conditions permit abnormally large concentrations of people. The motivation of such an emigration is social—to visit an allied band and to enjoy the company of its members [Silberbauer 1972: 296].

Again, the specific motives and functions of aggregations will not be examined here; it should be sufficient to recognize the generality of the desire for some periods of aggregation. Equally important is the realization that flexibility of group size must be maintained, not only for economic reasons of adjustment to specific resource conditions, but also for various social reasons. Such flexibility must include the allowance for group fission for conflict resolution. This model can deal only with the broad framework of economic opportunities and constraints influencing group size.

In summary, the objectives guiding decisions about population aggregation are:

1. Provision of food for the population.
2. Resource procurement in the predetermined proportions at low cost.
3. Resource procurement in the predetermined proportions with high security.
4. Insurance of reproductive viability.
5. Provision of social interaction.

Resources

In order to satisfy these objectives, decisions must consider various aspects of the interrelationship of resources and the human population. The provision of food for the population requires estimation of the carrying capacity of a region according to the cultural definition of resource needs. These needs are structured by the resource use decisions, and thus the biomass of different resources in relation to their proportional importance in the diet must be determined. For resource procurement at minimum cost, the most significant factor is the spatial distribution of resources—their general abundance and degree of concentration. The attainment of security in procurement as discussed here involves the group size of the exploiting population, as do the provision of social interaction and the insurance of reproductive viability. These last three objectives are theoretically further removed from considerations of food resources, although their actual attainment is indirectly affected by resource distribution.

Environment

Most of the factors of the environment of this system are specific features of the region inhabited and technology employed. Such features cannot be considered in a general model, but have a significant effect on the structuring of decisions. For example, the actual harvesting efficiency of a procurement activity serves as an intermediate filter between defined carrying capacity and supportable population density. Similarly, the degree of harvesting that a resource can biologically survive affects the long-range viability of the human population. The abundance and concentration of specific resources are important to cost minimization, but the actual pattern of overlap of the resources determines the realization of this goal. Since security of income has received consideration in the resource use decisions, the further significance of this goal in affecting group size depends on the general security level of the region inhabited. Marginal habitats of low resource abundance, low resource diversity, or great seasonal fluctuations in these factors would require the attachment of greater importance to security measures. In addition, the seasonal availability of a superabundance of resources provides the potential for cooperative exploitation, and in conjunction with contrasting lean periods, may provide the need for such cooperation as well. The insurance of reproductive viability depends, not only on the size of the mating network, but also on the actual population density, the area therefore occupied by the network, and the travel costs in this region as determined by topography, vegetation, snow, and water distribution. Finally, the strength of the desire for social interaction in any one season depends on the solutions of group size in other seasons, in other words, on the levels of social interaction in other seasons.

Measures of Performance

In order to estimate the culturally defined carrying capacity, it is necessary to calculate the biomass of each of the major resources. Then for each, given its proportional dietary contribution and an estimate of human caloric needs, the supportable human population can be determined. Since all the proportional utilizations must be fulfilled, the lowest figure for the population represents the maximum supportable. As an example, the data for the Round Lake Ojibwa will be used.

A rough estimate of 2000 kilocalories will serve as the daily dietary need per person. Thus, a yearly requirement of 365 × 2000, or 730,000 kilocalories per person may be assumed. As previously calculated, one moose provides approximately 320,000 kilocalories. At a density of .04 moose per square kilometer, an area of 100 square kilometers contains 4 moose, or a biomass of 1,280,000 kilocalories. Now assuming, as prescribed by the resource use decisions, that moose provide 35% of the yearly diet, then in this reference area of 100 kilometers, 1,280,000 kilocalories represent 35% of the carrying capacity. The total carrying capacity, therefore, is:

$$\frac{1,280,000}{.35} = 3,657,100 \text{ kcal}$$

The maximum supportable population, based on moose, is:

$$\frac{3,657,100}{730,000} = 5 \text{ people}/100 \text{ km}^2$$

Similar calculations may be performed for the other major classes of resources. The caloric yield of each individual can be estimated:

```
1 Beaver      = 20 kg × 4000 kcal/kg × 70% edible = 56,000 kcal
1 Fish        = 1 kg × 1300 kcal/kg × 50% edible = 650 kcal
1 Small game  = 1.6 kg × 1800 kcl/kg × 60% edible = 1,728 kcal
```

The number of individuals in 100 square kilometers, and the proportional contribution to the diet of each is:

Beaver:	130/100 km²	(.07)
Fish:	3,550/100 km²	(.23)
Small game:	13,600/100 km²	(.26)

Thus, the carrying capacity, in terms of total kilocalories available to a population, as defined by each resource is:

$$\text{Beaver:} \quad \frac{130 \times 56,000 \text{ kcal}}{.07} = 104,000,000 \text{ kcal}$$

$$\text{Fish:} \quad \frac{3550 \times 650 \text{ kcal}}{.23} = 10,032,608 \text{ kcal}$$

$$\text{Small game:} \quad \frac{13,600 \times 1728 \text{ kcal}}{.26} = 90,387,692 \text{ kcal}$$

And the population supportable according to each is determined by dividing the above figures by the dietary needs of 730,000 kilocalories per person per year, to yield:

Beaver:	142 people/100 km²
Fish:	14 people/100 km²
Small game:	124 people/100 km²
Moose:	5 people/100 km²

Thus, since the predetermined dietary contributions of all these resources must be attained, the lowest figure for population supportable represents the maximum feasible population density according to the resource use decisions. In this example, the importance of moose in the diet determines a limit of 5 people per 100 square kilometers. This and the other figures, however, are based on an assumption of 100% harvesting of the resources—an assumption which is technologically impossible and biologically not sustainable. At lower harvesting efficiencies, the size of the supportable population is also smaller. Using the larger estimate of 27% efficiency of moose hunting, a population density of 1.4 people per 100 square kilometers can be estimated.

The actual Round Lake population is 256 people in an area of 5000 square miles, or 12,800 square kilometers. The actual population density is therefore 2 people per 100 square kilometers. The predicted estimate is thus very close to the actual figure. The fact that the high-prestige moose resource is apparently the major limiting factor on population density is in agreement with Douglas' argument that people will tend to limit their populations according to prestige resources (Douglas 1966).

The goal of procurement at minimum cost determines that, other factors being equal, group size will be proportional to the abundance of spatially concentrated resources. This distribution of resources can be expressed in terms of the resource attributes previously discussed. The measure of a resource for low-cost population aggregation as used in the resource use decisions was *wna/m*. Since the abundance level of the concentrated resources is equally important in determining the *size* of such aggregations, this measure must be modified according to resource density. Thus, group size may be viewed as proportional to $(wna/m) \times d = wnad/m$. Since the total configuration of resource patterning affects groups size, this measure must be calculated for each resource. The sum of these measures in each month, then, represents a figure by which the potential for aggregation in each month can be compared.

Again, the data for the Round Lake Ojibwa will be used as an example. Using the figures for the various resource attributes presented in the discussion of resource use decisions, the value of *wnad/m* for each resource per month can be calculated. As mentioned earlier, the attributes of small game resources show either less pronounced seasonal changes, or changes whose significance to their utilization is less clear than that of other resources. As a result, these attributes of small game will be considered constant in the calculations. The values for the measures are given in Table 13, and the predicted potential for population aggregation is given in Figure 7.

The potential for population aggregation is clearly highest in the summer months (June, July, and August), according to these figures. The major determinant of this high potential is the seasonally abundant and concentrated fish

TABLE 13

Predicted Potential for Round Lake Population Aggregation

Month	Moose	Beaver	Fish	Small game	Total
			Resource		
January	53	675	300	87	1,115
February	53	650	300	87	1,090
March	44	650	357	87	1,138
April	19	675	560	87	1,341
May	11	135	1,800	87	2,033
June	7	80	31,800	87	31,974
July	7	85	25,000	87	25,179
August	10	85	25,000	87	25,183
September	30	85	5,000	87	5,202
October	28	85	1,800	87	5,200
November	27	150	533	87	797
December	32	725	417	87	1,261

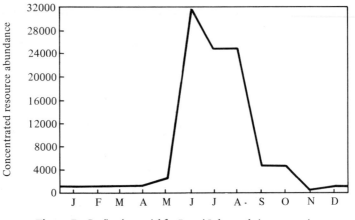

Figure 7 *Predicted potential for Round Lake population aggregation.*

resource. The actual pattern of group size changes among the Round Lake Ojibwa is one of aggregation at large lakes during the summer, and dispersal into smaller hunting and trapping groups in the other seasons. Thus, the actual pattern is in accord with the predicted potential. Among other groups, different resource configurations can induce other patterns of demographic behavior. For the Tuluaqmiut, for example, the spring and fall migrations of large caribou herds represent seasonally huge increases in groups size and overall density and a great decrease in relative mobility of this resource, so the general potential, as expressed by *wnad/m*, is extremely high in these seasons. In accord with this pattern, the Tuluaqmiut show their largest regular aggregations in these seasons (Campbell 1968).

According to the security considerations of this system, the larger the co-resident group, the greater the probability that some food will be brought into camp. The importance of this consideration, however, depends on the specific resource configurations. A measure of the overall security of an area might be expressed by a measure of resource diversity: As the diversity increases, the number of links in the food web increases, and thus the security of subsistence increases as well. Such a measure could be used to compare one region with another. More important is an estimation of the stability of the procurement schedule of each season in one area, allowing the seasonal security levels to be compared.

On this basis, an index of dominance can be calculated for the subsistence strategy of each season, allowing comparison of the stability of each seasonal strategy. The higher this index, the greater is the dominance of one procurement activity, and thus the less stable is this strategy (given the possibility of failure of any particular activity). It must be emphasized that this procedure examines the

TABLE 14

Predicted Round Lake Seasonal Resource Proportions

Resource	Months				
	JFM	AM	JJA	SO	ND
Moose	.63	.21	.14	.38	.40
Beaver	.13	.08	.01	.01	.10
Fish	.02	.07	.75	.14	.04
Small game	.11	.53	.01	.37	.36
Other	.10	.10	.10	.10	.10

stability of a strategy as expressed by diversification of activities. Hence, a large proportion of the procurement activity is viewed as potentially unstable, even though this particular activity may involve a resource judged to be very secure according to the measure used in the resource use decisions.

An index of dominance which may be used is:

$$\Sigma(ni/N)^2$$

in which ni is the importance value of each species, and N is the total of the importance values (Odum 1971: 187). For analyzing seasonal strategies, the proportional use of a resource will be used to express its importance value, and the total of these values will be 1.00.

From the calculations of the resource use schedule, five economic seasons for the Round Lake are predicted, and the proportional importance of the resources in each season (calculated by averaging the values of the component months) are given in Table 14.

The dominance indices for each resource and the sum of these per month are thus as presented in Table 15.

TABLE 15

Dominance Indices of Round Lake Seasonal Strategies

Resource	Months				
	JFM	AM	JJA	SO	ND
Moose	.3969	.0441	.0196	.1444	.1600
Beaver	.0169	.0064	.0001	.0001	.0100
Fish	.0004	.0049	.5625	.0196	.0016
Small game	.0121	.2809	.0001	.1369	.1296
Other	.0100	.0100	.0100	.0100	.0100
Sum	.4363	.3463	.5923	.3010	.3112

Thus, the dominance index is highest for the strategy of the summer season, with its great reliance on fishing. This season accordingly shows the least stable strategy, and if considerations of stability are operative in affecting group size, then the summer should witness the larger group size.

Another aspect of security which may influence group size decisions involves the existence of a great seasonal disparity in food abundance in conjunction with the technology for food storage. Given the prospect of a lean season and the capabilities of storing food, a group might choose to strive for maximum utilization of an abundant resource when possible, in order to provide for a later season. Such maximum utilization would require a large number of exploiters, and this factor might effect a population aggregation. Communal exploitation of seals, migrating caribou, and fish runs, and the big cooperative drives of rabbits or antelopes can all be seen as an attempt to maximize a seasonal procurement in order to provide greater security for later seasons. Such a tendency to maximize a seasonal yield can be an important factor modifying resource use decisions (as discussed in that section), and can affect resource proportions in both the season of abundance and the leaner periods. The evaluation of seasonal disparities might be accomplished by the same measure used for estimating the potential for population aggregation:

$$\Sigma\,wnad/m,$$

which expresses the concentrated abundance of resources.

The objective of insuring reproductive viability promotes group aggregation, when possible, up to a size equal to that of the mating network. According to Wobst, given some reasonable assumptions about demographic structure and mating behavior, the size of hunter–gatherer mating networks ranges between 175 and 475 people, with the higher figure more likely (Wobst 1974). Coresident groups of 475 hunter–gatherers are not seen, because the support of such a group requires an area too large to be exploited from one site. At a density of 2 people per 100 square kilometers, for example, 23,750 square kilometers provide support for 475 people. This would represent a circular catchment with a radius of 87 kilometers around a site, unless the resources were extremely concentrated. Assuming that a group of this size tried to remain together by moving about within this area, the local exhaustion of resources in most environments would require moves so frequent that their cost would be prohibitive. The importance of minimizing the cost of reproductive interaction, then, depends on the actual population density and the area thus inhabited by a mating network, in relation to the resource concentration and travel costs in the specific environment.

Finally, the goal of providing social interaction also prescribes a group size as large as possible in specific situations. The larger the number of coresidents, the greater the frequency and variety of social exchanges possible. The potential for coresidence is determined by the resource configuration; the desirability of coresidence in any one season depends on the general social opportunities in previous seasons. Among the Central Eskimo:

> While social factors may have influenced the size and location of summer and winter groupings, they must have been preeminent in the autumn aggregations; that is, after a period of fragmentation the desire to expand social contacts must have been the overwhelming motive for aggregations [Damas 1972: 23–24].

The strength of the desire for social interaction, then, varies according to the group size in previous seasons, as determined by the resource configurations and factors of cost and stability. The differential response of the two groups of Mbuti Pygmies to the honey season demonstrates the importance of previous group size to the immediate desires for group interaction:

> During this two-month period, the net-hunting and archer bands show a diametrically opposed socioorganizational response to essentially identical environmental conditions, namely, the abundance of the predilect honey. The net-hunting band fissions into territorially dispersed minimal sections, while the archers, usually dispersed, now unite. The honey season thus allows the net-hunters to relieve the tensions of living together by separating; conversely, the archers are given the opportunity to strengthen ties of friendship and lines of communication [Bicchieri 1969: 68].

The structuring of this goal, consequently, involves evaluating the resource potential for aggregation, not only in the immediate season, but in previous seasons as well.

Management Considerations

In the formulation of demographic decisions, all of the discussed goals are important, and each may seem most significant at any one time, depending on specific conditions. For this general model, all of the goals must be considered. On the basis of the last two goals, reproductive viability and social interaction, an initial assumption of the desirability of aggregation can be made. The limits of this aggregation, then, will be defined by consideration of the other three goals. The measures of carrying capacity can estimate population density; the changing resource potential for aggregation as expressed by $\Sigma wnad/m$ can reflect the expected pattern of group size changes according to criteria of minimum cost and stability.

Discussion

As the structure of these decisions has been presented, the major factors considered important are attributes of the natural environment. It would be expected, therefore, that identical natural environments would encourage identical or very similar solutions. Damas (1968, 1969) has examined three Central Eskimo societies who inhabit similar regions. Despite specific differences among the three in "social features," they do all show "highly similar or even identical patterns in the dispersal of people [Damas 1968:116]."

The Mbuti Pygmies, however, pose a problem in light of this general expectation Bicchieri 1969; Turnbull 1965, 1968. Within a broadly similar environment, two groups of Pygmies live, distinguished by the major hunting technology: net-hunters and archers. This technological difference is seen by the ethnographers as the major determinant of differences in group size and mobility between the two. This causal relationship is in accord with the principles of the present model. The problem arises from the successful practice of two different procurement technologies in the same environment. One would expect that one technology would eventually be more "adaptive," and thus would replace the other; in terms of decision making, one would expect that one technology would be chosen by all because it is more efficient, or secure, or both. As Turnbull (1968) says: "Regarding the Mbuti, there is no environmental reason why half of them should be net-hunters and the other half archers, although there may be some historical explanation [p. 134]." Two factors are stressed in the discussion of these technological differences: "Such differences seem more likely to be due to the human environment, that is to say, varying degrees of Pygmy association with different villager tribes [Turnbull 1965:243]. Part of the explanation may lie in the fact that in both cases, the environment is generous enough to allow alternative hunting techniques [Turnbull 1968: 135]."

Apparently, the physical environment of the two groups is very similar and rather secure, so that considerations of security and efficiency are not of paramount importance. Furthermore, the total environments of the two groups are evidently not identical, if one considers socio-political factors, the "human environment." Some differences between the two groups, as presented by Turnbull (1965) are summarized in Table 16.

From this table, one can see that the relationship of Pygmy archers to their villagers is very close and is reinforced by much ritual, as compared to that of the net hunters; the difference may be related to the differential influence of the Belgian officials.

These relationships with the villagers impose different constraints on, and stress different values for the Pygmies. The environments of the decisions for the two groups are distinctly dissimilar, and it is logical to assume that what is rational in one set of circumstances is not in another. Looking simply at the different technologies, net hunting is both more efficient and more secure and, on these grounds, would seem to be the more rational choice in the tropical forest environment. Consequently, it is interesting that the archers show the greater outside influence from non-hunting-and-gathering societies. The greater influence of, and dependence on the villagers may restrict the archers' mobility

TABLE 16

Differences between Pygmy Groups[a]

Relationship	Archers	Net hunters
Relationship with villagers villagers	Band to village	Individual to individual; family to family
Proximity to the village	Closer	Farther
Blood brotherhood with villagers	Present	Absent
Joint initiations with villagers	Identical association as the villagers	Means of acquiring status in alien community
Influence of the Belgians on the villagers	Great: bolstering of chief, who then deals with Pygmy "chief"	Less

[a]After Turnbull 1965.

away from the villages, and thus place a premium on lowering hunting yields so as not to deplete the local game. The choice of the less efficient archery, which requires smaller groups and less mobility is then a rational choice. Since this model deals with idealized and isolated hunter—gatherers, further examination of this choice is not relevant; it is sufficient to demonstrate that the two Pygmy groups do not occupy identical environments, and cannot be expected to make identical decisions.

PART TWO

ARCHEOLOGICAL APPLICATION

CHAPTER SIX

Overview of the Study

The purpose of this model is to provide an explanatory and predictive framework for archeological situations of hunter—gatherers. The model should be most useful when there is a lack of explicit evidence about subsistence and settlement patterns. Just such a situation seems to exist in the Mesolithic of southwestern Germany (see Figure 8). This area witnessed intensive investigation more than 40 years ago, with the result that two clear foci of Mesolithic occupation were delineated. In both of these foci, rather rich and dramatic findings were reported, and these have been cited frequently in subsequent discussions of the European Mesolithic (Clark 1958; Gulder 1953). One concentration occurs on the former shores of the Federsee Lake (Reinerth 1929, 1930). More than 80 "sites" have been located on these shores, most yielding only a few surface artifacts. Some, however, represent quite dense lithic concentrations, and one, Tannstock, was undisturbed by plowing and was excavated. From this site, Reinerth reported outlines of 38 oval huts, many with hearths, apparently representing at least two different occupations. No faunal material was preserved. The other major concentration of sites is located along the upper Danube, and consists of a series of cave and shelter sites yielding

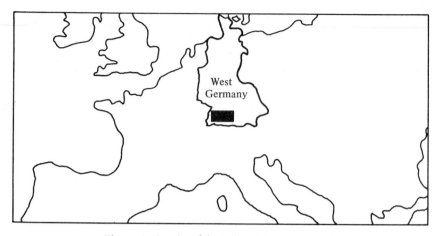

Figure 8 *Location of the study area in central Europe.*

rich stone and bone material (Peters 1934, 1935, 1941). These sites lie within 40 kilometers of the Federsee sites (see Figure 9).

Recently this region has been the focus of investigation by Wolfgang Taute of the University of Tübingen (Taute 1967a). Wherever possible he reexcavated portions of Peters' sites along the Danube. In addition, he located and excavated several new sites (Taute 1967b, 1972a,b, n.d. a). Not only was he able to provide new material and information for these sites, but he was also successful in establishing a chronology for the Mesolithic of this region based on microlithic

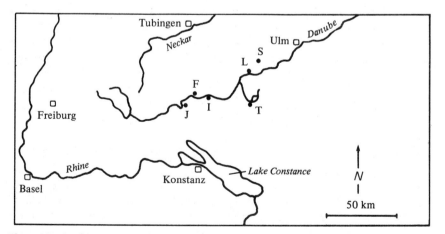

Figure 9 *Southwestern Germany with the location of major Mesolithic sites (J: Jägerhaus Cave; F: Falkenstein Cave; I: Inzigkofen Shelter; T: Tannstock; L: Lautereck Shelter; S: Schunters Cave).*

typology and supported by radiocarbon and palynological evidence. This chronological framework is most important in allowing temporal placement of nonstratified, open-air sites, such as those around the Federsee. His new findings from the older sites are especially critical, since much of Peters' and Reinerth's material was lost in the war and only poorly documented.

Discussions and interpretations of the Mesolithic economy in this region have been quite vague. Peters stressed hunting, fishing, and gathering in the Danube occupations, based on the faunal and floral material excavated, and inferred that fishing must have been more important here than up on the heights of the Swabian Alb mountains. A similarly diversified economy has been assumed for the sites around Federsee, and two authors have inferred an importance of fish and birds in the economy of these occupations greater than that of the Danube sites (Paret 1961; Rieth 1938). The actual *pattern* of subsistence and settlement in this region, however, has not been discussed, and, in particular, the relationship between these two focal areas remains unexplored. Taute touches upon this question in a general discussion of lithic assemblages of various sites. Based upon the observation that the Danube sites usually contain a greater proportion of microliths than the open-air Federsee sites, he suggests that the caves and shelters represent simply hunting camps rather than base camps (Taute 1973:144).

Implied in this suggestion is the possibility that the two foci might represent different components of a settlement system, with concomitant differences in economic activities. An implication of this interpretation is that the two areas should show evidence of intercommunication. Two such pieces of evidence seem to support this interpretation, and warrant its further investigation. First of all, the microlithic stylistic "types," as defined from the Danube sites, occur as well in the open-air sites of Federsee and other neighboring areas, and might indicate a broad zone of intercommunication (Taute, personal communication). Second, the bulk of the lithic raw material at the Federsee sites derives from the hills across the Danube, or from the Danube gravels (Reinerth 1929). While such evidence might be explained in terms of intergroup trade and communication, this explanation itself demands verification, for example, by the demonstration of a social boundary by the discontinuous distribution of some items, possibly those related to ritual and exchange (Wobst 1974). Since no such discontinuities are evident from the preserved material, the alternative hypothesis, that of different components of a seasonal round, will be investigated. The aim will be not to test this hypothesis, but rather to determine its probable implications for comparison with the archeological material.

There are various problems facing an investigation of this hypothesis. The sites themselves offer little unambiguous evidence of seasonality, and the structure of economic seasons during the Mesolithic remains unclear. Specific differences do exist among the sites—in lithics, location, and fauna—but their significance is not intuitively obvious. Lakeside occupation, for example, is known for summer (ethnographically for the Round Lake Ojibwa: Rogers 1962; archeologically for Holmegaard IV in Scandinavia: Becker 1945), for winter (again, the Round Lake Ojibwa; archeologically for Star Carr in Britain: Clark 1954), and for spring and fall (ethnographically for the Tuluaqmiut in Alaska: Campbell 1968). There is nothing inherent in the location which requires or favors one particular season of occupation. The potential of different locations must be evaluated in the framework of the total area and the changing seasonal configurations.

In order to permit this evaluation, the subsistence and settlement systems of this area will be approached through the decision model, and a necessary first task is to delineate the boundaries of the study region. A common observation in ethnographic reports is that territorial boundaries tend to follow natural boundaries, in particular, watersheds.

The Yuki habitat is, however, not defined, except incidentally, by limiting mountains and ranges, but is given in block by the drainage of such-and-such streams [Kroeber 1925: 160].

The concept of drainage and watersheds as forming territorial boundaries of tribes has proved applicable beyond California [Heizer 1958: 1].

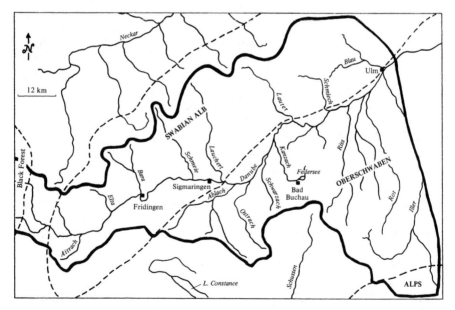

Figure 10 *Upper Danube watershed.*

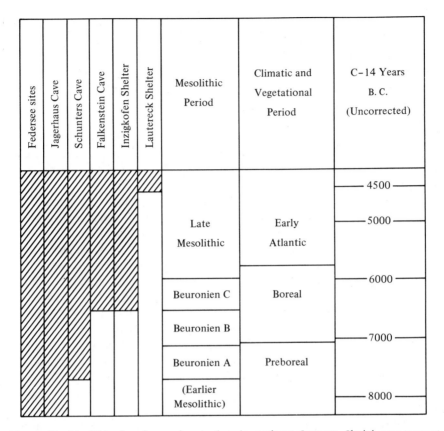

Figure 1. *Mesolithic chronology and occupations in southwest Germany. Shaded areas represent periods of occupation. (After Taute 1973.)*

Other ethnographies also substantiate this generalization:

> From existing evidence, the territories [of Indians of the Eastern Subarctic] coincided with parts or all of river basins [Rogers 1969: 43].

> For those interested in space orientation, it is noteworthy that Mathieu [a Montagnais—Naskapi informant] oriented his maps around interior water sheds [Leacock 1973: 99].

In light of this association of cultural boundaries with drainage basins, the study area here will be defined by the upper Danube watershed. The northern and western borders are thus clear: the heights of the Swabian Alb mountains and the Black Forest, respectively. The southern boundary is more problematic because no prominent height-of-land defines the watershed here; travel and communication south to Lake Constance encounters few substantial barriers. Support for the exclusion of the Lake Constance region, however, is provided by the pattern of lithic raw material distribution; the material occurring in the Mesolithic sites of Lake Constance comes primarily from the region near the town of Engen, which is in the Rhine drainage (Reinerth 1929). Since the Danube basin extends far to the east, the eastern boundary here must be rather arbitrary. The Iller River, running north into the Danube, and the Blau River, meeting this confluence from the north, form the present frontier between the states of Baden–Württemberg and Bavaria, and will serve as a convenient eastern boundary for the study region (see Figure 10). This line marks a dramatic change in the width of the watershed as well.

The time period for this study must also be specified. In his study of the postglacial chronology of the region, Taute was able to define four clear Mesolithic periods, which he called Beuronien A, B, and C, and Late Mesolithic (Taute n.d. a). These periods are associated with different types and proportions of microlithic tools. The approximate chronological positions of these periods are presented in Figure 11, along with the periods of occupation of the major Mesolithic sites. Of the primary sites to be discussed here, both Falkenstein Cave and Inzigkofen yield material from the Beuronien C and Late Mesolithic, Jägerhaus Cave and Schunters Cave contain levels showing occupation from Beuronien A through the Late Mesolithic, Lautereck Shelter has a very late Mesolithic occupation, and the Federsee sites show different combinations of the various periods. In order to allow comparisons of the sites, the period of Beuronien C through Late Mesolithic will be chosen, and thus the focus of attention will be the Boreal and Early Atlantic periods. Since the occupations at Falkenstein Cave and Inzigkofen Shelter could not be stratigraphically separated, no finer distinctions in the time period will be made.

CHAPTER SEVEN

The Study Area

The most striking aspect of this region is the contrast between the high hills of the Swabian Alb north of the Danube and the low, rolling area of Oberschwaben to the south. The distribution of physical and climatic features creates a distinct dichotomy of landscape types in this area (see Figures 12–17). The Swabian Alb is a limestone region characterized by marked karst conditions (Geyer and Gwinner 1968; Rieth 1938). Much of the rain which it receives is lost underground, resulting in quite dry conditions. Temperatures are relatively cool and high winds are common. The soils are predominantly rendzinas (Ganssen 1957). Cut into this limestone are the moist, deep valleys of the Danube and its tributaries, flanked by high cliffs and thus quite sheltered from wind. The low area of Oberschwaben is composed of morainic gravels and clays of the Würm and earlier glaciations, and contains many streams, bogs, and lakes. Brown soils predominate, and much groundwater is available. The low, moist character is in sharp contrast to the high, dry Alb.

It is certain that this contrast existed in Boreal and Atlantic times as well. No postglacial uplifts have significantly altered the topography; if Boreal temperatures in this region were somewhat higher than today (Firbas 1949),

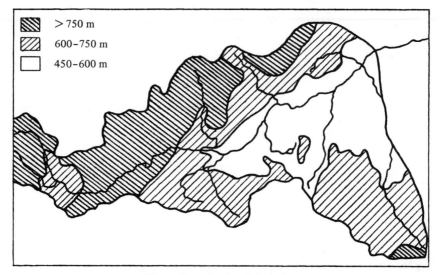

Figure 12 *Elevation of the study area.*

the temperature distribution would still have followed the elevational patterns. The Alb, running southwest—northeast, and with its highest parts in the west, would still have caught rain coming from the west and created a clinally decreasing precipitation pattern in its eastern shadow. The development of karst conditions in the Alb was certainly well advanced, as witnessed by the numerous caves already formed and inhabited during the Pleistocene. The

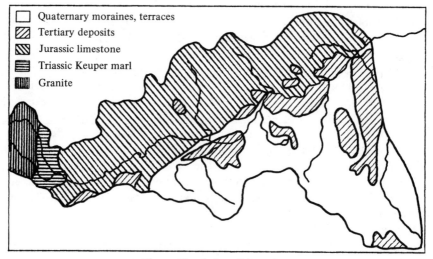

Figure 13 *Geology of the study area.*

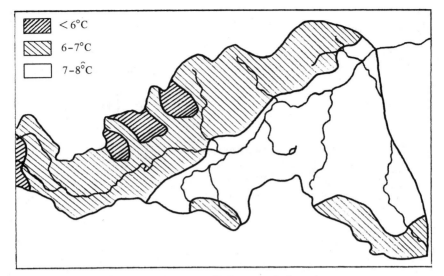

Figure 14 *Average yearly temperature in the study area.*

abundance of surface water in Oberschwaben, by contrast, was even greater
in the earlier Holocene than today. Federsee is but one of many lakes formed
as the ice retreated from this region. The Federsee basin was carved out during
the Riss advance, and subsequently dammed up by a Würm end moraine
(Wall 1961). During the Preboreal and Boreal periods, the lake was much
larger than today (Wall 1961). Many other lakes of this region have subsequently

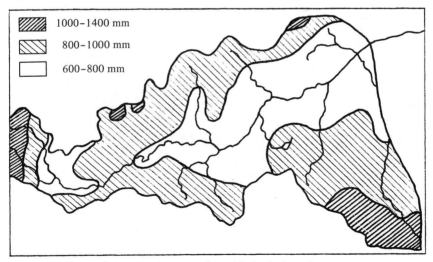

Figure 15 *Average yearly precipitation in the study area.*

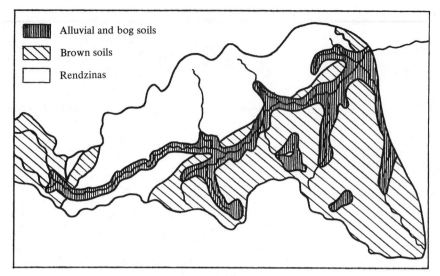

Figure 16   *Soils in the study area.*

disappeared altogether, but their location is clear from the wide distribution of peat deposits.

The basic contrast in soil types was also present in Mesolithic times. The development of rendzina soils is greatly dependent on substrates high in $CaCO_3$, such as the limestone of the Alb. The ground moraines and gravels of Ober-

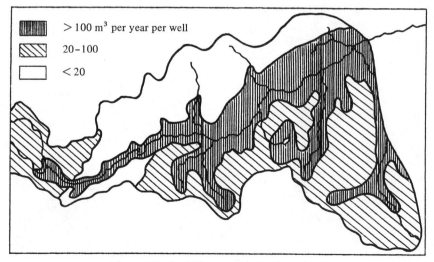

Figure 17   *Available groundwater in the study area.*

schwaben, on the other hand, probably favored the formation of pararendzinas, or in places, chernozems (during the drier Boreal), both of which usually precede the development of the brown soils which predominate today (Ganssen 1957). These soils of Oberschwaben are generally richer than those of the Alb.

One would expect that this contrast between the Alb and Oberschwaben would be reflected in the vegetational pattern as well. Such seems to be the case, both in present vegetational distribution and in reconstructions of the past. The Alb today shows mainly a forest dominated by beech and characterized by a great variety of species, including pine. Oberschwaben, on the other hand, bears a mixed forest of beech, spruce, and fir, interspersed with numerous remnant low and high moors (Figure 18). The reconstruction of past vegetational patterns rests largely on the work of Firbas (1949), and more recent studies have done little to alter his general conclusions (Frenzel, personal communication). During the Preboreal, all of south Germany carried a light pine—birch forest, with certain areas (Federsee, high elevations of the Alb) especially rich in birch (Figure 19). The upper forest limit approached that of today. Late in this period, trees of the mixed-oak forest (oak, elm, lime, ash, maple) began migrating into the area and would have been found especially along the larger river valleys. During the Boreal, and into the Atlantic periods, hazel and the trees of the mixed-oak forest showed strong increases. Hazel was most abundant in the west at high elevations, and in moist areas; it began as a shrub under pine, but may have formed true hazel forests in favored areas, displacing pine. The mixed-oak forest displaced pine on the richest soils and

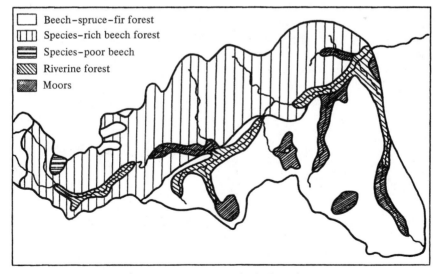

Figure 18 *Present vegetation in the study area.*

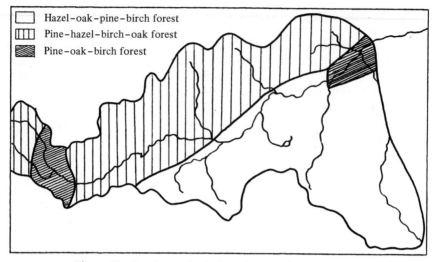

Figure 19   *Boreal vegetation in the study area. (After Firbas 1949.)*

in lower elevations. Birch was still quite abundant along lakeshores, together with willow and some alder. The upper forest limit in the Boreal was apparently somewhat higher than today. The forests were probably quite light, but there is no evidence of any large treeless areas. The rarity of alder in the Boreal would seem to indicate that lakes were not yet shrinking much, a conclusion that is supported by studies of Federsee lake levels (Wall 1961). During the Boreal–Atlantic, the Alb was probably characterized by pine–birch forests with some hazel underbrush, but only a few trees of the mixed-oak forest. Oberschwaben and the larger river valleys, on the other hand, were apparently dominated by the mixed-oak forest and hazel, with birch and willow along lakeshores, and pine only significant on the poorer soils.

The fauna of this region was evidently quite rich and diverse in Mesolithic times. Vogel (1940), and more recently Von Koenigswald (1972), have studied the spatial and temporal distribution of the animals of south Germany, based on archeological and paleontological finds. From their work, it appears that the following larger species (larger than 1 kilogram in weight) were present in the study region during the Boreal–Atlantic:

Red deer	Brown hare	Otter
Roe deer	Beaver	Wood marten
Wild boar	Brown bear	Stone marten
Moose	Wolf	Wild cat
Chamois	Fox	Lynx
Aurochs	Badger	

The differential abundance and distribution of these mammals will be considered later. Birds included various species of duck and grouse, while whitefish, carp, trout, hucho, perch, pike, and grayling comprised the major fish species. Thus, a great variety of food resources was available to a hunter—gatherer population; the pattern of their exploitation must now be considered.

CHAPTER EIGHT

Resource Use Schedule

Of these larger animal species, four will not be treated quantitatively: aurochs, moose, chamois, and brown bear. It is assumed here that these species were not sufficiently abundant during the Boreal–Atlantic to allow or warrant their regular patterned exploitation to any significant extent. Some suggestions can be made, however, about the most probable seasons of their exploitation. In south Germany, the aurochs is found in the glacial deposits of Petersfels (Mauser 1970) and Vogelherd (Hahn, Müller-Beck, and Tante, 1973), in the Mesolithic of Falkenstein Cave (Peters 1934) and Hohlstein in Bavaria (Freund 1963), and in the Neolithic of Federsee and Lake Constance (Reinerth 1929; Vogel 1940). Although in historic times the aurochs occurred in forests (Grzimek 1970), its original preferred biotope seems to have been grasslands and open parklands (Freeman 1973; Kurten 1968). According to Waterbolk (1968), Atlantic deciduous forests discouraged aurochs in northern Europe because of their shade and lack of grazing. In Denmark, the aurochs immigrated during the Younger Dryas, was numerous in the Boreal, but rare, and even absent from some areas, during the Atlantic (Degerbøl 1964). The Danish Boreal was characterized by a light hazel–pine forest, while the Atlantic saw the development of a climax deciduous forest (Flint 1971: 633). Because hazel and the deciduous trees migrated north from southern refuges during the Postglacial, however, their appearance and the development of a closed forest in south Germany occurred earlier than in northern Europe. Thus, Flint characterized the Boreal in southwest Germany, based on the work of Firbas, as a period of "hazel–elm–lime etc." forest (Flint 1971: 632). While pine was still quite abundant, as discussed previously, its focus during the Boreal–Atlantic was probably on the Alb heights. Consequently, the most favorable habitat for aurochs in this period would have been up on the dry Alb, with its light pine-dominated forest and greater grazing potential. Since aurochs, however, tended to restrict their movements to lowlands (Grzimek 1970), where the denser deciduous forest was predominant at this time, their density was probably not too great. One would expect that the Preboreal, with its overall lighter forest, and the late Atlantic and later periods, with the expansion of forest clearance for agriculture, would witness greater abundance of aurochs. Because the aurochs enters rut in August and September, and tends to restrict its movement in winter (Grzimek 1970), the consequent changes in weight, group size, and mobility would probably make their exploitation in fall and winter most desirable and efficient.

Similarly, it is probable that the Boreal–Atlantic did not offer ideal conditions for moose. This animal occurs in the late glacial site of Schussenquelle, and the Neolithic sites of Federsee and Lake Constance (Vogel 1940), but not in any Mesolithic faunas of southwest Germany. According to Peterson (1955): "The bases of a favorable habitat for moose is continual forest succession or regeneration. Moose populations apparently reach their maximum in the early stages of succession, and decrease as the forest reaches maturity [p. 153]." A survey revealed that the North American moose increases in density northward as the forest changes from deciduous through mixed to coniferous (Pimlot 1961). Based on vegetational cover, then, the most favorable habitat would have been on the Alb heights. But since moose require much surface water, the lake-rich area of Oberschwaben would probably have been the center of moose distribution, and its overall density in this denser, deciduous forest region would have been rather low. In Denmark, the moose, like the aurochs, was abundant in the Boreal, but rare, and in places absent, during the Atlantic (Degerbøl 1964). as previously discussed for the Round Lake Ojibwa, the most probable times of moose hunting, based on the animals' attributes, would be fall and late winter.

The chamois occurred in the Alb during the late glacial period, but they gradually withdrew into higher elevations as the ice retreated and temperatures rose. During the Neolithic, they were still present in the lower foothills of the Alps, and probably then, as now, occasionally wandered north in winter into parts of Oberschwaben (Vogel 1940). Thus, for most of the year, they were probably absent from the study area, and only present in small numbers during the winter. Consequently, any exploitation of this species would probably have been during the winter.

The brown bear was present in southwest Germany during the late glacial, as witnessed by finds at the sites of Petersfels and Schussenquelle, and persisted until the sixteenth century (Vogel 1940). For two reasons, however, this animal will not be treated quantitatively. First, its density is difficult to estimate, but is nowhere very high today and is likely to have been low in the past as well. Second, the importance of its habits to its exploitation is difficult to determine. From ethnographic examples, bears are hunted by different groups at different seasons: Some ignore this animal during hibernation, while others seek out the dens in winter. Late summer, during the berry season, finds bears rather localized, and many groups hunt them at this time. The spring emergence from the dens, when bears are sluggish, is another frequent period of hunting.

All four of these species, then, were probably too rare to support a significant pattern of planned exploitation. Hunting of these animals, when it occurred, is assumed to have been more opportunistic. For each, however, certain seasons would seem to have offered greater opportunities for encountering and killing them. It may be assumed that they would be pursued, once encountered, not only because of their relatively large meat yield, but also because of the probable high prestige value deriving from their size and scarcity.

The remaining major categories of food resources to be considered are: red deer, roe deer, wild boar, beaver, fish, birds, plants, and the various small game species. In estimating the weights of the animal resources, consideration must be given to age and sex differences, as well as to changes in weight which may have occurred since the Mesolithic.

In southwest Germay in modern times, male red deer range in weight from 80 to 180 kilograms (Von Raesfeld 1899). The weight of red deer stags in all of Germany today has been given as from 110 to 150 kilograms (Blase 1973), while a figure for all of Europe is 100 to 250 kilograms (Van den Brink 1957), and for the total area of distribution, 75 to 340 kilograms (Grzimek 1970). Swiss and British deer of Mesolithic times were larger than that of the present, more similar to the red deer of East Europe today (Bandi 1963; Clark 1954). The average weight of both sexes of red deer in East Europe has been reported at 255 kilograms (Southern 1964). Present female weights range from 46% (Blase 1973) to 63% (Van den Brink 1957) of male weight; a rough estimate of 55% will be used here. Applying this figure to the weight for East Europe, the stag weight would be about 330 kilograms, and female weight would average about 180 kilograms. These figures are in close agreement with those used by Clark for the Star Carr fauna of the Preboreal (Clark 1972). Based on a metrical analysis of the red deer bones of the site, he estimates an average deadweight of 190.5 kilograms for stags. Since the total weight of red deer is roughly 1.8 times the deadweight, this would represent an average stag weight of 343 kilograms, and consequently an average female weight of 189 kilograms.

For purposes of calculation, then, an average stag weight of 330 kilograms, and a female weight of 180 kilograms will be used for red deer. The average fawn weight through the year will be approximated by 100 kilograms. The proportion of fawns in a population ranges from 17 to 20%, and that of stags, from 30 to 36% (Lowe 1961). A ratio of 35% stags: 45% does: 20% fawns will be used here. Combining these age–sex proportions and the weight estimates gives an average figure for red deer weight of 217 kilograms.

The roe deer of Mesolithic times were also considerably larger than today (Boessneck 1956; Von Lehmann 1960). Present weights in Western Europe range from 15 to 32 kilograms (Von Raesfeld 1970; Von den Brink 1957), while for its total distribution, a range of 15 to 50 kilograms is cited (Grzimek 1970). From Clark's material at Star Carr, an average weight for both sexes in the Preboreal seems to be 41 kilograms (Clark 1954). Since female weight tends to average 90% of male weight (Anderson, 1953; Wandeler and Huber 1969; Blase 1973), this would represent an average male weight of 43 kilograms and an average female weight of 39 kilograms. Fawn weight will be estimated at 20 kilograms. Based on studies of modern populations, an age–sex ratio of 30% males : 35% females : 35% fawns can be estimated. Using this ratio, the average roe deer weight is 34 kilograms.

The prehistoric boar were also much larger than present animals: In the Neolithic of Switzerland, their size was comparable to present East European boar (Boessneck et al. 1963). Among present German boar, males average 150 kilograms (Blase 1973) and range up to 200 kilograms maximum (Van den Brink 1957). In east Europe, on the other hand, males range up to 350 kilograms and average 250 kilograms; females average 150 kilograms, and the young average 50 kilograms (Van den Brink 1957). From an age–sex ratio of 25% males : 35% females : 40% young (Heck 1950), an average boar weight of 135 kilograms can be calculated.

Beaver apparently have shown little diminution since Mesolithic times (Clark 1954), and hence a weight of 20 kilograms will be used for them. Similarly, many of the small game species underwent little significant change in size. Based on modern averages, the following weights will be used:

Brown hare	3.5 kg	Otter	9.0 kg
Wood marten	1.4	Badger	11.6
Stone marten	1.8	Lynx	12.0
Red fox	6.0	Wolf	38.0
Wild cat	6.5	[Jackson 1961; Southern 1964]	

The average weight of all fish can be estimated at 1.0 kilogram.

Of all the resource attributes, the animal densities are perhaps the hardest to reconstruct. The basis of estimation must be modern density figures. The use of these figures, however, is complicated not only by their great variation, but also by the many differences between the modern and prehistoric environments. In present-day Europe, the vegetational patterns have been completely altered by intensive clearance, agriculture, and forest monoculture. Most natural predators have been eradicated, and the intensity of hunting and culling varies with region and prey species. Competitive relationships are disrupted by the presence of domesticated animals. Consequently, the figures used will necessarily be only rough estimates which, it is hoped, will approximate the correct orders of magnitude.

Red deer presently inhabit a variety of habitats, from completely treeless heaths and grasslands to closed forests, from lowlands to high alpine areas. Most writers agree that this animal was originally and is primarily a woodland species (Darling 1964). Although Freeman stresses that its preferred habitat is a closed forest (Freeman 1973), many others suggest that deer show greater densities in more open forest-parkland (Blase 1973; Van den Brink 1957). According to Fleming (1972), the higher recorded densities come from more open forests. Waterbolk (1968) suggests that red deer decrease in abundance during the Atlantic period due to lack of grazing in the more closed deciduous forest. In the Swiss National Park, red deer utilize an area that is about 55% forest (Schloeth and Burckhardt 1961), but the percentage of grasses and herbs in their diet is 77% in summer and 61% in winter (Hegg 1961). The importance of grazing for German red deer has also been emphasized (Heck 1935). In addition to grasses, important items in the diet are bark, nuts, shoots, leaves, needles, mushrooms, and berries (Von Raesfeld 1899). Thus, an open and mixed forest would seem to be the habitat encouraging the greatest abundance of red deer.

As previously discussed, southwest Germany in the Boreal—Atlantic showed predominantly a mixed forest tending to become more closed and more deciduous through time. Consequently, it would have provided a habitat suitable, but not ideal, for red deer, and becoming less so as forest density and shade increased. The quality of this habitat must be kept in mind when considering red deer densities. Reported actual densities tend to show considerable agreement, as demonstrated by the figures in Table 17.

Thus, the range of densities is from .8 to 16.1 deer per square kilometer, with the higher figures for the more open or treeless areas. For the Boreal—Atlantic forests of southwest Germany, one would expect that the red deer density would be most similar to the lower end of this range: A figure of 4.0 deer per square kilometer will be used. This approximates the figure used by Clark for calculating deer biomass for the Star Carr population—despite his statement to the contrary (Clark 1972: 26—27).

Roe deer thrive in mixed woodlands with much underbrush and numerous

TABLE 17

Some Reported European Red Deer Densities

Density/km^2	Area	Source
14.8–16.1	Scotland (treeless island)	Lowe 1961
3.6–10.2	Scotland (all of mainland)	Lowe 1961
2.5–8.3	Scotland (deer forests)	Darling 1964
6.0	Germany (deer forest)	Baumann personal communication
5.0–6.0	Germany (deer forest)	Stahl 1972
.8–4.8	Germany (deer forest)	Ueckermann and Goepel 1973
4.5–5.8	Swiss National Park	Burckhardt et al. 1961
1.4–4.5	Eastern Carpathians	Philipowicz 1961

small clearings (Anderson 1962). Although, like the red deer, they can also adapt to treeless regions (Prior 1968), they tend to show very low densities in such areas, as opposed to red deer. On the other hand, completely closed forests also show much lower densities than the ideal habitat of mixed forests and clearings, as Darling (1964) makes clear. In contrast to red deer, roe are mainly browsing animals, preferring to feed on the shrub layer rather than grasses (Prior 1968). From rumen analysis, 62% of roe deer stomach content was parts of trees and shrubs (Holloway and Jungius 1973). Because of the importance of browse in the diet, deciduous woodlands with more undergrowth are preferred to coniferous forests (Roedelberger *et al.* 1960). In addition to the leaves and shoots of trees and shrubs, other important dietary items are twigs, nuts, grasses, and mushrooms (Von Raesfeld 1970).

According to research in game preserves, the suitability of an area as a habitat for roe deer increases with the length of the forest–clearing borders, the variety of tree species, and the proportion of deciduous trees, especially oak (Von Raesfeld 1970). The trends of forest development during the Boreal–Atlantic, then, were in conflict. The spreading mixed-oak forest, with its nut crops and abundant undergrowth, would have favored roe deer; the gradual closing of this forest, on the other hand, was unfavorable.

Important considerations, other than the vegetational pattern, that affect the density of roe deer are its competition with other herbivores and its culling by predators. Roe would have been in competition with both red deer and boar, especially for the nut crops of hazel and oak, and for browse in winter. Apparently, however, roe do not compete well with these species (Grzimek 1970; Hegg 1961) and their density would accordingly be lowered. Similarly, in relation to red deer and boar, roe deer seem to suffer much greater predation losses. The wolf, lynx, and fox, which prey on all three herbivores, take a greater proportion of the smaller roe. In addition, roe suffer predation by such animals as badger, marten, ermine, wildcat, and even boar. In the Mesolithic environment, then, roe deer would probably have shown densities lower, relative to red deer and boar, than today.

Table 18 gives some of the recorded densities of roe deer: The range of these figures is from 1 to 40 per square kilometer. In many cases, where they occur together, roe deer show a density from 2 to 5 times that of red deer, which is to be expected from the roe deer's much smaller body size. A figure of 12 per square kilometer, or 3 times that of red deer, will be used here.

Wild boar seem to have been most associated with rather closed forests, although in modern times they frequent agricultural fields. The ideal habitat is moist woods, especially mixed deciduous forests (Heck 1950). Higher elevations tend to be avoided by boar more than by deer, primarily because of the high snow cover. Coniferous forests, open grasslands, and dry soils all comprise unfavorable boar habitats. The major foods of boar are nut crops (acorns, hazelnuts, and beech nuts), followed by roots, herbs, grasses, worms, larvae, and occasional small mammals (Grzimek 1970). The boar's major predators are wolf and lynx, and occasionally fox and bear. The primary competition is with the other herbivores over the nut crops, but the boar appears to do very well in such competition; with the eradication of the main predators, boar populations often increase rapidly (Grzimek 1970).

Density figures for boar are not widely reported. Fleming mentions some extremely high figures—40 to 190 per square kilometer in eleventh century Essex (Fleming 1972). In one preserve in south Germany, present boar density is approximately 3 per square kilometer (Baumann, personal communication). This is on a red deer preserve, however, where boar are actively discouraged, so this figure is abnormally low. On a central German preserve, a density of 20

TABLE 18

Some Reported European Roe Deer Densities

Density/km^2	Area	Source
2.5	Bohemia (heavily wooded)	Darling 1964
10.0	France (deer forests)	Darling 1964
15.0	Germany (deer forest)	Ueckermann and Scholz 1970
7.0–15.0	Germany (deer forest)	Von Raesfeld 1970
10.0–20.0	Germany (deer forest)	Anderson 1953
15.0	Germany (deer forest)	Stahl 1972
28.7	England (uncontrolled community)	Prior 1968
11.0–21.2	England (less attractive woods)	Prior 1968
21.0–31.0	Denmark (deer forests and fields)	Anderson 1953
1.0–40.0	Switzerland (deer forest)	Burchkhardt et al. 1961

boar per square kilometer is reported, but this is said to be rather high and to have contributed to the outbreak of a disease epidemic among the boar (Sprecker 1969). The Atlantic forest would have offered a very favorable habitat for boar; the drier and more pine-dominated Boreal forest would have been less suitable. The density figure used here will be 12 per square kilometer, a rough average of the two German values reported for today.

The water area of Germany is approximately 2% of the total area, with most of it distributed in the previously glaciated north and east (Helfer 1949). In southwest Germany, the old morainic area of Oberschwaben is also quite water-rich, while the Alb is one of the driest regions in all of Germany. The study area is composed of about 50% of each of these two extreme regions, and thus the percentage of water in the study area probably approximates the national average of 2%, with the Alb having very little surface water, and Oberschwaben showing perhaps almost 4%, similar to Ontario (Rostlund 1952: 65). Because the beaver is so dependent on surface water, it would have occurred primarily in Oberschwaben, and there, perhaps, with a density similar to that in Ontario today (1.3 per square kilometer). Since it would have been virtually absent from about 50% of the study area, its overall density should have been roughly half of the above figure, or .65 per square kilometer.

The estimation of the fish resource density can follow two approaches. The first is by analogy with the work of Rostlund on North America (Rostlund 1952). The study area comprises the very upper end of the Danube Valley, which has no major anadromous fish. By comparison, then, this region should most closely resemble the upper Mississippi and Ohio Valleys, which, according to Rostlund, have an average annual production of 200 to 300 pounds of fish per square mile of total area. The second approach derives from reports on commercial harvests in south Germany. Report on the fisheries' catch in the German Danube indicate an average of 45 kilograms per hectare of water (Busnita 1967: 113). Assuming an average of 2% water area, this represents a catch of approximately 500 pounds per square mile of total area. In Rostlund's figures, commercial catches often comprise about 75% of his estimated annual production. Applying this ratio to the Danube data, annual production would be 667 pounds per square mile of total area. In North America, such high productivity is approached by the Great Lakes area, and surpassed only by the Atlantic and Pacific anadromous regions. The most important fish of the Danube fishery in Germany are several cyprinids which spawn in rather large schools; these apparently form a resource equal to the Great Lakes whitefish in importance. Since productivity of a river system tends to decrease up toward its headwaters, the portion in the study region would be less productive than the lower reaches in Bavaria. Consequently, a slightly lower figure, perhaps 550 pounds per square mile, should be used. This is equivalent to 98 kilograms per square kilometer, and assuming an average fish weight of 1.0 kilogram, this represents a fish density of 98 per square kilometer.

The density of the various small game species must be approximated from several modern sources (Holloway and Jungius 1973; Jackson 1961; Southern 1964). From these density estimates and the consequent biomasses, a figure for the density and weight of an average small game species can be calculated (see Table 19).

Thus, a square kilometer contains approximately 103 small game animals, each of which weighs $372/103 = 3.6$ kilograms average.

As nonfood products, red deer provide usable hides and large antlers, and beaver can supply pelts and large incisors (often used as chisels or knives). Roe deer hides would certainly be useful, while their antlers are generally too small to be very valuable. Boars' tusks appear to have been utilized as tools, and the various small game species provide useful pelts. Fish supply little in the way of useful nonfood products, although fish teeth jewelry is known for the Mesolithic. The value of n, the nonfood yield factor, can thus be approximated for each resource: red deer and beaver, 1.1 roe deer, boar, and small game, 1.05, and fish, 1.0.

The size of groups of red deer varies with sex, season, and vegetational cover. During most of the year, the sexes tend to remain separate, coming together primarily during the fall rut (Heck 1935). This separation of the sexes appears to be pronounced in heavily wooded conditions, but less so in open areas (Lowe 1966). Group size of both sexes also seems to be larger in regions of great eleva-tional differences which promote significant altitudinal migrations. Thus, among red deer in the Carpathians, groups of 100 to 200 are seen (Szederjei 1962), while in Holland, most groups are composed of 5 or less deer (Lowe

TABLE 19

Small Game Attributes

Species	Weight (kg)	Density/km^2	Biomass kg/km^2
Brown hare	3.5	100.00	350.0
Wolf	38.0	.13	4.9
Red fox	6.0	.75	4.5
Badger	11.6	.75	8.7
Otter	9.0	.02	.2
Wood marten	1.4	.25	.4
Stone marten	1.8	.25	.5
Lynx	12.0	.10	1.2
Wildcat	6.5	.25	1.6
Sum	—	102.50	372.0

1966). Among North American wapiti, average group size in summer and fall is about 21; winter groups are larger, and often number into the thousands (Martinka 1969; Altmann 1952, 1956). Old World red deer, by contrast, tend to show consistently smaller groups (Milne 1958). In Central Europe, male groups usually consist of from 1 to 10 deer; female young nursery groups are larger, averaging 4 to 30 (Grzimek 1970; Heck 1935; Schloeth 1961; Von Raesfeld 1899). Average male group size, then, will be estimated at 6, and that of females and fawns at 17. Allowing for the sex ratios, the average red deer group size would be about 13.

Roe deer, by contrast, show much smaller groups which are more stable through the year (Prior 1968; Von Raesfeld 1970). These are primarily family groups: The sexes show little separation. Group size usually ranges from 2 to 10, although groups of up to 50 are known (Grzimek 1970; Kurt 1966; Milne 1958). An intensive study of roe deer social behavior in Switzerland revealed an average group size of 1.4 to 3.5 through the year (Kurt 1968). A figure of 2.5 will be used here.

Boar group size is quite variable during the year. Most of the time, males are solitary, but during the rut in November and December, they join the female groups. Usually 2 to 3 females plus their young (6 to 12 per female) form groups (Haber 1961), and thus these groups range from 6 to 50. Apparently the most common size is from 10 to 30 (Heck 1950). Combining these averages with the approximate sex ratios, an average boar group size of 13.5 through the year may be estimated. Beaver group size will again be approximated by 5, the small game species by 2, and fish by 3 (slightly larger than was estimated for Canada, because of the importance of the schools of the cyprinids).

Figures expressing mobility of the resources will be estimated in relation to those figures used for the Round Lake resources. Beaver, small game, and fish will be assumed to show the same relative mobilities as in Canada: 1.0, .2, and .05 respectively. Moose was estimated to have a mobility of 1.15; since roe deer show very similar habits but are not so tied to open water, their mobility will be set at 1.2. Boar and red deer are much more mobile than roe deer, frequently traveling many kilometers in a day. Because red deer, in addition, may undertake long altitudinal migrations, they must be considered the most mobile resource. Red deer mobility will be estimated at 1.5, that of boar as 1.4.

Having formulated these estimates for the resource attributes (Table 20), the calculation of expected proportional utilization can be performed (Table 21).

Thus, the expected resource proportions can be estimated. Two resource categories, however, have been ignored until now: plants and birds. Since quantitative data for these is quite difficult to estimate for Mesolithic times, their proportional importance must be approximated by analogy with ethnographic groups, with consideration given to the Boreal–Atlantic in southwest Germany. In the coniferous forest regions of North America, plants vary in importance

TABLE 20

Southwest German Mesolithic Resource Attributes

Resource	Weight	Nonfood	Aggregation	Density	Mobility
Red deer	217.0	1.10	13.0	4.0	1.5
Roe deer	34.0	1.05	2.5	12.0	1.2
Boar	135.0	1.05	13.5	12.0	1.4
Beaver	20.0	1.10	5.0	0.65	1.0
Fish	1.0	1.00	3.0	98.0	.05
Small game	3.6	1.05	2.0	103.0	.20

from 0 to 20% of the hunter—gatherer diet (Lee 1968). Among the Flathead Indians of the Plateau and the Wintu and Achomawi of interior California, who live in areas of mixed woodland—grassland rich in nut crops, roots, and berries, 30% is the proportion of plants in the diet, although much higher values are known for richer areas of California. In southwest Germany, it is probable that plant foods became more important through the Mesolithic, as species recolonized the area and the pine—birch community gave way to hazel and the mixed-oak forest. As an approximation, it may be estimated that plants formed 20% of the diet in the mixed forest of the Boreal—Atlantic.

South Germany receives many scattered flocks of migratory waterfowl in the spring and fall, but is not part of a compact flyway. Some of these birds stay the winter, and fewer spend the summer in this area (Hölzinger 1970; Ricard 1969). The major regions frequented by these waterfowl are Lake Constance and the upper Rhine, while small lakes such as Federsee, and the broader, marshy areas of the Danube, receive far fewer. Various species of grouse inhabit the region year-round, some around the lakes and marshes, and others in the higher, dry Alb (Hölzinger 1970; Haas 1965). Because of the scattered distribution, rather low abundance, and short duration of presence of many of the species, it is improbable that birds formed a significant component of the diet; a figure of 2% will be used here.

TABLE 21

Predicted Partial Resource Utilization: Southwest German Mesolithic

Resource	wna/m	Percentage wna/m	wnd/m	Percentage wnd/m	Average percentage
Red deer	2069	56	637	10	33.0
Roe deer	74	2	357	6	4.0
Boar	1367	37	1215	20	28.5
Beaver	110	3	14	—	1.5
Fish	60	2	1960	32	17.0
Small game	38	1	1947	32	16.5

Thus, plants and birds together will be assumed to have comprised 22% of the total diet; the remaining resources would consequently have formed 78%, and their percentages, as calculated above, must be multiplied by this figure. As a result, the expected proportional contributions of the food resources to the Mesolithic diet would be as presented in Table 22.

In order to calculate the seasonally changing patterns of resource utilization, the behavior of the resource attributes through the year must be examined. As discussed previously, the most important factors influencing attribute changes are birth, rut, and the summer—winter dichotomous availability of food. For red deer, most births occur in May and June, and rut normally takes place in September and October. Stags attain their highest weights just before rut, but since they eat very little during the breeding period and expend much energy in defensive and combative behavior, they lose considerable weight by the end of rut (Von Raesfeld 1899; Heck 1935). Their lowest weight is in late winter. Females, on the other hand, are at their best weight in late fall, after rut, and show a secondary weight peak just before birth. The male groups tend to be largest in late winter and late summer; in spring and just before rut, these groups break up. During rut, they join with and defend a number of females, and these aggregations may be larger than any exclusively male groups, especially in heavily wooded regions. Female groups are also at a maximum in late winter, when they tend to concentrate in low-lying areas. During the spring calving period, female groups break up, to regroup somewhat once the newborn fawns can travel. The contrast between the winter concentration and summer dispersal of red deer is evident from maps of their distribution in Norway (Clark 1972) and central Germany (Schwerdtfeger 1968). The pattern of mobility shows a similar sharp contrast: During the winter concentration, mobility is quite

TABLE 22

Expected Dietary Importance of Resources in the Southwest German Mesolithic

Resource	Percentage of yearly diet
Red deer	26
Roe deer	3
Boar	22
Beaver	1
Fish	13
Small game	13
Birds	2
Plants	20

restricted, while in summer, quite large distances may be traveled. During rut, mobility is also relatively restricted.

The nonfood yields of red deer, being strongly dependent on the condition of the antlers, is higher from September to March, when antlers are carried and free of velvet. Density will be treated as constant. Thus, the pattern of the changing attributes for red deer, taking the age—sex ratios into account, may be approximated as follows:

Red deer attribute	J	F	M	A	M	J	J	A	S	O	N	D
w	205	197	209	218	207	203	221	230	242	216	225	218
a	21.7	21.7	21.5	11.4	4.9	5.7	12.3	14.1	10	10	11.6	11.4
m	1	1	1	1.5	1.7	2	2	2	1.3	1.3	1.7	1.5
n	1.15	1.15	1.15	1.05	1.05	1.05	1.05	1.05	1.15	1.15	1.15	1.15

From these values, the pattern of scores for each of the two goals can be determined:

Goal	J	F	M	A	M	J	J	A	S	O	N	D
wnd/m	944	908	960	612	512	428	464	484	856	764	608	668
wna/m	5121	4926	5160	1744	627	610	1427	1706	2140	1910	1763	1904

And the fraction of the total in each month is:

Goal	J	F	M	A	M	J	J	A	S	O	N	D
wnd/m	.12	.11	.12	.07	.06	.05	.06	.06	.10	.09	.07	.08
wna/m	.18	.17	.18	.06	.02	.02	.05	.06	.07	.07	.06	.07

The average of these two figures for each month, and thus the proportional distribution of the red deer utilization is:

	J	F	M	A	M	J	J	A	S	O	N	D
Red deer	.15	.14	.15	.065	.04	.035	.055	.06	.085	.08	.065	.075

The predicted distribution of red deer utilization is shown in figure 20.

Roe deer show similar patterns of behavior, but their attributes tend to vary within a smaller range. Births occur in May and June, and rut takes place in August and September. The rut is rather subdued, so that the male weight loss is not so great; also, because of the earlier timing of rut, the male has longer to regain weight before winter (Wandeler and Huber 1969). Antlers are free of velvet in April and shed in October, on the average. In winter, roe tend to be

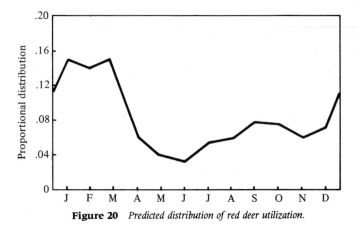

Figure 20 *Predicted distribution of red deer utilization.*

more concentrated and less mobile than in summer (Kurt 1968). Allowing for sex ratios, the attribute behavior can be estimated:

Roe deer attribute	J	F	M	A	M	J	J	A	S	O	N	D
w	35	32	35	31	27	31	34	33	35	37	37	35
a	4	4	4	3	2	1.5	1.5	1.7	1.7	2	2	3
m	1	1	1	1.2	1.2	1.4	1.4	1.2	1.2	1.3	1.2	1.1
n	1	1	1	1.09	1.09	1.09	1.09	1.09	1.09	1.09	1	1

The scores and fractions for each of the goals, and the proportional use of roe deer are:

Goal	J	F	M	A	M	J	J	A	S	O	N	D
wnd/m	420	384	420	336	288	288	312	360	384	372	372	384
	.10	.09	.10	.08	.07	.07	.07	.08	.09	.08	.08	.09
wna/m	140	128	140	84	48	36	39	51	54	62	62	96
	.15	.14	.15	.09	.05	.04	.04	.05	.06	.07	.07	.10
Roe deer	.125	.115	.125	.085	.06	.055	.055	.065	.075	.075	.075	.095

The predicted distribution of roe deer utilization is shown in Figure 21.

Boar enter rut primarily in November and December, and births occur from February to May (Heck 1950). Males tend to be solitary except during rut, when they join the female groups. In addition to the rut concentration, secondary aggregations, mainly of the female–young groups, occur in late winter and in fall with the nut ripenings. Female dispersal is greatest in spring during birth. Mobility is lowest in late winter, rather high in summer, and may be greatest during fall, when boar will often travel many kilometers to concentrations of nut crops. Nonfood yields and density will be treated as constants. Consequently, the pattern of attributes, scores, and fractional scores may be estimated:

Boar attributes	J.	F	M	A	M	J	J	A	S	O	N	D
w	149	125	126	95	102	118	128	139	147	161	165	160
a	14.5	14.5	14.5	5.8	5.7	11.9	11.8	11.6	15.1	15.1	21	21
m	1	1	1	1.4	1.5	1.6	1.6	1.6	1.8	1.8	1.2	1.2
Goal												
wnd/m	780	655	660	355	355	390	420	455	430	470	720	700
	.12	.10	.10	.06	.06	.06	.07	.07	.07	.07	.11	.11
wna/m	2262	1900	1914	412	405	928	991	1056	1299	1419	3024	2940
	.12	.10	.10	.02	.02	.05	.05	.06	.07	.08	.16	.16
Boar	.12	.10	.10	.04	.04	.055	.06	.065	.07	.075	.135	.135

The predicted distribution of boar utilization is shown in figure 22.

The fisheries' catch in the German Danube includes about 70% carp, bream, barbel, and other cyprinids, 5% salmonids, and 5% pike (Busnita 1967, 121). Because the cyprinids tend to show the largest schools, it is probable that their catch surpasses their proportional importance. These cyprinids are spring spawners, mainly from April to July (Schindler 1953). The salmonids of this region include spring spawners (grayling, hucho) and fall spawners (trout). Pike spawn in the spring, especially April and May. Other important fish in this area are perch and catfish, both of which are spring spawners. In nearby Lake Constance, the most important fish commercially is the true whitefish, but this species seems to be rare in the Danube drainage (Kiefer 1972). During a recent severe winter, many of the Federsee fish were killed by freezing: census of the bodies revealed about 50% cyprinids and 50% catfish, but this sample is apparently biased toward those fish living in the shallows (Haas 1964). Thus, the majority of the fish in the study area spawn in the spring, with May apparently the peak month; a small proportion spawn in the fall, from September to December. Fish

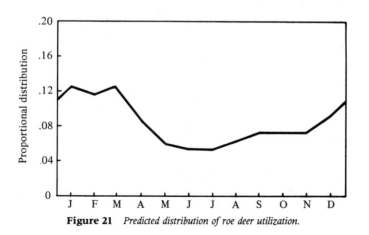

Figure 21   *Predicted distribution of roe deer utilization.*

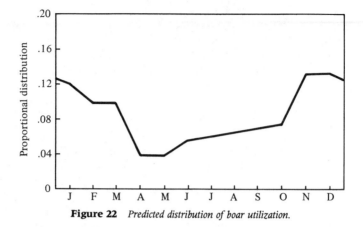

Figure 22   *Predicted distribution of boar utilization.*

attain their best weights just before and during spawning, and at this time their group size is largest and their mobility least. The spring spawners tend to remain rather inactive in shallow water during the summer and into early fall.

The estimation of the fish attributes must be very rough, but based on the above discussion, the following attributes, scores, and fractional contributions may be approximated for the general fish resource.

Fish attributes	J	F	M	A	M	J	J	A	S	O	N	D
w	.6	.7	.8	1.2	1.5	1.4	1.3	1.3	1.4	1.1	.9	.8
a	1	1	2	4	6	5	5	5	5	1	1	1
m	.08	.07	.06	.04	.02	.03	.03	.03	.03	.06	.07	.07

Goal												
	675	900	1197	1980	6750	4203	3897	3897	4203	1647	1161	1026
wnd/m	.02	.03	.04	.09	.21	.13	.12	.12	.13	.05	.04	.03
	8	10	27	120	450	234	217	217	234	18	13	11
wna/m	.01	.01	.02	.08	.29	.15	.14	.14	.15	.01	.01	.01
Fish	.015	.02	.03	.085	.25	.14	.13	.13	.14	.03	.025	.02

The predicted distribution of fish utilization is shown in Figure 23.

The distribution of beaver utilization will be estimated as was calculated for the Round Lake Ojibwa; the altered density figure does not change the pattern of scores. Since birds are in greatest abundance during the spring and fall migrations—March–April and October–November are the peak periods—their utilization will be defined as equally distributed among these 4 months, with their significance at other times being negligible. Similarly, the differential distribution of plant utilization cannot be estimated, and so will be assumed to be equally distributed from April to November.

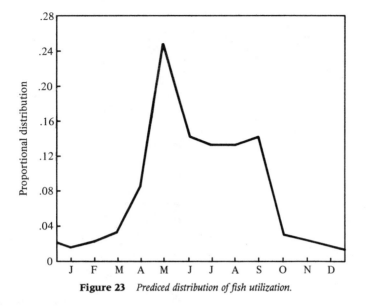

Figure 23 *Prediced distribution of fish utilization.*

In order to calculate the distribution of the contribution of each resource, these figures representing the patterned utilization of each must be multiplied by its total percentage of the yearly diet (see Table 23).

Since each month contains 1/12, or .083, of the yearly diet, small game use will be calculated so as to bring each monthly total up to the figure shown in Table 24 (see also Table 25).

TABLE 23

Predicted Proportional Resource Contribution to Total Yearly Diet of the Southwest German Mesolithic

Resource	Month											
	J	F	M	A	M	J	J	A	S	O	N	D
Red deer	.039	.036	.039	.017	.010	.009	.014	.016	.022	.021	.017	.020
Roe deer	.004	.003	.004	.003	.002	.002	.002	.002	.002	.002	.002	.003
Boar	.026	.022	.022	.009	.009	.012	.013	.014	.015	.017	.030	.030
Beaver	.002	.002	.002	.002	—	—	—	—	—	—	—	.002
Fish	.002	.003	.004	.011	.033	.018	.017	.017	.018	.004	.003	.003
Birds	—	—	.005	.005	—	—	—	—	—	.005	.005	—
Plants	—	—	—	.025	.025	.025	.025	.025	.025	.205	.025	—
Sum	.073	.066	.076	.072	.079	.066	.071	.074	.082	.074	.082	.068

TABLE 24

Predicted Proportional Contribution of Small Game to Total Yearly Diet

Resource	J	F	M	A	M	J	J	A	S	O	N	D
Small game	.010	.017	.007	.011	.004	.017	.012	.009	.001	.009	.001	.015

TABLE 25

Predicted Distribution of Small Game Utilization of the Southwest German Mesolithic

Resource	J	F	M	A	M	J	J	A	S	O	N	D
Small game	.09	.15	.06	.10	.04	.15	.11	.08	.01	.08	.01	.13

The predicted distribution of small game utilization is shown in Figure 24.

From these figures expressing the proportional contribution to the total yearly diet, the relative monthly importance of each resource can be calculated (Table 26 and Figure 25). An examination of the configurations of resource proportions reveals four economic seasons, with two further possible subdivisions. That is, there seem to be at least four general time periods which differ in their proportional importance of the various resources. The first of these is composed of the late winter months, January through March, with a preponderance of red deer, followed by boar, then small game. April seems to stand alone as a transitional month, with the big game declining in importance, plants and fish increasing, and birds and small game also significant. The summer months of May through August are similar in their emphasis of plants and fish and their relatively low importance of big game. September through December show an emphasis of big game during rut—first red deer, then boar—while fish and plants are declining

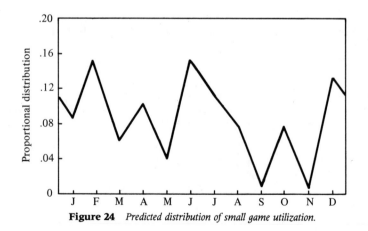

Figure 24 *Predicted distribution of small game utilization.*

TABLE 26

Predicted Resource Contributions to Monthly Diets of the Southwest German Mesolithic

Resource	Month											
	J	F	M	A	M	J	J	A	S	O	N	D
Red deer	.47	.43	.47	.20	.12	.11	.17	.19	.27	.25	.20	.24
Roe deer	.05	.04	.05	.04	.02	.02	.02	.02	.02	.02	.02	.04
Boar	.31	.27	.27	.11	.11	.14	.16	.17	.18	.20	.36	.36
Beaver	.02	.02	.02	.02	—	—	—	—	—	—	—	.02
Fish	.02	.04	.05	.13	.40	.22	.20	.20	.22	.05	.04	.04
Birds	—	—	.06	.06	—	—	—	—	—	.06	.06	—
Plants	—	—	—	.30	.30	.30	.30	.30	.30	.30	.30	—
Small game	.11	.18	.07	.12	.05	.18	.13	.10	.01	.10	.01	.16

in importance. The summer season might be further subdivided between May and June, because of the great emphasis on fish during the May spawning. Similarly, the fall—early-winter season might be divided into two parts: September—October aimed at red deer in rut and fall-spawning fish, and November—December focused on boar in rut. Whether these subdivisions have any relevance to site location or population arrangement depends on the changing

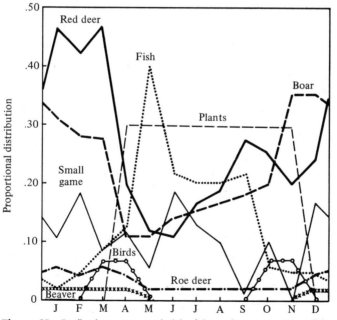

Figure 25   *Predicted resource use schedule of the southwest German Mesolithic.*

TABLE 27

Predicted Seasonal Resource Percentages: Southwest German Mesolithic

Resource	Season					
	JFM	A	M	JJA	SO	ND
Red deer	46	20	12	16	26	22
Roe deer	5	4	2	2	2	3
Boar	28	11	11	16	19	36
Beaver	2	2	—	—	—	1
Fish	4	13	40	21	14	4
Birds	2	6	—	—	3	3
Plants	—	30	30	30	30	15
Small game	12	12	5	14	6	8

spatial distribution of the pertinent resources, and their consequent differential spatial "pulls" (see Tables 27 and 28).

There is no ethnographic record of southwest Germany with which this proposed scheme of economic activities may be compared. The best basis for comparison, therefore, should be provided by a hunting-and-gathering group living in similar conditions and utilizing similar resources. The Salishan Indians of the North American interior represent rather similar groups for whom some economic information is available (Teit 1930; Turney-High 1937). These groups include the Flathead, Okanagon, and Coeur d'Alene Indians of western Montana, Idaho, and eastern Washington. The country ranges from 1000 to 3000 meters in elevation, and the vegetation included mixed forests dominated by cedar, hemlock, fir and pine, some dry grasslands, and subalpine communities. Salmon reach the region in the Pacific drainage, but the runs are quite weak east of Washington. Game animals include wapiti, mule deer, mountain sheep, bear, and many smaller species. A variety of vegetable foods are available, including camas root, berries, and hazelnuts. Antelope are important in the grasslands of eastern Washington, and bison in the grasslands of western Montana. With the introduction of the horse, bison became important to the Flathead,

TABLE 28

Predicted Southwest German Mesolithic Economic Seasons

JFM	A	M	JJA	SO	ND
Red Deer	Plants	Fish	Plants	Plants	Boar
Boar	Deer	Plants	Fish	Deer	Deer
Small game	Fish	Deer	Deer	Boar	Plants
			Boar	Fish	

TABLE 29

Salishan Economic Seasons

		Summer		Fall	
Winter	Spring	Early	Late	Early	Late
Elk, deer	Roots	Fish	Berries	Elk, deer	Big, small game
(Bison)	Big game	Roots	Fish	Berries	Some Fish
Small game	Fish	Big game	Some game	Fish	Some roots
Some fish			(Bison)		

and long hunting expeditions were undertaken to the grasslands to the east. Formerly, however, they were much less significant, and only those animals that wandered into the forested foothills were hunted. "The divisions of the Flathead year were quite simple, as they were primarily based on the economic pursuits which the changing seasons dictated [Turney-High 1937:23]." Depending on the report consulted, there seem to have been from four to six economic seasons among these groups. In discussing the Flathead activities, Teit indicates the following six seasons (Table 29).

In the discussion of the Okanagon and Coeur d'Alene groups, five seasons are indicated, with the summer considered as one season. Finally, as Turney-High presents the Flathead economy, four seasons are represented: winter, spring, summer, and fall; the activities which he describes are similar to those discussed by Teit (Turney-High 1937). Thus, the seasonal configuration of these Salishan groups, based on similar resources, are similar to that derived for the Mesolithic of southwest Germany, including the possible seasonal subdivisions.

CHAPTER NINE

Site Location

As discussed previously, the major determinant of site location is resource distribution. Given the structure of economic seasons as just derived, the location of the various resources in these seasons must be considered. Red deer distribution will be examined first, since this is the single most important resource, and because it seems to show the most extreme changes in location through the year. A most significant aspect of red deer behavior is its tendency to undertake altitudinal migrations. In the Carpathians, distances of 150 kilometers may be traveled (Szederjei 1962). In the Swiss Alps, average summer range lies 600 meters above the winter grounds (Schloeth and Burckhardt 1961). In the Rocky Mountains, wapiti have a summer range 1000 meters above the winter territory (Altmann 1956). In regions of less extreme elevational differences, seasonal changes in distribution are nevertheless still evident. Among the red deer studied by Darling in Scotland, winter grazings were primarily between sea level and about 500 meters, while in summer and fall, most grazing took place between 500 and 1000 meters (Darling 1964). Similarly, on the Scottish island of Rhum, the average elevation of different age—sex classes ranged from 86 to 113 meters in spring, and between 251 and 280 meters in summer (Lowe 1966).

119

The factors most important in conditioning these movements seem to be the spring thaw and the first snow of winter, with their consequent effects on food availability (Altmann 1952, 1956; Roedelberger 1960; Schloeth and Burckhardt 1961. Red deer food habits show marked seasonal changes: much grass and herbs in summer, and mainly buds of birch and willow and other browse in winter (Hegg 1961; Von Raesfeld 1899). Both German and Scottish deer show similar timing of the altitudinal shifts: Winters are spent in protected lowlands, especially river valleys and around reed swamps; births and rut tend to occur in small openings in forests at middle elevations; summers and the period between rut and the first snowfall are usually spent in meadows or stands of pine at higher elevations (Heck 1935; Darling 1964). North American wapiti show similar behavior, except that rut tends to take place in the high summer range, rather than at middle elevations Altmann 1952; Orr 1970; Murie 1951).

The study area contains sufficient variation in physical factors to warrant the expectation that the prehistoric red deer of this region showed similar behavior patterns. In accord with differences in temperature, elevation, precipitation, and vegetation, the region shows a patterned distribution of wind, frost, and snowcover. On the average, there is snow on the Alb heights for 80 days, on the rolling hills of Oberschwaben for 70 days, and in the river valleys for 60 days (Grube 1972; 197). The Alb heights and most of Oberschwaben have heavy winds, while the narrow valleys in the Alb are quite sheltered. First frost occurs around September 30 on the Alb, October 17 in Oberschwaben, and October 21 along the lower Danube. The frostfree season begins around April 27 along the lower Danube, May 2 in Oberschwaben, and May 17 up on the Alb.

Following this differential distribution of physical factors, suggestions may be proposed concerning the probable location of red deer in the different seasons. The winter months of January through March should find most deer concentrated in the river bottoms, especially in the sheltered narrow valleys of the Alb; the willow and birch of the riverine forests would provide most of the diet at this time. April still witnesses frosts and snows, but the average minimum temperature in most of the region now rises above freezing. Since deer movements in spring often anticipate the spring thaw, and because of a possible exhaustion of food supplies in the valleys, it may be expected that the deer begin to move out onto the nearby slopes and perhaps around the low swamps and lakes of Oberschwaben. By May, the valleys and Oberschwaben are free of frosts and snow; the deer would probably be spreading out over much of Oberschwaben and moving up into the middle elevations of the Alb, and many females should be isolated as they give birth. The summer months of June through August would find most of the deer in the highest elevations of the Alb and Oberschwaben, where the openings of the light pine—birch forest would offer good grazing. During rut in September and October, the deer should still be at rather high elevations, although the frosts in October should gradually drive them down. With the first snows of late October—early November, the downward migration should assume greater magnitude, and the middle and low elevations of the Alb and Oberschwaben should be occupied by most of the deer during November and December.

Roe deer show a much smaller tendency to undertake altitudinal migrations: In contrast to red deer, they are very site-attached (Holloway and Jungius 1973). In general, winter grounds and summer territories are not necessarily separate, especially if cover and browse are present in all seasons (Prior 1968). Roe deer which range above the tree-line in the Alps in summer tend to shift downward into the protected forest for winter (Holloway and Jungius 1973). For roe deer in deciduous forest areas in summer, leaf-fall is usually a stimulus for autumn movements in order to seek greater shelter (Prior 1968). In mixed and coniferous forest regions, however, roe deer may very likely remain at higher elevations in winter if food is available, since the evergreens would provide protection. Because of the greater demands of winter, consequently, summer territories in most habitats should cover a wider area than winter grounds, but the seasonal contrast would probably not be so great as with red deer. Winter concentrations tend to begin in November, and spring dispersal and territory formation in April and May (Von Raesfeld 1970).

The Boreal—Atlantic forests of both the Alb and Oberschwaben had much hazel underbrush, which would be suitable food for roe deer. In addition, Oberschwaben had more deciduous browse and nut crops, and so would be a rich habitat in most seasons. In winter, however, this primarily deciduous forest region would offer less protection, and one might expect the deer to shift to stands of pine and to the thickets around bodies of water. In the Alb, on the other hand, pine was in much greater abundance and would have offered greater protection in winter. Roe deer in this season might be expected to remain at middle elevations in this forest, with only a slight tendency to concentrate on lower slopes and valley bottoms. The distribution of roe deer, consequently, would tend to be rather homogeneous through the year, in contrast to that of red deer. Any concentration would occur from November to March, and would occur in valleys, low slopes, and the edges of lakes and swamps.

Boar movements are also rather restricted and are guided by the need for food and cover (Grzimek 1970). Because of the importance of nut crops in the diet, the mixed-oak and hazel forests of Oberschwaben and the river valleys would have been the preferred habitat, especially in fall and winter. The Alb forests would have offered hazelnut crops, but their dry soils and the higher snow cover would have discouraged boar. It is likely that summer would find boar rather widely dispersed, but consistently more abundant in the moist deciduous forests of Oberschwaben. Fall and early winter should see a tendency for boar to shift even more to this area, while the great sensitivity to cold and stormy weather would favor winter concentrations in the protected forests of the valleys (Heck 1950). In spring, the pattern of dispersal should find boar again in lower elevations of the Alb and throughout much of Oberschwaben.

Beaver show no great changes in distribution: They are consistently tied to open water, and would have occurred in lakes and all but the fastest and most shallow rivers. The center of density, then, would have been in Oberschwaben, while the Alb would have beaver only along the lower watercourses. The small game species each have their own pattern of distribution, but it would seem that the thickets and cliffs of the valleys of the Alb would have been consistently richest in these animals. Red fox, lynx, badger, marten, and wildcat thrive in such rocky, overgrown areas, and, according to Vogel, were probably always less abundant in Oberschwaben and on the Alb heights (Vogel 1940). Otter are tied to water, and would have occurred along the rivers, lakes, and marshes of the area. Hare tend to favor dry grasslands and forests up to about 1600 meters; hence they may have been more abundant on the Alb.

The fish species of this region can be grouped according to their habits (Busnita 1967; Mills 1971; Schindler 1953). Trout and whitefish are the major fall spawners; they tend to migrate upstream in rivers and into tributaries, and from lakes into their feeder streams. Hucho, or Danube "salmon," which are confined to the Danube river system, go upstream and into the tributaries in spring, and at all other times of the year are deep in the main river. Grayling and cyprinids such as chub and barbel inhabit running water; during the spring, they cluster around the mouths of streams tributary to lakes and rivers. In summer, they tend to occupy shallows, while in fall and winter, they are deep and inactive. Pike and perch spawn in the spring in river and lake shallows, and remain in shallow water during the summer. Finally, the catfish and cyprinids such as carp, bream, ide, and tench are normally found in very slow water; their spring spawning occurs in the floodplain of the lower reaches of the Danube and lake shallows. Throughout the summer, they remain near the surface along the water edges; in fall and winter, they are deep.

Thus, the centers of distribution of the fish resources change with the seasons. In spring, the major foci are: in the tributaries of the Danube upstream; in the floodplain of the lower reaches of the Danube; and around lakeshores, especially at the mouths of their feeder streams. In summer, the centers of distribution shift to the lower Danube edges and the shallows of lakes. The focus in fall again shifts to the tributaries of the Danube and of lakes. The winter distribution is primarily in deep water of the lakes and the main river.

Although hazelnuts were available throughout most of the study area, it is probable that Oberschwaben and the river valleys were much richer than the Alb in other plant foods. The greater richness and variety of deciduous forests in general would offer more possible foods, including acorns. The abundant lakes and streams provide additional habitats potentially rich in food plants, especially assorted root plants and greens, along the shores and in the water. Thickets in the riverine forests would be the center of distribution of various berry crops. It might be expected that Mesolithic populations would have followed a pattern of plant exploitation similar to that of the Ojibwa of the Great Lakes region (Yarnell 1964). If so, then roots would have been most important in spring and late fall, greens in late spring and summer, berries in summer and early fall, and nut crops in fall. Actually, nuts might have been utilized throughout the winter as well, since rodent burrows could be robbed for these, as they were among the Ojibwa. In addition, nuts lend themselves to easy storage after the fall harvest. In most seasons, then, the focus of plant food distribution would have been around the lakes, rivers and streams; nut crops would have tended to be located on drier slopes away from the water.

The waterfowl of southwest Germany include many species, most of which pass through in late fall and early spring. Some stay the winter; very few are present in summer. The centers of their occupation are Federsee and other lakes of Oberschwaben, and the Danube Valley, especially its broad lower reaches (Hölzinger, 1970). Among the year-round residents are several species of grouse. The black grouse tends to inhabit moist marshy regions, and hence would be found around the lakes, rivers, and marshes (Haas 1965; Zettel 1972). The capercaillie, or wood grouse, inhabits higher elevations, especially pine-covered hills; it would be found in greatest abundance, consequently, on the lower slopes of the Alb. The hazel-hen has a similar distribution to that of the wood grouse, but also occurs in lowlands and among predominantly deciduous forests as well; it would be rather evenly distributed throughout the study area away from the water edges.

Given these changing patterns of resource distribution, the general regions of site location for each season may be considered. Based on the discussion of the considerations guiding decisions about settlement placement, it may be postulated that sites would be located closest to the least mobile resources—in this case, plants and fish. The plants in this area would probably be most densely concentrated along water edges in all seasons except autumn, when the distribution becomes more homogeneous due to the wide availability of hazelnuts. Consequently, locating close to plant resources would accomplish a proximity to fish resources as well. Since fish are expected to be utilized to some extent in all seasons, it is likely that base camps throughout the year are located close to bodies of water productive of fish.

The formulations of the gravity model agree with this expectation. Using the formula $R^2 = wna/p$, and the seasonal averages of the resource attributes and use proportions, the relative distances from base camp to the centers of distribution of each resource can be calculated (Table 30). From these figures, it can be seen that a location closest to the fish resource is predicted for every season.

An examination of the map of resource distributions for the late winter

TABLE 30

Relative Distance from Camp to Resource Centers Based on Gravity Model

Resource	Season					
	JFM	A	M	JJA	SO	ND
Red deer	10.5	11.4	9.4	12.4	10.1	11.5
Roe deer	5.2	5.0	5.4	5.4	6.1	5.5
Boar	0.5	7.3	7.3	10.0	11.4	10.0
Beaver	7.1	7.2	—	—	—	10.8
Small game	.8	.8	1.2	.7	1.1	1.0
Fish	.5	.6	.5	.6	.5	.5

months of January through March (Figure 26) reveals one area of overlap of all four major resources: the narrow upper Danube Valley in the Alb. It is probable, therefore, that sites for this season would be located in this area of overlap, not only for the most efficient procurement of these resources, but also because this region offers the greatest shelter as well. Due to the high cliffs and rather dense vegetation, a site located within the deep valley would be protected from the wind—a factor important in these winter months. In addition, the valley has the least snowcover during the year of any part of the study area.

If one assumes occupation within this focal area, then the region of potential site catchments can be approximated. Arguing from ethnographic examples, Jarman has estimated an average hunter–gatherer site catchment to be defined

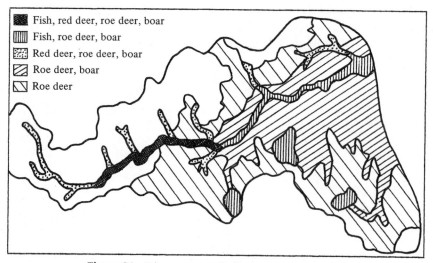

Fish, red deer, roe deer, boar
Fish, roe deer, boar
Red deer, roe deer, boar
Roe deer, boar
Roe deer

Figure 26 *Primary resource distributions: January–March.*

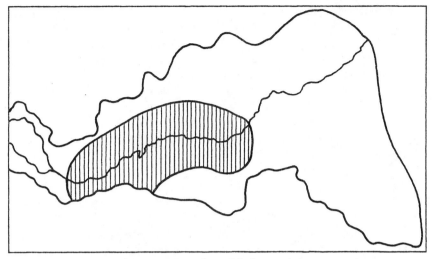

Figure 27   *Zone of potential winter catchments.*

by a radius of a 2-hour walk, roughly 10 kilometers in flat terrain (Jarman 1972). Using this estimate (and ignoring the terrain for the moment), a zone encompassing catchments of all sites within the upper Danube Valley can be constructed (Figure 27).

A contrasting situation exists in the summer months of June through August (Figure 28). In this season there is no zone of overlap of all four major

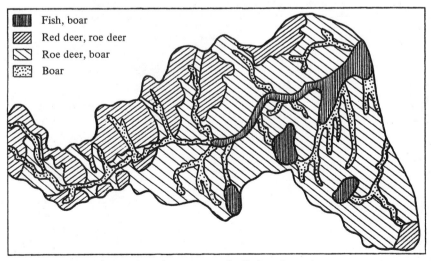

Figure 28   *Primary resource distributions: June–August.*

resources. Site location is expected to be in proximity to the main distribution of the fish resource, which centers around the lakes of Oberschwaben and the lower, quieter reaches of the Danube. In this fair season, shelter from wind is of less significance, so that a location in this flatter, more unprotected terrain poses no problem. The zone of potential site catchment can be constructed around this region of fish concentration, again using a radius of ten kilometers (Figure 29).

An interesting feature of this zone is that it contains none of the region of primary red deer distribution in this season. During the summer, it is expected that most red deer would be found in the higher elevations of the Alb. A location so far from the red deer distribution is supported by the gravity model formulation, which predicts a distance far greater than that to the fish center (and also the greatest distance to red deer of any season). Satellite red deer hunting camps would be necessary.

A comparison of the potential exploitation zones for summer and winter reveals almost no overlap; the summer and winter territories seem to be quite distinct (Figure 30). This separation makes sense, not only because of the different resource distributions and shelter requirements in the two seasons, but also because high mobility and changes of exploited areas are characteristic of a hunting-and-gathering economy in most cases, due to local resource exhaustion. A basic pattern, then, of seasonal movement between these two regions may be postulated.

More specific location of settlement in each region depends on two further considerations. First, the size and yield of catchments, and suitability of shelter,

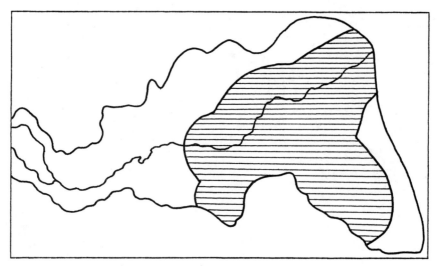

Figure 29   *Zone of potential summer catchments.*

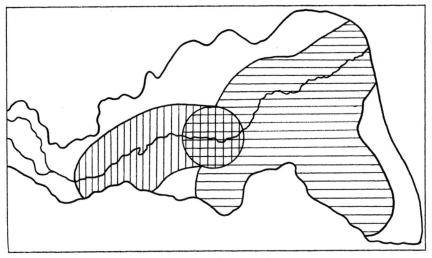

Figure 30 *Comparison of winter and summer zones.*

view, and ground surface would differ due to specific local features not evident in these broad distribution maps. Second, just two locations during the year might not be suitable (in terms of resource distribution) or provide sufficient yield; if more frequent change of site location is necessary, then considerations of effort and catchment overlap will structure the decisions about areas utilized. If just two sites, winter and summer, are necessary, then the least travel effort, without any overlap of the site catchments, is required by a situation in which the two catchments are adjacent:

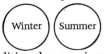

On the other hand, if an additional move is necessary—for a fall site, for example—then the least-effort solution with no overlap is:

But if the sites are confined to a linear pattern, such as a river valley, the more costly arrangement would be:

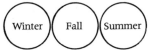

Similarly, the two solutions for a four-site system would be:

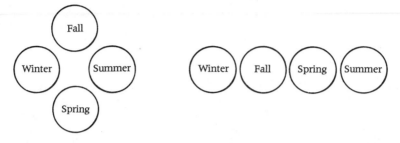

From these considerations, the following suggestion may be made: The sites of the winter and summer seasons should be located as close to each other as possible, while allowing for additional catchments of other seasonal sites in between.

The resource distributions for April (Figure 31) indicate a region of overlap of all four major resources all along the Danube and around the lakes of Oberschwaben. No relocation of the winter site is necessary, consequently, from these distributions. If, however, a move is necessary because of resource exhaustion, or desired simply for a change, then the spring site should also be along the Danube (near one of the tributary months where the fish are most abundant) in between the winter and summer catchment zones.

The distributions in May show no one zone of overlap of all four resources (Figure 32). The fish resource is widely distributed in the lake shallows and tributaries, the Danube floodplains and its upper reaches and tributaries. Locations suitable for winter, April, and summer would all be adequate for this

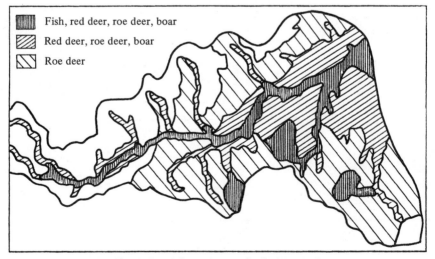

Figure 31 *Primary resource distributions: April.*

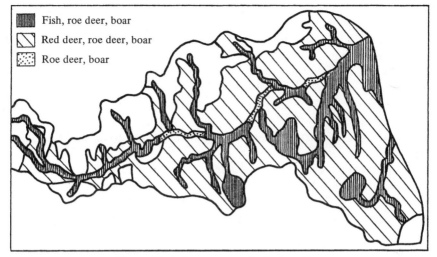

Figure 32 *Primary resource distributions: May.*

month as well. Since this month is only a possible subdivision of the broader summer season, there seems to be no reason, based on resource distribution, to separate it from the June—August site.

The September—October distributions are quite different from those of the summer months (Figure 33). The fish distribution shifts to the upper Danube and its tributaries. Red deer again become accessible from some of these shores.

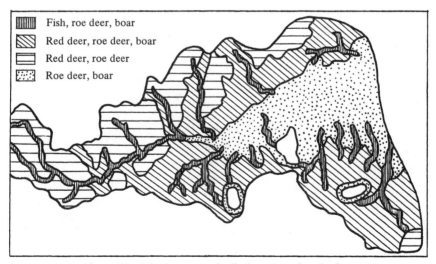

Figure 33 *Primary resource distributions: September—October.*

Sites in the winter catchment zone would all be suitable, but those in its eastern part would have more productive catchments than those farther upriver. The fish distribution for November–December is along most of the main Danube (Figure 34), and therefore the catchment zone of this season also includes that of the winter months and is richer in the eastern part of this region. Based on resource distributions, then, one location could feasibly serve for the period from September to March. If a 7-month period, however, is too demanding on local resources (as is probable), then the fall months of September to December would favor a separate location, downriver from the winter camp in the more productive eastern part.

From these considerations of resource distributions, it may be concluded that the Mesolithic settlement system included at least two base camps during the year, with four being perhaps more likely. The seasons of these camps would be:

> Summer (May–August)
> Fall (September–December) ⎫ Possibly only
> Winter (January–March)   ⎬ one camp
> Spring (April)   ⎭

The relative spatial arrangement of these camps, based on least effort within the linear watershed, is shown in Figures 35 and 36.

The seasonal pattern of movement, then, is postulated to be from winter camps in the sheltered Danube Valley in the Alb to summer camps out in the

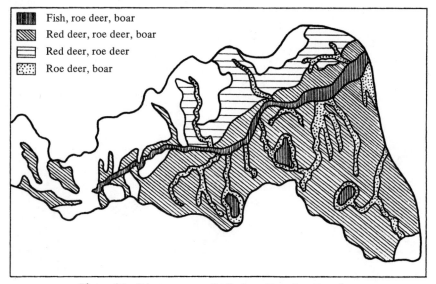

▦	Fish, roe deer, boar
▨	Red deer, roe deer, boar
▤	Red deer, roe deer
▦	Roe deer, boar

Figure 34 *Primary resource distributions: November–December.*

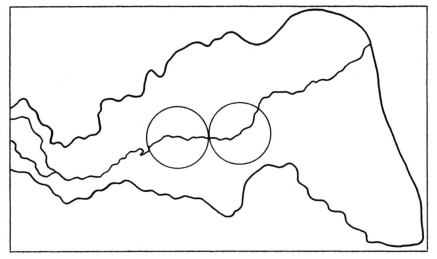

Figure 35 *Least-effort arrangement of two catchments.*

more unprotected area of Oberschwaben, along either lakes or the edges of
the lower Danube. Possible sites for spring and fall would be intermediate between these two, probably also along the Danube, near months of tributaries.
The need for shelter in these two intermediate seasons would be less than in
winter, but greater than in summer, and should be reflected in the choice of
campsites. Whether, in fact, these two additional seasonal camps would be

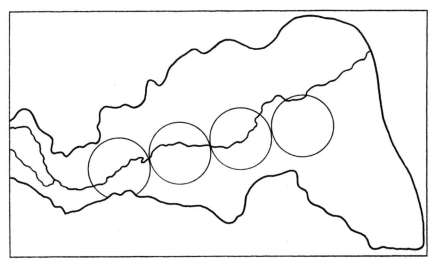

Figure 36 *Least-effort arrangement of four catchments.*

necessary from local resource exhaustion depends on the populations of the camps, a consideration that will be treated in the next section. Similarly, it is possible that base camps within each season were necessarily shifted among several locations; this possibility also requires consideration of population size and potential local resource exhaustion.

CHAPTER TEN

Demographic Arrangement

The overall carrying capacity of the study region and the size of seasonal coresident populations are defined by the cultural choices of resource use and by the spatial arrangement of these resources. As discussed earlier, some estimations of these demographic figures can be formulated. The carrying capacity will be limited to the minimum figure supportable by the various resources when used in the chosen proportions. A red deer, with a weight of 217 kilograms, a caloric content of about 2000 kilocalories per kilograms, and an edibility of 50%, yields 217,000 kilocalories per animal. At a density of four animals per square kilometer, red deer provide 4 × 217,000 = 868,000 kilocalories per square kilometer. This is 26% of the diet; the total diet is 868,000/.26 = 3,338,462 kilocalories. With an average requirement of 730,000 kilocalories per person per year, this diet would support 4.57 people per square kilometer at 100% harvesting efficiency. At a 20% harvest, a population of .91 people per square kilometer could be supported.

Similar calculations may be performed for the other resources. The caloric yield of each individual is:

HUNTER–GATHERER SUBSISTENCE AND SETTLEMENT

```
1 Red deer    = 217   kg × 2000 kcal/kg × 50% edibility = 217,000 kcal
1 Roe deer      34         2000           50%              34,000
1 Boer         135         4000           70%             378,000
1 Beaver        20         4000           70%              56,000
1 Fish           1         1300           50%                 650
1 Small game    3.6        1800           60%               3,888
```

The number of individuals per square kilometer, and the proportional contribution to the diet for each is:

```
Red deer        4      per km²    26% of the diet
Roe deer       12                  3
Boar           12                 22
Beaver          0.65               1
Fish           98                 13
Small game    103                 13
```

The carrying capacity in kilocalories as defined by each is:

```
Red deer       (217,000 × 4)/.26 =   3,338,462 kcal
Roe deer       (34,000 × 12)/.03 = 13,600,000
Boer           (378,000 × 12)/.22 = 20,618,181
Beaver         (56,000 × .65)/.01 =  3,640,000
Fish           (650 × 98)/.13 =        490,000
Small game     (3,888 × 103)/.13 =   3,080,492
```

And the maximum supportable human population density at 100% and 20% harvest is given in Table 31.

Thus, it seems that the population would be limited to a density of .13 per square kilometer by the fish resource, even though the actual fish productivity of this region was estimated to be rather high. For comparison, densities less than or equal to this figure were maintained in much of North America (Kroeber 1939). Densities of .05 to .12 people per square kilometer were charac-

TABLE 31

Supportable People per Square Kilometer Based on Different Resources

Resource	100% Harvest	20% Harvest
Red deer	4.57	.91
Roe deer	18.63	3.73
Boar	28.24	5.65
Beaver	4.99	1.00
Fish	.67	.13
Small game	4.22	.84

teristic of hunter—gatherers of much of the Great Lakes and St. Lawrence drainage and parts of the western Plateau, including some of the interior Salishan groups. Higher densities existed in coastal areas, among groups practicing agriculture, and among the Wisconsin wild-rice gatherers. Lower densities characterize most of the Arctic, Subarctic, and interior continental regions of the Plains. The estimate for the Mesolithic of southwest Germany, therefore, lies within the range of most ethnographic examples, and seems to be in accord with the relative productivity of the environment. It should be stressed that this is an estimate of the culturally defined limit to population density, as determined by the choices of resource utilization. The population feasibly supportable from the available biomass would be much higher, but would require a different set of values guiding resource decisions. Furthermore, the figure estimated represents an upper limit: The actual population density may have been significantly lower. In this respect, it is interesting to note that the best estimate of a Mesolithic population density, Clark's estimates for the Preboreal population density of Britain, range from 15 per 600 square kilometers to 20 per 300 square kilometers, that is, from .03 to .07 per square kilometer (Clark 1972: 38). These figures are certainly in accord with the upper limit determined for southwest Germany for the somewhat later time period.

The area of the study region is approximately 6700 square kilometers; the upper limit to the total population, then is 871 people. Because of the dichotomous nature of this region, the Alb heights, which form almost 50% of the area, are relatively unproductive in most seasons. Furthermore, occupation would seem to be concentrated along the linear watercourse, imposing a strain on the maintenance of a large mating network, and thus perhaps discouraging occupation of the narrow tail-end of the watershed (Wobst 1974). For these reasons, the total population of the study area may have been a good deal less than the maximum as calculated.

The potential for population aggregation may be estimated for each month by calculating the sum of the figure *wnad/m* (Table 32 and Figure 37).

The most striking feature of these calculations is the relatively constant potential for aggregation through the year, as compared with the Round Lake Ojibwa. The potential in April is lowest, and would seem to indicate a fragmentation of the winter group at this time, and thus the establishment of new camps by smaller groups. October also has a low potential, but this month is not a season by itself, but forms part of the postulated 4-month fall season. The other three seasons are roughly comparable, and each begins with a period of high potential. Aggregation for maximum procurement in each of these peak months, September, January, and May, would be encouraged in order to provide support during the somewhat leaner months that follow each. Because the potential, and hence the probable group size, is relatively low in April, it may be expected that the desire for aggregation following this month would be

TABLE 32

Predicted Potential for Population Aggregation of the Southwest German Mesolithic

Month	Red Deer	Roe deer	Boar	Beaver	Fish	Small game	Total
January	20,484	1,680	27,144	338	784	3,894	54,323
February	19,704	1,536	22,800	325	980	3,893	49,238
March	20,640	1,680	22,968	325	2,646	3,893	52,152
April	6,976	1,008	4,944	338	11,760	3,893	28,919
May	2,508	576	4,860	68	44,100	3,893	56,005
June	2,440	432	11,136	40	22,932	3,893	40,873
July	5,708	468	11,892	43	21,266	3,893	43,270
August	6,824	612	12,672	43	21,266	3,893	45,310
September	8,640	648	15,588	43	22,932	3,893	51,744
October	7,640	744	17,028	43	1,764	3,893	31,112
November	7,052	744	36,288	75	1,274	3,893	49,326
December	7,616	1,152	35,280	363	1,078	3,893	49,382

great, and would lead to the largest aggregations in summer. That the highest potential of the year occurs in May supports this tendency for aggregation, especially since most of this potential is provided by the very localized fish resource. Furthermore, the plant resources have not been considered: They would provide additional support from spring to fall. Since they would be simultaneously most abundant and concentrated (near water edges) in the summer, larger aggregations in summer could be supported.

Beginning in fall, the plant distribution becomes less concentrated by water edges. In addition, the desire for aggregation for social reasons would be low

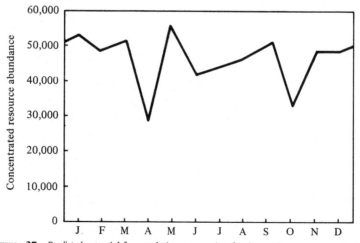

Figure 37　*Predicted potential for population aggregation for the southwest German Neolithic.*

following the larger summer groupings. Thus, although the potential is relatively high, it might be expected that some fragmentation would occur at this time. The fact that much of the calculated potential derives from the more mobile and higher risk big game resources would support this assumption of some fragmentation.

The potential in the late winter months is also relatively high, but most of this derives from big game. The more secure plants and fish are of little importance. Thus, although aggregation may be desirable for social reasons, it would not seem to be supportable because of the risky nature of the resource base at this time. In addition, greater snowcover is probable in this season, imposing limits on mobility and hence on the catchment exploitable. Greater demands for fuel, coupled with this limited mobility, would also seem to militate against large aggregations at this time. Tentatively, then, it may be suggested that the largest aggregations would occur in the summer, the smallest in spring, and groups of intermediate size in fall and winter.

An index of dominance for the seasonal strategies may also be calculated, allowing an estimation of the general economic stability of each season. The formula used is $\Sigma(ni/N)^2$, where ni is the proportional utilization of each resource, and N is 1.00. The dominance indices for each resource and the sum of these for each season are given in Table 33.

The index is highest in late winter, and thus the economic strategy is least stable in this season, followed by that of summer. If group size increases in order to compensate for an unstable strategy by increasing the number of exploiters coresiding, then winter should witness the largest aggregations, followed by summer, then fall and spring. It was argued above, however, that the winter season could probably not securely support a large aggregation, and it is likely

TABLE 33

Dominance Indices of Seasonal Strategies of the Southwest German Mesolithic

Resource	Season			
	JFM	A	MJJA	SOND
Red deer	.2116	.0400	.0225	.0576
Roe deer	.0025	.0016	.0004	.0006
Boar	.0784	.0121	.0225	.0784
Beaver	.0004	.0004	—	.0001
Fish	.0016	.0169	.0961	.0081
Small game	.0144	.0144	.0144	.0049
Plants	—	.0900	.0900	.0506
Birds	.0004	.0036	—	.0009
Sum	.3093	.1790	.2459	.2012

that the increase in camp food yield from increasing the number of exploiters could not adequately or reliably compensate for the extra food requirements. The value of this calculation of a dominance index, therefore, may be to indicate that extreme fragmentation during winter is not to be expected: Winter group size should be less than or equal to that of summer, but greater than that of spring.

Further indications of group sizes during the various seasons may be derived from consideration of yields of catchments in these seasons. Since fish seems to be the limiting resource, its yield will be considered. In comparing catchment yields between winter and summer, a major assumption is that exploitable areas in winter will be smaller due to limited mobility. Two factors in winter would tend to restrict mobility. First of all, snowcover in this season makes traveling quite difficult. Even with aids such as snowshoes, walking at a given rate requires an energy expenditure at least twice as great as walking on dry ground (Spector 1956: Table 315). Walking on snow without snowshoes requires an average of 3.5 times the energy of walking on dry ground. For the Mesolithic of Central Europe there is no evidence of snowshoes. Thus, it may be that an average winter catchment radius would be only 10/3.5, or approximately 3 kilometers, assuming equal energy outputs. A second limit to mobility would be posed by the cliffs and steep slopes of the narrow valley in which winter sites are expected to be located. Walking up a 10% grade, for example, is about twice as costly as walking on level ground (Spector 1956: Table 316). Consequently, the radius of exploitation perpendicular to the valley would be at most only half as great as that parallel to the river. In winter, this would mean a distance from the site of only 1.5 kilometers, assuming a constant energy output. The winter catchment, consequently, would probably resemble a rectangle of 6 × 3 kilometers, or an area of 18 square kilometers. In summer, on the other hand, there is no snow cover, and sites are expected to be located in the flatter region of Oberschwaben or along the lower Danube. Summer catchments, therefore, may be approximated by a circle with a radius of 10 kilometers and an area of 314 square kilometers.

The tremendous discrepancy in catchment areas suggests that a smaller population should be supportable from winter sites. Because of the relatively great concentration of resources in winter, however, a small catchment may be quite productive, so that the difference in group sizes may not be so great. In addition, the assumption of constant energy output through the year may not be warranted; greater exertion may be a feature of the winter months. Thus, the difference in group sizes may not be so large. Calculation of the average fish yields may indicate the magnitude of this difference.

The winter season lasts 3 months, or about 90 days. One person would require 90 × 2000, or 180,000 kilocalories during this season. If fish are expected to contribute 4% of this diet, then 7200 kilocalories should be provided by fish. If an average fish has about 650 edible kilocalories, then approximately 11 fish are required by each person during the winter season. An average density of 98 fish per square kilometer would mean that 11/98, or .11 square kilometers are needed to support each person. A winter catchment of 18 square kilometers would support 18/.11, or 164 people. This figure, however, represents 100% harvesting efficiency; at a 20% harvest, 33 people could be supported by an average territory for the winter. Since fish at this time of year tend to be rather dispersed, local density might actually be less than the average. If it were half the average, then the supportable population would be 17 people.

In the 4-month summer season, 1 person would require 240,000 kilocalories. Of this total, 31%, or 74,400 kilocalories are expected to be provided by fish. This represents a requirement of 114 fish per person in the summer. At a fish density of 98 per square kilometer, 1.16 square kilometers are needed to support 1 person. A summer catchment of 314 square kilometers could support 271 people at 100% harvesting efficiency, or 54 people at a 20% harvest. Since fish tend to be relatively concentrated around the shores of a few areas in this season, the actual local density might be higher than the average. If it were twice as great, then 108 people could be supported by an average summer catchment at a 20% harvest.

From these calculations, it is expected that winter group size might range between 17 and 33 people, and summer groups from 54 to 108. These sizes are in accord with the previous discussion of aggregation potential. These estimates, together with the proposed pattern of aggregation and fragmentation, suggests the following scheme: The largest groups should occur in the summer at lakes or along the lower Danube; for fall and winter, these aggregations should separate into two or three units which disperse into the most protected parts of the valleys, occupying perhaps two base camps each during these seasons. In spring, these winter groups should further subdivide and relocate at months of tributaries intermediate between summer and winter sites.

The calculation of the winter catchment yield of fish indicates that this 3-month period could be spent in one base camp by a group of 17 to 33 people. Since no extreme fragmentation of the group is expected in either fall or winter, it is doubtful that group size would have been much smaller in either of these seasons. Consequently, it might be expected that fall groups would be of the same size as those of winter. Fall mobility, and hence catchments, would be greater than in winter; with the prospect of the very restricted movement in winter, it seems unlikely that a fall group would choose to settle in the region to be so intensively exploited in the next season. Thus, it seems probable that fall camp would be separate from that of winter. Similarly, the spring increase in mobility and its probable group fragmentation would favor occupation of sites different from that of winter. A system of four base camps during the year seems to be the most likely for the Mesolithic of this region.

CHAPTER ELEVEN

Summary and Predictions of Site Characteristics

The results of the consideration of these three subsystems of the subsistence and settlement in Mesolithic southwest Germany may now be summarized. It seems probable that a series of four base camps would have been occupied during the year; the expected characteristics of each may be discussed. The winter site should have been occupied from January through March by a group whose maximum size ranged from 17 to 33 people. The site should be deep in the protected Danube Valley, with specific locational attributes affording great protection from the elements. The dietary proportions of the different resources during this season should be:

Red deer	46%
Roe deer	5
Boar	28
Beaver	2
Fish	4
Small game	12
Birds	2

141

Faunal remains should approximate these proportions. Plants are expected to have been of little importance, although some nuts could have been stored and utilized at this time. The overwhelming importance of hunting in the economy should be reflected in the lithics.

The summer camp should be occupied from May through August, and should be located in the more exposed region of Oberschwaben or along the lower Danube. It should be situated by a lake or by the main river. Maximum group size may have ranged from 54 to 108 people. The diet should comprise:

Red deer	15%
Roe deer	2
Boar	15
Fish	31
Small game	12
Plants	30

Satellite hunting camps aimed principally at red deer would be very likely in this season, probably in the higher elevations. The lithics of the base camp should reflect the lesser importance of hunting, and the diversity of economic activities.

Base camp in spring would be occupied in April, and would likely be located along the Danube near a tributary, somewhere in between the summer and winter sites. Shelter in this season would not be so important, and locational attributes of the site should reflect this. Group size should be smaller than that of winter. Dietary proportions would be approximately:

Red deer	20%
Roe deer	4
Boar	11
Fish	13
Small game	12
Birds	6
Plants	30

The fall site should be occupied from September through December by a group similar in size to that of winter, that is, a maximum of 17 to 33 people. Its location should also be intermediate between the summer and winter camps, probably with greater shelter available for these colder months than that of the spring site. Hunting activities should be relatively important, as witnessed by the expected dietary importance of the resources:

Red deer	24%	Fish	9%
Roe deer	3	Small game	7
Boar	28	Plants	23
Beaver	1	Birds	3

In addition, skin-dressing activities in preparation for winter should be quite important.

Besides these general characteristics of each site, some further suggestions may be made. The less abundant resources, such as moose and aurochs, would be most likely procured during the fall and winter, when they are most susceptible. Chamois would probably have been available only in winter. Hucho, more than any other fish, is limited in availability to the late winter and spring. Boar piglets would be available in late winter and spring, deer fawns in spring and summer.

Finally, although all the camps would be close to water, the relative proximity would seem to depend on the importance of fishing and the need for shelter. The more important the need for shelter, the more likely that camp would be set back from the open water's edge. Furthermore, many ethnographic examples seem to indicate that, as fishing becomes more important, sites are moved closer to the water. For example, both the Canadian Dogrib and the Ainu move from the river terrace to the banks with the onset of a period of greater fishing importance (Helm 1961; Watanabe 1968). Thus, it might be assumed that summer camps here should be closest to the shore, followed by spring, fall, and winter respectively.

CHAPTER TWELVE

The Sites

The sites to be discussed here do not represent all of the Mesolithic sites in the study area, but only the best documented. The publication *Fundberichte aus Schwaben* has reported Mesolithic finds over a number of years, and although most of these have been lost or are in the hands of private collectors, the location of most of these finds can be determined. Figure 38 presents the location of reported finds of Mesolithic artifacts in the study area. As can be seen from this map, there are apparently three different focal areas of Mesolithic occupation: *(1)* along the Danube in the western Alb; *(2)* around the former shores of Federsee Lake; *(3)* along the lower Danube, its tributaries, and on the heights of the eastern Alb. The possible significance of these different areas, as well as of the poorly documented finds, will be discussed after a consideration of the major sites.

Jägerhaus Cave

Jägerhaus Cave (Figure 39) is situated at the foot of a steep cliff in the narrow Danube Valley near the town of Fridingen. The Danube follows a north–south loop at this spot in its otherwise predominantly eastwest course; the

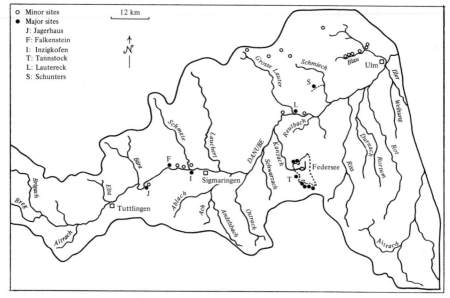

Figure 38 *Mesolithic sites in the study area.*

location is thus quite well protected from westerly winds. The cave lies about 70 to 80 meters above the valley floor, which is approximately 250 meters wide. The horizontal distance from cave to Danube is about 300 meters. The cave faces southeast, and has a maximum width of 13 meters and a maximum depth of 12 meters. A freshwater spring surfaces nearby and, in spring, runs partly through the cave; during the rest of the year, the cave was probably dry (Taute n.d. a). The spring deposits of travertine are important in that they sequentially sealed off cultural deposits so that fifteen different cultural levels could be discerned. This cultural sequence provides the basis for Taute's chronology of the Mesolithic in this area (Taute 1967, 1972, n.d. a).

The excavation, carried out between 1964 and 1967, revealed eight levels definitely assigned to the Mesolithic. For the purpose of comparing this site with others in the region, only those levels belonging to the Beuronien C (Levels 9 and 8) and the Late Mesolithic (Levels 7 and 6) will be considered. Because separate occupation levels cannot be distinguished at the other sites, the most fruitful comparisons may be provided by considering all of these levels at Jägerhaus Cave together. Consequently, the lithics and fauna of Levels 9 through 6 will be treated as a single unit, to be compared to the undifferentiated material of the other sites, which span the same time period.

Table 34 shows the faunal material from these levels of Jägerhaus Cave, as identified by Boessneck (n.d. a). Over 8000 pieces of bone were found at the site, of which only about 15% could be identified. The boar are distinguished by a high

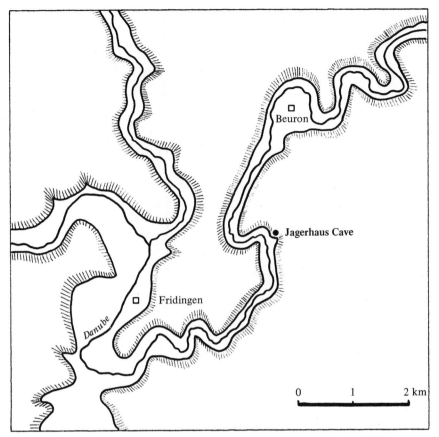

Figure 39 *Location of Jägerhaus Cave.*

percentage of young individuals, both piglets and yearlings. In addition to these faunal remains, many carbonized hazelnuts and shells of freshwater mussels were found in these levels.

Table 35 presents a summary of the flaked stone tools in these levels of Jägerhaus Cave, based on Taute's typology. In addition to these tools, there were many worked pieces of other materials, including:

Antler double-barbed harpoon fragments	3
Worked antler fragments	1
Worked bone fragments	25
Worked boar tusk	2
Perforated bone	1
Perforated fossil snailshell	1
Groundstone axe fragments	2
Hammerstones	1

TABLE 34

Jägerhaus Cave Fauna, Levels 9—6[a]

Animal	#[b]	MNI[c]
Red deer	341	24
Roe deer	125	20
Boar	418	34
Beaver	6	3
Fox	14	5
Badger	22	9
Wood marten	55	14
Otter	7	4
Wildcat	29	8
Hare	3	3
Chamois	10	3
Brown bear	1	1
Duck	1	1
Wood grouse	5	3
Cyprinid fish (carp family)	12	5

[a] After Boessneck n.d. a.
[b] Number of bones.
[c] Minimum number of individuals.

TABLE 35

Lithics of Jägerhaus Cave, Levels 9—6[a]

Tool class	Number
Microlithic points, triangles, crescents, trapezes	62
Bladelets (backed and blunted)	8
Atypical and fragmentary microlithics	24
Backed blades	1
Notched blades	12
Saws	10
Other retouched blades	43
Borers	1
Burins	1
Scrapers	33
Atypical and fragmentary pieces	6
Microburins	4
Cores	46
Blades, flakes, waste	4021

[a] After Taute n.d. a.

Falkenstein Cave

Falkenstein Cave (Figure 40) measures 15 meters maximum width and 10 meters maximum depth, and is situated in the Danube Valley to the east of Jägerhaus Cave, near the town of Thiergarten. It is some 300 meters from the river, 35 meters above the valley floor on an unusually gentel slope in the otherwise steep-sided valley. It faces southwest. Leading down from the slopes is a gully which occasionally carries meltwater over the roof of the cave; in winter, seepage through the roof often causes the formation of icicles in the cave.

The 1933 excavation by E. Peters was written up in preliminary reports, but the final manuscript, together with most of the material, was lost during the war (Peters 1934, 1935). The manuscript of the faunal analyses survives. W. Taute carried out new excavations in 1963 and 1964, in which he was able to locate a 9 square meter area that was undisturbed. The material from this excavation and Peters' surviving reports form the basis of this discussion. The Mesolithic deposits range from 45 to 85 centimeters thick; in neither excavation were any natural stratigraphic subdivisions evident. As a result, Taute imposed arbitrary levels by dividing the deposits into thirds. Based on radiocarbon,

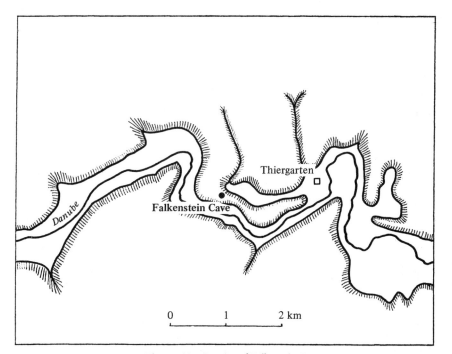

Figure 40 *Location of Falkenstein Cave.*

TABLE 36

Falkenstein Cave Fauna: Both Excavations

Animal	Peters (1933) #	MNI	Taute (1963–1964) #	MNI	Total #	MNI
Red deer	85	6	63	3	148	9
Roe deer	100	10	67	3	167	13
Boar	285	?	157	6	442	6 +
Beaver	22	3	3	1	25	4
Wolf	4	2	—	—	4	2
Fox	12	2	2	1	14	3
Badger	12	2	—	—	12	2
Wood marten	150	21	53	4	203	25
Otter	29	4	—	—	29	4
Wildcat	97	7	2	1	99	8
Hare	—	—	5	2	5	2
Brown bear	5	?	—	—	5	?
Aurochs	3	2	—	—	3	2
Cyprinid fish					194	9 +
Whitefish					2	?
Grayling			(studied together)		5	?
Pike					3	2

palynological, and stylistic studies, the upper third is attributed by Taute to the
Late Mesolithic and the lower third to the Beuronien C (Taute n.d. a).

Table 36 presents the fauna as reported by Boessneck (n.d. b). In addition,
635 pieces of bone were not identifiable from the 1963–1964 excavations, and
an unknown number from the 1933 excavation. The boar are represented by all
ages from yearling to strong adults, but there are no piglets. In addition to these
resources, carbonized hazelnuts and musselshells were found.

TABLE 37

Falkenstein Cave Lithics: Both Excavations

Tool class	Number
Microliths	211
Blade points	9
Notched blades	37
Retouched blades and bladelets (backed, truncated, etc.)	251
Saws	68
Borers	35
Burins and "burin-like" pieces	50
Scrapers	201
Cores	282
Blades, flakes, waste	ca. 7000

The relative proportions of the flaked stone tools are difficult to estimate, since they must be based on the preliminary reports of the 1933 excavation. Since Peters' types are not congruent with, or easily translated into Taute's typology, comparison among sites is problematic. Based on several reports and illustrations (Peters 1934, 1935, 1946; Taute n.d. a), the approximate tool counts shown in Table 37 may be estimated.

Additional finds at Falkenstein Cave include:

Antler harpoons, fragments	4	Worked boar tusk	4
Antler hafts	2	Sandstone grinding stone	1
Worked antler pieces	11	Sandstone hammerstone	1
Bone points and awls	6	Polished stone axe with antler haft	1
Worked bone pieces	25	Perforated shells and teeth	14
Boar tusk awl	1	Painted pebble	1

Inzigkofen Shelter

Inzigkofen (Figure 41) is a small shelter situated in the Danube Valley to the east of Falkenstein Cave, just before the river exits from the Alb near the town of

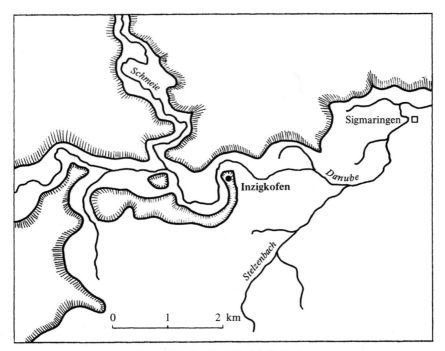

Figure 41   *Location of Inzigkofen Shelter.*

Sigmaringen. It faces west–southwest and has maximum dimensions of 8 meters width and 3 meters depth. Situated at the base of a cliff, the shelter is 70 meters from the river and 5 meters above the valley floor.

Peters excavated part of this shelter in 1938 and reported a rich assemblage similar to that of Falkenstein Cave, although lacking in antler harpoons (Peters 1946). Unfortunately, all of his material plus the manuscripts of his reports were lost during the war. Much of this site, however, was left unexcavated, in contrast to Falkenstein Cave. Taute conducted a new excavation in 1965, and was able to recover a large amount of material, which forms the basis of discussion here. In both excavations, no natural stratigraphic subdivisions of the Mesolithic deposits were evident. Again, Taute imposed arbitrary levels, which he was able to date to the Beuronien C and Late Mesolithic (Taute n.d. a).

Table 38 presents the fauna of Inzigkofen Shelter, as reported by Boessneck (n.d. c). For this site, as for Falkenstein Cave, estimates for minimum number of individuals are not available for some of the species, in this case, some of the fish. An additional 1545 bones were not identifiable. Here, as at the other sites already discussed, all body parts are represented for most animals. The proportion of young is rather high, and both infantile red deer and piglets were present. Musselshells were also found.

TABLE 38

Inzigkofen Shelter Fauna (1965 Excavation Only)[a]

Animal	#	MNI
Red deer	211	5
Roe deer	416	8
Boar	305	7
Beaver	68	3
Wolf	2	1
Fox	16	2
Badger	10	1
Wood marten	58	7
Lynx	24	1
Wildcat	37	4
Ducks	10	2
Grouse	9	4
Cyprinid fish	25	7 +
Hucho	39	9
Grayling	2	2
Pike	17	6
Whitefish	8	4
Other fish	44	?

[a]After Boessneck, n.d. c.

TABLE 39

Inzigkofen Shelter Lithics: 1965 Excavation[a]

Tool class	Number
Microliths	14
Notched blades	3
Retouched blades, bladelets (backed, truncated, etc.)	41
Saws	12
Borers	2
Burins	1
Scrapers	20
Microburins	5
Cores	46
Blades, flakes, waste	802

[a]After Taute n.d. a.

The number of the different categories of flaked stone tools are presented in Table 39.

In addition, this excavation revealed a bone and antler industry similar to that of the other sites, which had not been reported by Peters. The finds included:

Antler harpoons and fragments	5
Worked antler pieces	3
Bone points and fragments	5
Bone awl	1
Worked bone pieces	2
Worked boar tusk pieces	6
Perforated bone pieces	2
Perforated teeth	1
Sandstone hammerstones	2
Sandstone "chopping-tool"	1

Lautereck Shelter

Lautereck shelter (Figure 42) is situated on the Danube at the mouth of a large tributary, the Grosse Lauter. This small shelter lies to the east of the other Danube sites, due north of Federsee. Measuring a maximum of 7.5 meters wide and 2 meters deep, the shelter is 3 to 4 meters above the valley floor at the foot of a cliff, and faces southwest. A spring emerges nearby.

The site, excavated by Taute in 1963, yielded five cultural levels, the lowest of which (Level E) was attributed to a very late Mesolithic (Taute 1967a,b). This excavation covered some 40% of the floor area of the site; the other 60% was disturbed previously. A total of 1294 bones were re-

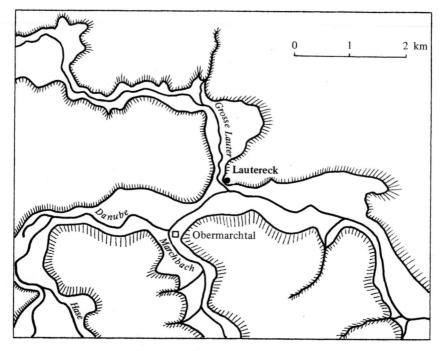

Figure 42   *Location of Lautereck Shelter.*

covered from this level, of which 844 were identifiable (Boessneck n.d. d; Lepik-saar n.d.). The number of bones and individuals for each species are given in Table 40.

The scant lithic assemblage is presented in Table 41.

In addition, the following artifacts were found:

Bone double points	2
Bone point fragments	1
Perforated bone pendant	1
Worked boar tusk piece	1

Schunters Cave

Schunters Cave (Figure 43) lies in the narrow, presently dry Briel Valley in the Alb north of the Danube, to the north and east of Lautereck Shelter. The cave faces southsoutheast and is 7 meters above the valley floor. Its maximum width is 12.5 meters, and maximum depth is 6 meters. The site was partially excavated by A. Kley in 1938—1939 (Kley 1951, 1952). He was able to distinguish two Mesolithic levels with stone and bone assemblages, but these findings were not fully published. The faunal assemblage was since lost during the war, but most

TABLE 40

Lautereck Shelter Fauna

Animal	#	MNI
Red deer	29	1
Roe deer	23	3
Boar	12	3
Beaver	1	1
Wolf	1	1
Fox	21	2
Badger	1	1
Wood marten	2	2
Wildcat	26	3
Otter	3	1
Ducks	5	4
Grouse	3	3
Cyprinid fish		22
Hucho		3
Grayling	703	3
Pike		4
Perch		1

of the stone artifacts survived. In 1954, working with Kley's notes, A. H. Nuber published a study of the southwest German Mesolithic, in which he discussed the finds at Schunters Cave, but his emphasis was on stylistic changes through time, especially in microliths (Nuber 1954). Taute conducted new excavations in 1961–1962 of the undisturbed portions of the cave (Taute 1967a, n.d. a). He was able to confirm the existence of two separate stratigraphic levels of Mesolithic occupation: Level 4, which he dated to the Beuronien A, and Level 3, spanning the periods from Beuronien B to Late Mesolithic. In addition, he found a lower, late Paleolithic Level 5.

A very sparse faunal assemblage was found in this excavation: Finds included one bone each of roe deer, a bovid (possibly aurochs), and wood grouse, but these were not attributable specifically to either Level 3 or Level 4 because of

TABLE 41

Lautereck Shelter Lithics

Tool class	#
Microliths	1
Blade points	1
Notched blades	6
Retouched blades	2
Scrapers	6

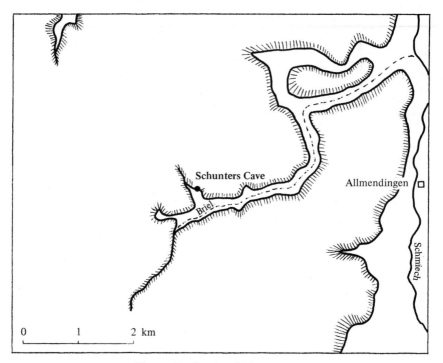

Figure 43   *Location of Schunters Cave.*

the disturbed nature of the deposits (Soergel n.d.). The small lithic assemblage of Level 3 is given in Table 42 (Nuber 1954; Taute n.d. a).

In addition, two bone needles and two pieces of worked bone were found in Level 3 of Schunters Cave.

TABLE 42

Schunters Cave Lithics, Level 3

Tool class	
Microliths	8
Blade points	1
Retouched blades	2
Saws	1
Burins	1 +[a]
Scrapers	6
Microburins	3
Cores	7
Flakes, waste	39

[a]"numerous" acc. to Nuber.

Federsee Sites

The present Federsee Lake measures approximately 2.5 by 1.0 kilometers, but this size is the result of both natural shrinkage during postglacial time and artificial drainage in recent centuries. The lake basin was carved out by a branch of the Rhine Glacier during the Riss and subsequently blocked off by an end moraine of the Würm (Wagner 1961). The basin measures roughly 10 by 5 kilometers and is the largest of Oberschwaben. In 1928, H. Reinerth began a survey along the former shorelines, in which he located 81 different Mesolithic sites (Reinerth 1929). Intermittent collecting since that time has increased the number of sites reported, especially by amateur collectors. Most of these sites, however, yield one or a few stone tools, and many cannot be dated with certainty to the Mesolithic. Occupation of the lake shore began in the Late Paleolithic and intense settlement is known for the Neolithic, Bronze and Iron Ages, and later times as well.

The major problem in dealing with the Mesolithic at Federsee is that all the sites show mixed occupations, not only within the Mesolithic, but from earlier and later periods as well. Since these are surface sites disturbed by plowing, the artifacts are intermixed and cannot be separated stratigraphically. The basis of Taute's chronological differentiation of the Mesolithic is a series of microlith forms; using these, some degree of dating within the Mesolithic is possible. But the vast majority of macroliths are common to all Mesolithic, plus earlier and later periods, so that their time of deposition cannot be determined. Hence, proportional tool counts from these sites are of little value. As will be discussed later, some categories of tools show general proportional changes from the Late Paleolithic through the Mesolithic in south Germany, and such changes should be kept in mind when considering the assemblages of Federsee.

Most of the material from these sites is in the state museum in Stuttgart; other collections occur at Federsee, Tübingen, and with private collectors. Of the large number of sites reported, only 21 can be assigned with any certainty to the Mesolithic and will be considered here; the rest have, for the most part, either cores and flakes only, or nondiagnostic tools such as scrapers and burins.

In order to discuss site locations, consideration must be given to changes in lake levels and shorelines since the late glacial period. Reinerth (1929) and Bertsch (1949) have published maps of the Mesolithic shorelines along with the distribution of sites. Both maps represent the Boreal situation, and are very similar. The lake level, however, apparently showed significant changes during the early Postglacial. Based on numerous studies, Wall (1961) has published a diagram of lake level changes; from this diagram, the following average levels can be taken:

Allerød—Younger Dryas	581—582 meters above sea level
Preboreal	579
Boreal—Early Atlantic	580—582

The lowest levels, then, occurred during the Preboreal, and not in the drier Boreal as one might have expected. These figures are supported by independent studies; Blank reports a Preboreal level of between 578.7 and 579.4 meters (Blank 1961); Göttlich (1961) gives the Preboreal level as 576.8 meters. During these early periods, the process of peat growth and lake shrinkage made few significant gains: In the Preboreal, some peat growth occurred in small parts of the south and southwest of the basin, but during the frequent changes in lake level of the Boreal, alternate land growth and erosion led to little overall progress (Wall 1961).

Figure 44 presents the maximum limits of the lake basin, based on the distri-

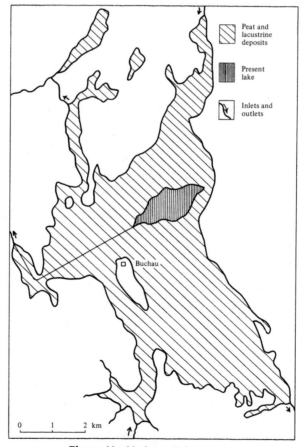

Figure 44   *Maximum Federsee Basin.*

bution of peat and lacustrine deposits. It will be noted that there were three major outlets—to the west, northwest, and southeast—all draining into the Danube, and two primary inlets, from the north and south. According to Wall (1961), all the outlets were apparently functional throughout Mesolithic times. The present lake is fed mostly by underground springs and drains to the west through the Kanzach Canal.

For the purpose of estimating the actual shorelines during the different periods, consideration must be given to the various sediments and their time of deposition, as well as to the changes of lake level. Wall (1961) has published a contour map of the "solid underground," that is, of the main glacial deposits. Similarly, Göttlich (1965) published a contour map of the "mineral underground," or of lacustrine sediments deposited mainly in the late glacial, especially during the Allerød. It is these late glacial deposits, then, which floored the

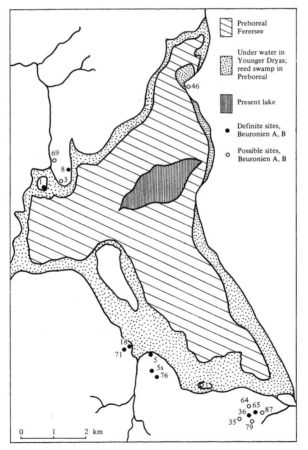

Figure 45   *Preboreal Federsee.*

basin at the beginning of the Postglacial, and whose contours should represent
the maximum lakeshores at the various water levels. Using the figures for lake
levels and sediment contour, the approximate lakeshores during the Mesolithic
have been drawn. Figure 45 presents the lake during the low stage of the Preboreal together with sites that were occupied during the Beuronien A and B.
In Figure 46, the situation in the Boreal–Early Atlantic is represented by the
maximum and minimum shorelines, together with sites of the Beuronien C and
Late Mesolithic.

It will be noticed that the sites tend to cluster around the stream inlets and
outlets, and especially those in the southern and western parts of the lake. When
all of the "sites," that is, all of the locations of artifact finds are plotted, this
clustering around the south and southwest shores becomes even more distinct.

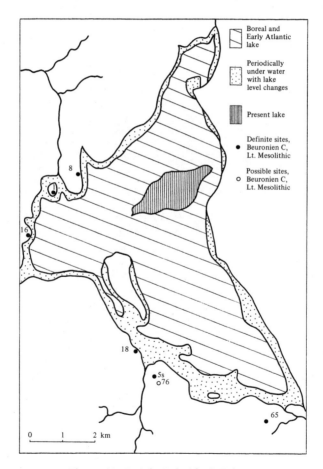

Figure 46   *Boreal–Early Atlantic Federsee.*

TABLE 43

Periods of Occupation of Federsee Sites

Site	Late Paleolithic	Beuronien			Late Mesolithic	Neolithic
		A	B	C		
1	X		X		X	X
5		?	X		X	
8	X	?	X		X	X
18	X	X	X	X	X	X
36	X		X			X
65	X	X	X		X	X
76			X		?	

In this respect, it is significant that the south and southwest are the shallowest parts of the basin and witnessed the earliest and greatest horizontal displacement of the shoreline.

Of the 21 sites showing certain Mesolithic occupation, 7 yielded more than 50 retouched tools and will be considered further. These sites are known by numbers based on Reinerth's original report. The sites and their datings are given in Table 43. Most of these sites were occupied, not only during the Mesolithic, but during the Late Paleolithic and the Neolithic as well.

All of these sites except #18, "Tannstock," are represented by flints only. The counts of the various tool categories are given in Table 44.

In general, the Federsee sites cover large expanses, usually circular or oval areas of 50 × 50 or 50 × 100 meters (Reinerth 1929). Since they occur on a limited number of favorable higher spots, and witnessed repeated reoccupation, it is not surprising that their areal expanse is quite large.

TABLE 44

Lithics of the Federsee Sites

Tool class	Site						
	1	5s	8	18	36	65	76
Microliths	20	30	37	60	32	78	21
Blade points	5	—	2	5	2	7	—
Notched blades	4	3	6	—	2	4	3
Retouched blades	3	2	6	10	1	12	1
Burins	20	5	24	11	30	55	4
Borers	—	1	8	2	9	8	—
Scrapers	43	19	22	32	44	63	30

Tannstock, site #18, is situated on a heavy clay substrate, in contrast to the loose morainic gravels and sands underlying most of the other sites. On this site, Reinerth reported finding stains and depressions of 38 oval huts ranging from about 2 × 2 to 6 × 3.5 meters. Each supposedly had a hearth marked by circular charcoal concentrations, some enclosed by stone rings. Based on the alignment and depth of these stains, he distinguished at least two occupations (Figure 47). In one hut, traces of a wall of brushwood were found, supported by stronger posts. Charcoal in the hearth areas was identified as ash, alder, hazel, willow, birch, oak, and sycamore (Reinerth 1929). In addition, one smooth bone point was found at this site.

Unfortunately, no further details of these finds were ever published, so that important details, such as the nature of the fill of these hut depressions or the distribution of the artifacts relative to the huts, are not known. Reinerth reports the occurrence of potsherds on this site, and artifacts diagnostic of the Late Paleolithic occur as well, so that a mixture of occupations is clear. Paret (1961) tends to discount the report of huts at this site on the basis of the apparent placement of some hearths immediately adjacent to the hut wall. A similar cluster of hut depressions was found by Reinerth at the Swiss Mesolithic site of Schötz 1, and is similarly poorly documented (Bodmer-Gessner, 1950).

Some further finds in the Federsee region should be mentioned. Among these are the so-called "dam-ways" (Figure 48). These consist of raised ridges which closely follow the old shorelines but tend to cut across former bays, connecting points of higher ground. They are all of roughly the same height, between 582

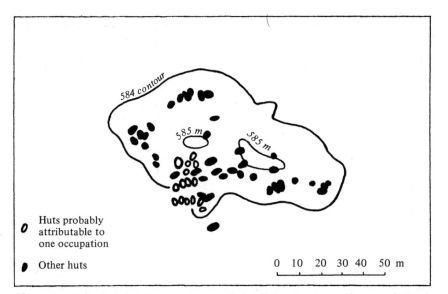

Figure 47 *Federsee site #18 ("Tannstock"): Distribution of the hut outlines. (After Reinerth 1929.)*

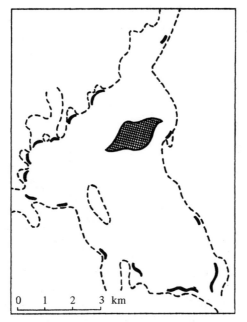

Figure 48   *Federsee "dam-ways." (After Paret 1951.)*

and 583 meters above sea level (Wall 1961). Various interpretations have been given these ridges: Roman roads, Mesolithic paths built over the marshy ground, and roads of a Germanic Mesolithic State (Paret, 1951). Based on an analysis of one of these ridges in the southern part of the basin, Paret (1951) determined that they represent natural beach deposits, and consist primarily of fine sands and gravels. According to his reconstruction, they were formed during a high water period of the later Mesolithic following a period of low water and beginning peat growth in the earlier Mesolithic. This reconstruction agrees with the postulated lake level rise from Preboreal to Boreal—Early Atlantic, and thus these shoreline segments probably date to the Boreal—Early Atlantic.

Similarly, Göttlich (1965) conducted a probe of one of these ridges in the northwestern part of the basin that connects a small island to both sides of the bay in which it sits. This island is the location of Site #1, which shows relatively intense occupation (Figure 49). In contrast to the ridge studied by Paret, this ridge is not composed simply of sands and gravels; resting on a base of peat is a 15-centimeter-thick layer of birch poles, which in turn is covered by sands and gravels. The poles are not in any systematic arrangement, but rather lie in random disarray. Radiocarbon analysis of one of these poles dates it to the Boreal Period. Göttlich sees this ridge as having been laid down purposefully, in contrast to the natural origin of the ridge studied by Paret. The exact diameter of these poles, and the condition of their ends—whether cut or gnawed—are

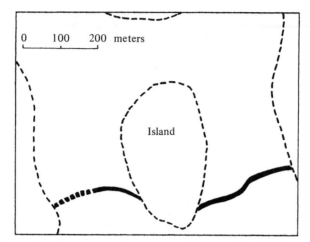

Figure 49   *Dam-way in northwestern part of Federsee. (After Göttlich 1965.)*

not discussed by Göttlich, so that the possibility that they derived from beaver dams cannot be ruled out. The architects are assumed by Göttlich to have been the Mesolithic occupants of the island. Such a construction could have had two possible functions. First, it might have served as a dry path connecting the island to shore across marshy ground or open water. Second, it may have had the alternative or additional function of blocking off a shallow bay frequented by fish during spawning and summer, thus trapping the fish in a vulnerable location.

An additional find in Federsee relates to this second interpretation. In the southwestern part of the basin, near the shore close to the sites #5 and 76, J. Eberhard found several inclusions in otherwise fine-grained Boreal lacustrine sediments. These finds included stones and pieces of wood which must have been brought there by man (Wall 1961). In addition were found a 2-meter-long, smoothed and sharpened hazelwood spear and the remains of two large fish. These were found in a small, shallow bay which was partially blocked off from the open lake by a low gravel bank. Wall's interpretation is that fish sought out these protected shallows during spawning, where they could be driven toward a spear-holder with stones and sticks.

CHAPTER THIRTEEN

Comparison of Data and Expectations

As was stated previously, the purpose of the model of subsistence and settlement decisions is to provide a coherent set of expectations which can be compared to archeological data. Its greatest value should be the generation of such expectations about many different classes of data, so that material—which may intuitively seem uniformative or perhaps ambiguous—can be organized and made to yield the greatest amount of information possible. The data presented above certainly seems to be lacking in clear-cut indications of patterned differences in subsistence activities: All sites are more or less close to water; all the faunas show emphasis of big game hunting; and all show fish which spawn in the spring. There are, however, a significant number of differences among the sites which, when examined in light of the expectations of the model, appear to form a coherent pattern. In order to analyze these differences, the data can best be organized into categories of: resources, location, size, and artifacts.

Resources

The information contained in the resource assemblages of the sites consists of two categories of data: presence–absence and relative proportions of various resource classes. Arguments based on contrasting presence or absence of any material are, of course, risky, since chance factors of preservation and discovery are so important. When, however, an otherwise rich faunal industry lacks certain species or age classes, such lacks should be examined for any consistent and meaningful patterning. The sites with large faunal assemblages are Jägerhaus and Falkenstein Caves and Inzigkofen and Lautereck Shelters, and these will be considered here.

Boar young are born between February and May, with most occurring in March and April. One would expect, therefore, that piglets could occur among the faunas of the winter, spring and summer sites. Both Jägerhaus Cave and Inzigkofen Shelter contain piglets; the others do not.

	Winter	Spring	Summer	Fall
Piglets: (Jägerhaus, Inzigkofen)	+	+	+	−

Red deer young are born between April and July, with most occurring in May and June. Infantile red deer should thus be found among the prey of the spring and summer sites. Inzigkofen is the only site for which red deer fawns are reported.

	Winter	Spring	Summer	Fall
Red deer fawns: (Inzigkofen)	−	+	+	−

Hucho are among the spring-spawning fish, migrating in April into tributaries of the main river. This species, however, more than any other of this region, tends to be deep and rather inaccessible at other times of the year. Consequently, its presence among the fish catch should be not only most probable in spring, but also most likely confined to this season. Both Inzigkofen and Lautereck Shelters show hucho among their faunas.

	Winter	Spring	Summer	Fall
Hucho: (Inzigkofen; Lautereck)	−	+	−	−

As discussed previously, chamois was probably absent from the study area for most of the year, and most likely present during the winter, if at all. Hence, this animal would occur with greatest likelihood in the faunal assemblage of winter sites. Jägerhaus Cave is the only site containing chamois.

	Winter	Spring	Summer	Fall
Chamois: (Jägerhaus)	+	−	−	−

Similarly, the aurochs was probably relatively rare in the study area in the Boreal–Early Atlantic. Because of its habits, one would expect that this animal would most likely have been exploited during fall and winter. Falkenstein Cave is the only one of these four sites in which aurochs occurs.

Aurochs:	Winter	Spring	Summer	Fall
(Falkenstein)	+	–	–	+

Hazelnuts ripen in late August and September, but would be available on the ground and in rodent burrows for much of the rest of the fall. They may have been stored for use in the winter. The probability of their occurrence, then, should be greatest in fall (and perhaps very late in summer), decreasing through the late fall and winter. Hazelnuts are reported for Jägerhaus and Falkenstein Caves.

Hazelnuts:	Winter	Spring	Summer	Fall
(Jägerhaus; Falkenstein)	+	–	–	+ +

The relative proportions of different resource groups may also be informative about seasonality. Specifically, the ratio of different resource classes can be compared among the various sites. The ratio of fish to other animal resources is expected to vary greatly during the year. From the figures for expected utilization, this ratio for the different seasons is:

Fish–other animals:	Winter	Spring	Summer	Fall
	.04	.23	.79	.13

Thus, winter has the lowest, summer the highest, and spring and fall are intermediate.

Since these figures reflect the relative contribution to the diet, then the data from the faunal assemblages should take meat yield of the different animals into account. Ideally the figures representing minimum number of individuals would be used, and corrected for weight and edibility. Unfortunately, these figures are not available for all species for all the sites. Only for Jägerhaus Cave and Lautereck Shelter are complete lists of minimum numbers of individuals given. The only possible approach to a comparison of sites, consequently, would seem to be to use the less meaningful number of bones for each species. The proportion of each resource, based on number of bones and adjusted for weight and edibility, for the four sites is given in Table 45. From these figures, the ratio of fish to other animals at the four sites is:

Fish–other animals:	Jägerhaus	Falkenstein	Inzigkofen	Lautereck
	.00008	.0016	.0011	.0718

TABLE 45

Proportional Meat Contribution at Mesolithic Sites of Southwest Germany[a]

Animal	Jägerhaus	Falkenstein	Inzigkofen	Lautereck
Red deer	46.5	25.0	37.9	59.7
Roe deer	2.7	4.4	11.7	7.4
Boar	49.7	65.0	47.7	21.5
Beaver	.1	.5	1.6	.3
Small game	.5	1.5	.9	4.3
Aurochs	—	2.1	—	—
Chamois	.3	—	—	—
Brown bear	.2	1.4	—	—
Ducks	.001	—	.02	.13
Grouse	.009	.002	.02	.08
Fish	.008	.16	.11	6.70

[a]In percentages.

Thus, Jägerhaus has the lowest, followed by Inzigkofen and Falkenstein, and then Lautereck. These figures are of much smaller magnitude than those predicted, but since fish bones would be preserved and recovered in much smaller proportion than larger and sturdier mammal bones, this is not surprising. The rank order of this ratio among the sites is important here.

The ratio of ducks to other animals may also be considered. For the different seasons, the expected ratios are:

Ducks–other animals:	Winter	Spring	Summer	Fall
	.02	.09	—	.04

Thus, summer has the lowest, followed by winter, fall, and spring. In the four sites, these ratios are:

Ducks–other animals:	Jägerhaus	Falkenstein	Inzigkofen	Lautereck
	.00001	—	.0002	.0013

This ratio is lowest at Falkenstein Cave, followed by Jägerhaus, then Inzigkofen and Lautereck.

Significant seasonal changes occur also in the importance of the big game species, red deer, and boar, relative to other resources. The expected ratios are:

Big game–other animals:	Winter	Spring	Summer	Fall
	3.8	1.0	.8	2.5

These resources are most important in winter, followed by fall, spring, and summer. The ratios for big game (including aurochs, bear, and chamois, whose capture may be expected to result from expeditions after the other big game) are:

Big game—other animals:	Jägerhaus	Falkenstein	Inzigkofen	Lautereck
	124.0	46.6	36.6	7.8

The ratio is highest at Jägerhaus, followed by Inzigkofen, Falkenstein, and Lautereck. Again, the rank order, not the absolute magnitude of this ratio, must be examined here, since the large mammal bones would show the best preservation.

Finally, the relative importance of the two major species, red deer and boar, can be considered. The expected ratios of boar to red deer are:

Boar—red deer:	Winter	Spring	Summer	Fall
	.61	.55	1.00	1.17

Boar are the relatively more important in fall, followed by summer, winter, and spring. These same ratios for the sites are:

Boar—red deer:	Jägerhaus	Falkenstein	Inzigkofen	Lautereck
	1.07	2.60	1.26	.36

Falkenstein Cave has the highest ratio, followed by Inzigkofen, Jägerhaus, and Lautereck.

From these considerations of resource proportions, some suggestions may be made. Jägerhaus Cave has the lowest proportion of fish and the highest of big game, a low proportion of ducks, and an intermediate relative importance of boar: This constellation of traits agrees most closely with the expectations for winter. Falkenstein Cave agrees most with the fall expectations for both boar and general big game importance; its fish proportions resemble the relative importance in spring; and its lack of ducks agrees most with summer expectations. Inzigkofen resembles spring or summer in its big game importance, spring or fall in the proportion of ducks, summer in the importance of boar, and fall in the importance of fish. Finally, Lautereck most approximates the spring or summer expectations for the relative importance of fish and big game, and spring for the importance of boar and ducks.

The results of these considerations of resource assemblages may be summarized by a table for each site (see Tables 46—49).

The total configuration of these seasonal indications tends to suggest that Jägerhaus Cave most reflects a winter subsistence strategy, Falkenstein Cave one of fall, and Inzigkofen and Lautereck Shelters a spring strategy. These suggestions must be considered in conjunction with other evidence.

TABLE 46

Seasonal Indications for Jägerhaus Cave

Evidence	Winter	Spring	Summer	Fall
Piglets	+	+	+	
Chamois	+			
Hazelnuts	+			+ +
Fish	+			
Ducks	+			
Big game	+			
Boar	+			

TABLE 47

Seasonal Indications for Falkenstein Cave

Evidence	Winter	Spring	Summer	Fall
Aurochs	+			+
Hazelnuts	+			+ +
Fish		+		
Ducks			+	
Big game				+
Boar				+

TABLE 48

Seasonal Indications for Inzigkofen Shelter

Evidence	Winter	Spring	Summer	Fall
Piglets	+	+	+	
Red deer fawns		+	+	
Hucho		+		
Fish				+
Ducks		+		+
Big game			+	
Boar			+	

TABLE 49

Seasonal Indications for Lautereck Shelter

Evidence	Winter	Spring	Summer	Fall
Hucho		+		
Fish		+	+	
Ducks		+		
Big game		+	+	
Boar		+		

Location

Specific expectations about site locations in the various seasons were generated by the model. These include statements about immediate shelter provided, situation in relation to resource distributions, and location relative to one another. In general, the need for protection from wind and precipitation was probably greatest in winter, followed by fall, spring, and summer.

There are various factors to consider about the sites in terms of the protection offered. The sites fall into three categories according to the natural shelter provided: caves, rock shelters, and open-air sites. Caves not only provide protection from wind and precipitation, but also tend to maintain temperatures more moderate than external extremes. Rock shelters offer protection in accord with their size and orientation relative to wind direction. Open-air sites provide the least natural protection, only that of topography and vegetation.

The orientation of the cave and shelter sites affects the degree of shelter they offer: Southern exposures tend to receive greater insolation and thus to be warmer and more comfortable during the colder months. Most commonly, winds of this region come from the west and southwest, so that exposures away from these directions would be more protected. Based on these observations, southeast should be the most protected and insolated orientation, followed by south, and then either southwest or east, depending on the relative importance of wind and insolation. The orientation of each site is:

Jägerhaus	Falkenstein	Schunters	Inzigkofen	Lautereck
SE	SW	SSE	WSW	SW

Thus, Jägerhaus Cave has the most protected orientation, followed by Schunters Cave, then Falkenstein Cave and Lautereck Shelter, and finally, Inzigkofen Shelter.

Other factors important in affecting the degree of protection offered by a site through their influence on wind flow are the relative width and depth of the valley and the shape of the valley around the site. The approximate width of the valley floor at each site is:

Jägerhaus	Falkenstein	Schunters	Inzigkofen	Lautereck
250 m	300 m	250 m	400 m	550 m

Thus, the caves are located in narrower segments of the valleys than the two shelter sites. Jägerhaus Cave is situated deep in the Alb valley of the Danube, while Schunters Cave is also deep in the Alb, in a tributary valley. Falkenstein Cave is further downstream on the Danube, but still well within the Alb. Inzigkofen, on the other hand, is on the Danube just before it leaves the Alb; just downstream of the site, the valley floor widens considerably. Lautereck Shelter, too, is on the edge of the Alb, where the Danube runs along its southern edge; to the south of the river are lower rolling hills of Oberschwaben.

Jägerhaus Cave is further protected by being situated on a north–south loop of the Danube, so that westerly winds coming down the valley are blocked before they reach the site. Similarly, Schunters Cave is located in a small side-arm of its valley, out of line of any windcourses in the valley. The other sites are more directly in the main courses of the valley. In addition, Jägerhaus Cave lies in the path of a spring which surfaces in the springtime, so that this site may not have been inhabitable in the springtime. Falkenstein Cave may have been less suitable for habitation in winter and spring, due to the icicles formed by seepage and the spring runoff partially through the roof.

From all these considerations, it appears that Jägerhaus Cave provides the greatest shelter, followed by Schunters Cave, Falkenstein Cave, and the two rock shelters. These rankings, together with the seasonal periods of unsuitability for occupation for Jägerhaus and Falkenstein Caves support the provisional suggestion of seasonality of the sites derived from the resource assemblages:

Jägerhaus:	winter
Falkenstein:	fall
Inzigkofen:	spring
Lautereck:	spring

Schunters Cave seems to offer shelter intermediate between that of Jägerhaus and Falkenstein Caves, so that a fall or winter occupation is suggested. The Federsee sites, providing the least natural shelter, would appear to suggest a summer occupation.

Based on resource distributions discussed earlier, the following expectations were derived: Winter camp should be deep in the Danube Valley; spring camp would probably be downriver near a tributary mouth; summer camp should be either farther down along the wider parts of the main river, or on a lake in Oberschwaben; and fall camp should again be on the upper river or one of its tributaries. From these expectations, together with considerations of limiting effort, it was further suggested that the main axis of movement was east–west: from deep in the Alb in winter, east to the lower Danube or Oberschwaben in summer; and the spring and fall sites should be intermediate between these two locations. It may be here suggested that, if indeed there was some degree of aggregation in summer and separation for fall and winter, then there may in fact have been two such patterns of movement along different axes. The other fall–winter locations may have been, not to the west of the summer camp, but to the north or northeast, into the eastern Alb for its protection. The expected pattern of movement, then, is:

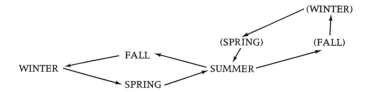

Figure 50 presents again the relative locations of the sites discussed here. These relative positions are also in accord with the suggested seasonality of the sites. Jägerhaus Cave lies at the extreme west of this series of sites, deep in the upper Danube Valley, as expected for a winter camp. Falkenstein Cave and Inzigkofen Shelters are roughly intermediate along the axis between Jägerhaus Cave and Federsee, while Federsee itself lies at the eastern end of this east–west axis. Lautereck and Schunters Cave may represent the spring and fall (or winter) components of a second, northward axis leading out of Federsee, with Lautereck somewhat closer and more exposed, while Schunters Cave is deeper in the Alb.

The immediate proximity to water of each of these sites agrees with this suggested seasonality. As discussed earlier, it is assumed that distance to water may correlate with the importance of fishing. That is, in seasons of great fishing importance, sites closer to the fish-productive waters would be chosen. The horizontal and vertical distances to water for each of the sites are:

	Jägerhaus	Falkenstein	Schunters	Inzigkofen	Lautereck
Horizontal:	300 m	300 m	300 m	70 m	50 m
Vertical:	75 m	35 m	7 m	5 m	4 m

The two shelters are thus much closer to the rivers, in accord with their probable occupation during spring, when fishing was significant. No precise figures for the Federsee sites can be given, but they were apparently quite close to the shores.

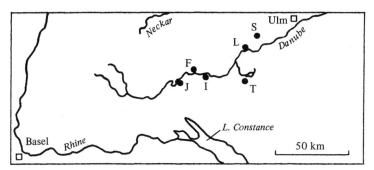

Figure 50   *Location of major sites. J: Jägerhaus Cave; F: Falkenstein Cave; I: Inzigkofen Shelter; T: Tannstock; L: Lautereck Shelter; S: Schunters Cave.*

Furthermore, both Inzigkofen and Lautereck Shelters, in contrast to the cave sites, are located close to broad floodplains and numerous tributaries, probably the focus of fishing activities in spring. The location of the Federsee sites along lakeshores, especially their concentration around the shallower south and west shores and around inlets and outlets, is in agreement with the probable focus of late spring and summer fishing activities in shallows and stream mouths. In addition, the scant evidence of fish spearing in the shallows of Federsee (and perhaps the damming of these shallows) is in accord with summer occupation, when many fish tend to be located in shallow water close to shore.

All of the above evidence seems to support the following settlement scheme:

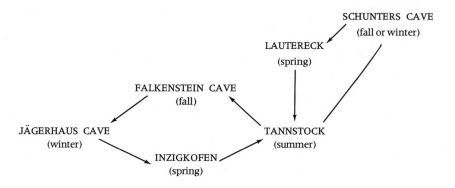

Size

The pattern of settlement as presented thus far must be compared to the expectations about group size in the various seasons. It was suggested that summer aggregations were largest, with a maximum perhaps in the range of from 54 to 108 people. Fall and winter groups should have been smaller, perhaps in the range of from 17 to 33 people maximum. In spring, group size should have been even smaller.

If the cave and shelter sites were chosen, at least in part, because they offered some protection, then the population should be able to be accommodated within the site (at least in times of inclement weather, since many of the activities may have occurred at the mouth or outside altogether). The relative size—under the roof—of each site, therefore, should be proportional to the maximum population which could be accommodated. From the dimensions for each, a figure for floor area under roof can be calculated for each site:

	Jägerhaus	Falkenstein	Schunters	Inzigkofen	Lautereck
Area:	123–156 m²	118–150 m²	59–75 m²	19–24 m²	12–15 m²

Jägerhaus and Falkenstein Caves are the largest, and quite similar in size, followed by Schunters Cave, and then the two rock shelters.

Estimates of the population corresponding to these floor areas are difficult. Naroll's figure (10 square meters per person) correlating the two is derived from artificial housing of agricultural communities, and thus is not directly applicable (Naroll 1962). For lack of better figures, it might be used to provide an estimate, in this case probably a low one, since the natural shelters may have housed the whole population only occasionally. Using this figure, the population estimates for the sites are:

	Jägerhaus	Falkenstein	Schunters	Inzigkofen	Lautereck
Population:	12—16	12—15	6—8	2	1—2

These figures are in accord both in absolute and relative magnitude with the expectations generated from the model. The probable fall and winter sites, Falkenstein and Jägerhaus Caves, have roughly the same areas, and could accommodate populations of similar size. The shelter sites, probably representing spring occupations, could house, by contrast, small groups, although perhaps not as small as suggested by the estimates here.

Figures for the Federsee sites, on the other hand, are even more difficult to determine. The average areas quoted by Reinerth are quite large, from 2500 to 5000 square meters, but as mentioned, probably result from overlapping but not congruent occupations. Furthermore, the area of an open-air occupation may be much larger than that confined in, or geared to a natural shelter. One approach to this problem may be to utilize Reinerth's data on the hut outlines at Tannstock. Specifically, if the 15 huts that are purported to represent one occupation are assumed actually to do so, then these may be used to formulate population estimates. If each hut is assumed to have housed one family, or from 3 to 5 people, then the population would range from 45 to 75 people.

An alternative approach also utilizes this assumption that the 15 huts represent one occupation, but deals with the area covered by this cluster of huts, which is approximately 600 square meters. Draper has reported figures of population size and camp area for four !Kung Bushman camps (Draper, 1973), which are as follows (Table 50). Using these figures as estimates of the magnitude of the area of open-air camps of hunter—gatherers, estimates for the camp at Tannstock are:

m^2/person:	3.9	14.7	16.4	32.4	//	16.8 average
Population:	154	41	37	19	//	36 average

63 average

TABLE 50

!Kung Camp Population Densities[a]

Camp	m²/person
1	3.9
2	14.7
3	16.4
4	32.4
	16.8 average

[a]After Draper 1973.

Thus, a range of from 19 to 154 people, or using the average area or the average of the four population estimates, a smaller range of from 36 to 63 people is suggested. This range is in close agreement with the estimate derived from assuming one family per hut (45–75). The range for Tannstock may be summarized as from 36 to 75 people. The assumed summer occupancy of this site is supported by these figures, since the expected summer maximum population was 54 to 108 people.

The expected and estimated actual populations for the different seasons may be summarized in Table 51.

If the family of 3–5 people was a coresident unit in the Mesolithic, then summer camp would have been occupied by up to 15 families, fall and winter camps by 2–6 families, and spring camp by perhaps 1 family.

Artifacts

Finally, the differences in artifact assemblages among the sites may be considered in conjunction with their probable seasonality. Because of all the unknowns intermediate between site activities and archeological artifact analy-

TABLE 51

Population Estimates for the Mesolithic Sites

Season	Seasonal estimate from model	Estimated relative site population	Site
Spring	(17–33)	2	Inzigkofen
Spring	(17–33)	1–2	Lautereck
Summer	54–108 (max.)	36–75	Tannstock
Fall	17–33 (max.)	12–15	Falkenstein
Winter	17–33 (max.)	12–16	Jägerhaus
Fall or winter	17–33 (max.)	6–8	Schunters

TABLE 52

Percentages of Lithic Tool Classes at the Mesolithic Sites

Tool class	Jäg	Fal	Sch	Inz	Lau	1	5s	8	18	36	65	76
Microliths	43	25	40−	15	7	21	50	35	50	27	34	36
Blade points	—	1	5−	—	7	5	—	2	4	2	3	—
Notched blades	6	4	—	3	37	4	5	6	—	2	2	5
Saws	5	8	5−	13	—	—	—	—	—	—	—	—
Retouched blades	26	29	10−	44	13	3	3	6	8	1	5	2
Borers	1	4	—	2	—	—	2	8	2	8	4	—
Burins	1	6	5+	1	—	21	8	23	9	25	24	7
Scrapers	16	23	30−	22	37	45	32	21	27	37	28	51

sis, only a few observations may be made. Table 52 presents the relative percentages of the surviving assemblages, grouped so as to allow site comparison.

For a variety of reasons, these artifact proportions in most cases are not necessarily reliable reflections of originally deposited artifact percentages. For Falkenstein Cave, only rough approximations could be made of the proportions from Peters' excavations, since his material was lost. The artifacts from Peters' excavation of Inzigkofen were also lost and, in addition, not reported, so that these counts represent only that portion excavated by Taute. The Lautereck figures represent the excavated material, but these derive from only part of the site, since the rest was disturbed. Since this site is dated only to the very late Mesolithic, it is not representative of the same time periods as the other sites. The material from Schunters Cave represents a very small assemblage, but even so, one which spans the time from the Beuronien B through the Late Mesolithic; thus it also is not strictly comparable in time with the other sites. The Federsee material derives from surface collecting over a number of years by different people, including many amateur collectors. Furthermore, virtually all the sites show mixed occupations including Paleolithic and Neolithic, in addition to several stages of the Mesolithic.

These observations on chronological differences among the sites introduce the necessity of considering chronological changes in tool frequencies. Within the Mesolithic, there were apparently significant changes in tool proportions through time. An examination of the proportions of major artifact classes in the different periods of occupation at Jägerhaus Cave indicates the nature of these changes (Table 53).

Thus, within this site, microliths and burins tend to decrease through time, while the other artifact classes all tend to increase. The decrease in microliths is coincidental with the appearance of antler harpoons, which may represent

TABLE 53

Percentages of Tool Classes at Jägerhaus Cave in Different Mesolithic Periods[a]

Period	Microliths	Burins	Notched blades	Scrapers	Retouched blades
Late Mesolithic	16	—	9	31	38
Beuronien C	61	1	5	5	27
Beuronien B	85	—	3	2	6
Beuronien A	88	3	1	3	5

[a] After Taute n.d. a.

a functional replacement of composite projectiles utilizing microliths. In this connection, it is interesting that burins, commonly associated with bone and antler working, do not increase with the apparent increase in antler working associated with harpoon manufacture. It may be that other artifacts, perhaps the notched blades, were primarily used to make these harpoons. In any event, if one assumes that the relative importance of various activities at this site remained roughly the same through time, that is, that Jägerhaus Cave retained its functional role in the yearly settlement system, then the changes in artifact proportions represent functional replacements which should have occurred throughout the study area.

Support for this assumption is found in the evidence of similar changes occurring during the Mesolithic of other regions. At Birsmatten-Basisgrotte in Switzerland, the proportions of these tool classes for Levels 5 through 1 are given in Table 54.

Thus, most of the artifact classes show similar changes, except that scrapers tend to decrease rather than increase through time. Wyss (1973) characterizes the later Swiss Mesolithic, represented in Levels 2 and 1 of Birsmatten, as a "Notched Blade–Transverse Arrowhead–Antler Harpoon Horizon," stressing the increased abundance of both notched blades and harpoons in this period as compared to earlier times.

TABLE 54

Percentages of Tool Classes at Birsmatten-Basisgrotte by Level[a]

Level	Microliths	Burins	Notched blades	Scrapers	Retouched blades
1 (Upper)	14	4	32	17	33
2	30	5	18	20	24
3	40	6	9	21	19
4	51	4	11	20	13
5 (Lower)	37	9	12	31	9

[a] After Bandi 1954.

The importance of these changes to the present discussion is that differences among sites in artifact proportions may be related to chronological, not functional, differences. Falkenstein Cave, Inzigkofen Shelter, and Levels 9–6 of Jägerhaus Cave all show occupations spanning the Beuronien C and Late Mesolithic and should be roughly comparable. But different admixtures of these two stages could produce different proportions of tools unrelated to functional differences. Lautereck Shelter, lacking the Beuronien C component entirely, could be expected a priori to contain fewer microliths and burins and more of other tool classes than a functionally similar site occupied in both periods. Schunters Cave, on the other hand, having been occupied during the Beuronien B in addition to the later periods, would probably contain more microliths and burins, and fewer of the other tool classes than a functionally similar site occupied only in the Beuronien C and Late Mesolithic.

These considerations are further complicated when one considers the mixed occupations of the Federsee sites, since Paleolithic and Neolithic occupations are common here as well. Compared to the Mesolithic, the Late Paleolithic tends to show more burins, backed blades, and blade points, and fewer microliths (Taute n.d. a). Mesolithic sites with a Late Paleolithic component, consequently, would probably show a higher frequency of these macrolithic categories than a similar, purely Mesolithic site. It is therefore consistent that Federsee sites #5s and #76, the only two not occupied in the Late Paleolithic, are the two with the lowest proportions of burins and blade points, and among the highest proportion of microliths.

The result of these considerations is that comparison of lithics among these sites cannot be too rigorous, that too much significance should not be attached to any specific proportional differences. The greatest comparability should be among the three sites occupied during the Beuronien C and Late Mesolithic only. In accord with these conclusions, only tentative suggestions can be proposed. The majority of microliths were probably used as points and barbs for arrows, and would have been most important in big game hunting (with the possible exception of transverse arrowheads which may have been used for birds). Finds of mounted microliths (Petersson 1951) and of microliths lodged in the bones of big game species (Hallam et al. 1973; Noe-Nygaard 1973; Ströbel 1959) support this association. Consequently, one would expect the relative importance of big game and proportion of microliths to show a pattern of covariation. Table 55 indicates that such a pattern does exist.

Furthermore, since red deer antlers are in best condition in fall and winter, one might expect that burins, if associated with antler working (other than the manufacture of harpoons?), should be relatively more important during these seasons. Both Falkenstein and Schunters Caves show relatively high proportions of burins, but Jägerhaus Cave has few. As discussed previously, the high fre-

TABLE 55

Comparison of Big Game Importance and Percentage Microliths

	Jägerhaus (Winter)	Falkenstein (Fall)	Inzigkofen (Spring)	Lautereck (Spring)
Expected				
big game–other animals	3.8	2.5	1.0	1.0
Actual				
big game–other animals	124.0	46.6	36.0	7.8
Percentage microliths	43	25	15	7

quency of burins at the Federsee sites probably reflects the Late Paleolithic and earlier Mesolithic occupations.

In addition, it was suggested earlier that the fall site should show a significant amount of skin-dressing and clothing-manufacture activities in preparation for winter. If this is so, then one should expect relatively higher proportions of associated artifacts, such as borers, scrapers, and needles at a fall site. Falkenstein Cave has the highest proportion of borers of any site except for some of the mixed occupations at Federsee; Schunters Cave, however, has no borers, but has the only needles reported. Both sites have relatively high proportions of scrapers, but are surpassed by the Federsee sites and Lautereck Shelter. Since this latter site, however, represents a very late Mesolithic occupation, its high frequency of scrapers may reflect the trend toward an increase in scrapers through the Mesolithic. The high proportion of scrapers at Federsee, on the other hand, may actually be of functional significance, since the two sites with neither Paleolithic nor Neolithic occupations, #5s and #76, also show very high scraper percentages. The possibility of functional differences within this broad category of scrapers is suggested by a study of the edge angles of these artifacts at several sites. For the Federsee sites #5s (17 scrapers) and #76 (30 scrapers) the average angle in each is 72°, while for the scrapers of Jägerhaus Cave, Levels 9–6 (25 scrapers), the average angle is 65°. Furthermore, the most common type of scraper at both of these Federsee sites is Taute's type #F–6, round scrapers. At both Jägerhaus and Falkenstein Caves this is one of the rarest types; most common at these sites are Taute's type #F–2 (short), #F–3 (broad), #F–7 (nosed), and #F–8 (side-scrapers). The significance of these differences, however, remains unclear.

Conclusions and Discussion

The results of these considerations support the application of the general model to the Mesolithic of southwest Germany, and help elucidate the probable functional role of the various sites in the subsistence–settlement system. A pattern of seasonal movement of base camp coupled with sequential fission and fusion of the coresident group is proposed. The major axis of movement apparently connected the deep valleys in the Alb with the more open lakeside areas of Oberschwaben. Several such axes may have radiated out from the larger summer occupations at Federsee, one leading westward, the other to the north. At the end of these axes would be the sheltered winter sites—Jägerhaus Cave, for example—while the spring and fall occupations would be in intermediate locations. Both Inzigkofen and Lautereck Shelters apparently represent spring camps, and Falkenstein and perhaps Schunters Caves seem to have been fall occupations.

Such a pattern was probably not rigid, but remained flexible enough to respond to specific conditions of a particular season or year. Response flexibility is an important characteristic of hunter–gatherer subsistence and settlement behavior and population arrangements, and the significance of opportunistic behavior should not be minimized. Yearly variations in nut crops, oscillations of prey populations, and deviations from seasonal climatic norms all determine a particular constellation of environmental conditions requiring specific immediate responses. Over the long run, however, these conditions and the human behavioral responses should tend to show clustering around average configurations, and it is this average pattern that the model attempts to approximate.

Because the base camps for the various seasons are expected to have been of different sizes, reflecting a pattern of seasonal aggregation and dispersal of the population, then the sites assigned to these seasons should be represented in different proportions. The largest summer sites should be least abundant, followed by the fall and winter sites, with the small spring sites being the most abundant. As was mentioned earlier, the vast majority of the "sites" around Federsee contain only a few nondiagnostic artifacts, and cannot be taken to represent base camps. The number of sites sufficiently rich, and datable with certainty to the Mesolithic, is seven. Furthermore, these are rather thin surface sites, and may represent only a relatively few reoccupations at different periods of the Mesolithic. By comparison, the Mesolithic deposits at the cave and shelter sites are quite thick, from 45 centimeters to 1 meter in places, and apparently result from numerous reoccupations. It may well be, consequently, that the number of occupations represented at Federsee, and the cave and shelter sites, respectively, are inversely proportional to the number of different sites involved.

Nevertheless, it is expected that the number of *different* nonsummer sites be relatively high: greatest in spring, intermediate in fall and in winter. The fall and winter populations, for example, may have been half of that in summer, so that these cold-weather sites should be twice as numerous. If Schunters Cave indeed represents a fall or winter camp, and indicates a second, northerly axis of movement from Federsee, then such a segmentation of the summer population into two groups is suggested. The study area may have contained two cold-weather territories, one in the western Alb, the other in the east.

The distribution of other Mesolithic sites in the study area (Figure 38) supports the possibility of two separate cold-weather territories in the Alb. In addition, the location of these other sites may permit some suggestions regarding their season of occupation. Along the western, upper Danube or four additional cave–shelter sites. Less than 1 kilometer from Jägerhaus Cave is the site of Probstfels, while further downriver, between Falkenstein Cave and Inzigkofen Shelter, are Teufelsloch Cave and Bernaufels Shelter. These three sites were mentioned by Peters as containing material similar to Falkenstein and Inzigkofen, and were all grouped together in his "Upper Danube Mesolithic [Peters 1934, 1941]." It may be that Probstfels represents an alternative winter camp, Teufelsloch Cave a fall site, and Bernaufels another spring site. Another site in this region, which is better documented, is Zigeunerfels. This small shelter (approximately 24 square meters maximum floor area) is about 1.5 kilometers from Inzigkofen on the Schmeie River just before it joins the Danube. It was excavated by Taute, who found Mesolithic levels dating to the Beuronien A and B, and thus it is not contemporary with Inzigkofen (Taute 1972b). From its size and location, it seems likely that it served as a spring camp, similar to Inzigkofen.

In the eastern part of the Danube and Alb are more reported Mesolithic finds. Along the Danube itself are two reported sites near Lautereck, one 3 kilometers to the east, the other 3 kilometers to the west. Because nothing further is known of these sites, it is difficult to discuss them, although from their location alone, it may be that these, like Lautereck, represent spring occupations. Alternatively, it is possible that they are locations of satellite hunting camps, perhaps originating from Lautereck. A cluster of six different reported sites occurs along the Blau River in the eastern Alb (Figure 51). Along the lower Blau, at the mouth of a tributary stream, occur two adjacent open-air sites which yielded microliths, scrapers, retouched blades, borers, and cores (*Fundberichte aus Schwaben* 1950–1965). From the exposed position and location at a stream confluence, it is possible that these sites represent spring camps. Farther upriver, along the middle Blau, are four sites, including two caves which contained a variety of tools, and one shelter that had a burial plus an assemblage which included two bone needles. This portion of the Blau Valley is rather wide (500–900 meters) and steep-sided, and apparently formed a long, narrow lake during the Mesolithic, until a new, larger exit of the Blau out of the Alb was formed in the Late Atlantic Period (Zürn 1958). This sheltered lake area would have been a suitable winter habitat for big game, and would have offered greater fishing potential than a simple tributary river valley. Consequently, this part of the Blau, with its caves, may have been the winter focus for the group moving out

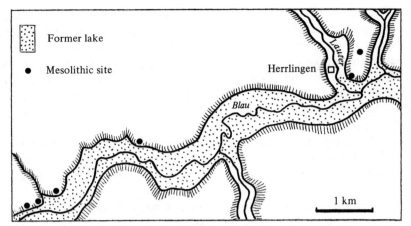

Figure 51 *Mesolithic sites in the Blau Valley.*

along the second axis to the north from Federsee. Lautereck may be a spring camp, and Schunters Cave a fall camp associated with this axis.

An additional five sites are reported: one on the Alb heights above the headwaters of the Blau, the others on the heights above the headwaters of the Grosse Lauter. The exposed position of these sites and their distance from watercourses suggest that they may have been satellite hunting camps rather than base camps. These most likely would have been associated with summer, spring, or fall base camps.

These various sites and their distribution suggests that the spring, fall, and winter sites may indeed be rather numerous, and furthermore, that there were two separate axes of movement radiating out of Federsee. The Federsee, located roughly in the middle of the study area, would have been an appropriate point of aggregation for these two groups in summer.

It must be emphasized that the sites presented here represent archetypes of the seasonal camps postulated: Neither rigid adherence to a fixed seasonal schedule nor yearly reoccupation of each site is to be expected. Specific seasonal conditions would show yearly variation, so that a site may not be suitable each year. For example, animals may change their winter focus from one year to the next, because the time might not be sufficient for the regeneration of their food supply. Given the periodicity of good yields of nut crops, their location from one fall to the next would be expected to change. Furthermore, intensive harvest of firewood around a site in one year might preclude reoccupation in the subsequent year. The necessary shifts of human occupation would have to allow for these variations, but should be in accord with the principles developed here.

The discussion of these Mesolithic sites has stressed their locational attributes. In the case of open-air occupations, the population was free to select sites suiting the seasonal requirements, but the cave and shelter sites would seem to offer more limited choices. That is, once the choice of a natural shelter was made, it might be questioned whether other characteristics, such as exposure or distance from water, were of any significance. An affirmative answer to this question appears to be supported by an examination of those cave and shelter sites *not* occupied during the Mesolithic. Only those sites with reported prehistoric oc- cupations will be considered here; caves and shelters with no reported archeological deposits may suffer from lack of investigation or may have been totally emptied of deposits in recent times. Figures 52 and 53 present the western and eastern parts of the Danube Valley and Alb, with the distribution of Paleolithic (primarily Magdalenian) occupations of caves and shelters as reported by various sources (Paret 1961; Peters 1946; Rieth 1938; Wagner 1973). For comparison, the Mesolithic sites are shown as well.

Most striking from these figures is the difference in patterning of the site distributions for the two time periods. Occupations of both occur together only at one site (Zigeunerfels). The Paleolithic sites tend to be higher up along tributary streams, farther from the Danube, and deeper in the Alb. Mesolithic occupations in the Alb tend to lie along the main river or along the one tributary which apparently formed a narrow lake. A close-up view of this tributary, the Blau (Figure 54), shows the differential distribution of Paleolithic and Mesoli- thic sites: The Mesolithic occupations occur along the former lake shores, while the Paleolithic sites are farther upstream, before it widens into a lake. Thus, it appears that different factors conditioning site location were operating in

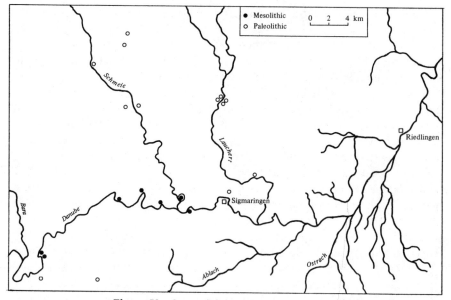

Figure 52   *Cave and shelter sites in the western Alb.*

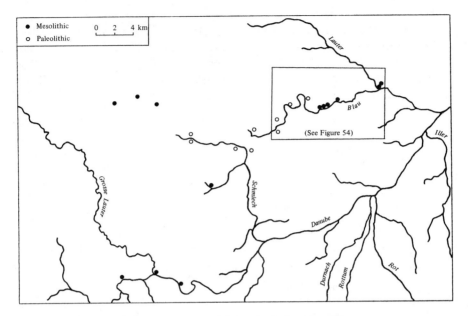

Figure 53 *Cave and shelter sites in the eastern Alb.*

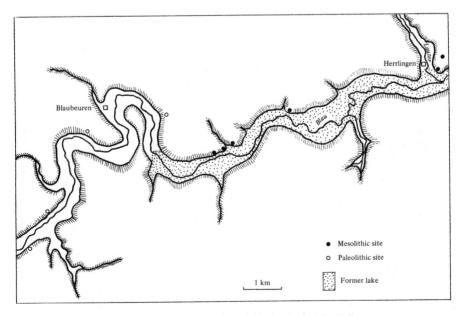

Figure 54 *Paleolithic and Mesolithic sites in the Blau Valley.*

these two periods. The Mesolithic choice of a lake and the larger river in the Alb, rather than the smaller tributaries, may reflect their greater fish potential in winter, when fish would have been, not of great numerical importance, but a significant emergency food. It is clear that choices were made among the various caves and shelters available, and it is suggested here that the characteristics of site location discussed were considered in these choices.

CHAPTER FOURTEEN

Concluding Remarks

The model presented here is very general; its application, however, should be quite specific. The patterns of subsistence and settlement formulated for the later Mesolithic of southwest Germany are adapted to this region and time period, and should not be generalized. Elements of topography, vegetation, and animal resources in other environments could encourage a different set of choices and result in different strategies of subsistence and settlement.

For example, to the west of the study area is the region of the Upper Rhine, whose main valley is extremely wide (up to 30 kilometers) and has a very moderate climate almost as far south as Basel. Adjacent to the valley are the granite hills of the Black Forest in Germany and the Vosges in France, and the limestone Jura in Switzerland. Lakes are almost absent from this region; a few lie high in the Black Forest. Resources during the Mesolithic would have been similar to those of the study area, with two exceptions. Atlantic salmon migrated each year up the Rhine as far south as Schaffhausen and would probably have been extremely important and have exerted a strong pull on settlement toward the river and its tributaries. In addition, migratory waterfowl pass through the region in great numbers along the Rhine corridor; the relatively mild climate

187

encourages many to spend the winter in its low, marshy floodplain. Consequently, waterfowl may have been of much greater importance in this area as compared to the Danube drainage. A consideration of subsistence and settlement in this region would require an investigation of the attributes of these resources (especially density and aggregation size) and the timing of their appearance. The subsequent patterns of resource distribution could then be used to predict patterns of human distribution over the landscape. In this manner, the significance of such sites as Isteiner Klotz Cave on the Rhine (Lais 1929; Schmid 1962, 1965), Birsmatten and other Mesolithic sites in the tributary Birs Valley (Bandi 1956; Bandi et al. 1963; Sarasin 1918; Sedlmeier 1968; Wyss 1957), and the numerous low-lying sites of Mittelbaden to the north (Gersbach 1951) may be elucidated.

To the east of the study area, in North Bavaria, is the hilly region of the Frankish Jura, a continuation of the limestone formation of the Alb. Much of this region lies in the Rhine watershed, and thus may have had significant amounts of salmon. The low areas contain very few lakes or bogs, so that there were probably few waterfowl available. The summer focus of Mesolithic occupation may have centered on the salmon in the rivers. The numerous Mesolithic sites in this area (Freund 1963; Gumpert 1929; 1933; 1938; 1942; Schönweiss 1965a,b, 1967a,b,c, 1968) might be placed in perspective by a consideration of this total resource configuration.

Even within the study area, changes in the resource environment through time doubtless had a strong influence on subsistence and settlement. The contrasting site distribution in the Paleolithic has already been mentioned. Within the Mesolithic, however, there may have been significant differences. If, for example, the moose and aurochs were indeed more abundant during the Preboreal, then these may have been more systematically exploited. Implications of this exploitation might include: lesser significance of the other resources; greater overall resource "pull" toward the low-lying Oberschwaben; and possible lower human population densities if these probably high-prestige resources were more limiting in their utilized proportions.

The environmental differences discussed above would have important consequences for an exploiting population of hunter—gatherers. Such specific conditions must be taken into account when considering the archeological record. The model developed here is capable of investigating these differences and should be a valuable aid to archeological research.

References

Altmann, M.
  1952   Social Behaviour of Elk in the Jackson Hole Area of Wyoming. *Behavior* **IV**(2).
  1956   Patterns and Herd Behavior in Free-ranging Elk of Wyoming. *Zoologica* **41**(2).
Anderson, J.
  1953   Analysis of a Roe Deer Population. *Danish Review of Game Biology* **II**(2).
  1962   Roe Deer Census and Population Analysis by Means of Modified Marking Release Technique. In *The Exploitation of Natural Animal Populations* (British Ecological Society Symposium 2).
Bandi, H. G.
  1956   Sauveterrien im Birstal. *Ur-Schweiz* **XX**(1/2).
Bandi, H. G., R. Bay, C. Gfeller, C. Graffenried, C. Lüdin, E. Müller, H. Müller-Beck, K. Oakley, E. Schmid.
  1963   *Birsmatten-Basisgrotte* (Acta Bernensia I). Bern: Verlag Stämpfli & Cie.
Balikci, A.
  1968   The Netsrlik Eskimos: Adaptive Processes. In *Man the Hunter*, edited by R. B. Lee and I. DeVore. Chicago: Aldine.
Baumhoff, M. A.
  1963   Ecological Determinants of Aboriginal California Populations. *University of California Publications in American Archeology and Ethnology* **49**(2).
Beardsley, R. K.
  1956   Functional and Evolutionary Implications of Community Patterning. Society for American Archeology *Memoir 11*.

189

Becker, C. J.
1945   *Fra Nationalmuseets Arbejdsmark.* Copenhagen: National Museet.
Bergerud, A. T., and F. Manuel
1969   Aerial Census of Moose in Central Newfoundland. *Journal of Wildlife Management*
        33(4).
Bertsch, K.
1949   *Geschichte des Deutschen Waldes.* Jena: Gustav Fischer.
Bicchieri, M. G.
1969   The differential Use of Identical Features of Physical Habitat in Connection with
        Exploitative, Settlement, and Community Patterns. National Museum of Canada:
        Bulletin 230.
Binford, L. R.
1973   Interassemblage Variability—the Mousterian and the "Functional" Argument. In
        The Explanation of Culture Change: Models in Prehistory, edited by C. Renfrew. London:
        Duckworth.
Birdsell, J. B.
1953   Some Environmental and Cultural Factors Influencing the Structuring of Australian
        Aboriginal Populations. *American Naturalist* **87.**
Blank, W.
1961   Sedimentgeschichte. In *Der Federsee,* edited by W. Zimmermann, Stuttgart: Verlag des
        Schwäbischen Albvereins.
1973   *Die Jägerprüfung.* Melsungen: J. Neumann-Neudamm Verlag.
Bodmer-Gessner, V.
1950   Provisorische Mitteilungen über die Ausgrabung einer mesolithische Siedlung in
        Schötz ("Fischerhäusern") Wauwilermoos, Kt. Luzern, durch H. Reinerth im Jahre
        1933. *Jahrbuch der Schweizerischen Gesellschaft fü Urgeschichte* **40.**
Boessneck, J.
1956   Zur Grosse des mitteleuropäischen Rehes in alluvial-vorgeschichtlicher und früher
        historischer Zeit. *Zeitschrift für Säugetierkunde* **21**(3–4).
n.d. a Die Tierknochenfunde aus den mesolithischen Kulturschichten der Jägerhaushöhle.
        In *Untersuchungen zum Mesolithikum und zum Spätpaläolithikum in südlichen Mitteleuropa:
        Naturhistorische Studien,* edited by W. Taute. Tübingen: Manuscript.
n.d. b Die Tierknochen aus der mesolithischen Kulturschicht der Falkensteinhöhle. In
        *Untersuchungen zum Mesolithikum und Spätpaläolithikum in südlichen Mitteleuropa:
        Naturhistorische Studien,* edicted by W. Taute. Tübingen: Manuscript.
n.d. c Tierknochenfunde aus der mesolithischen Kulturschicht unter dem Felsdach Inzigkofen.
        In *Untersuchungen zum Mesolithikum und Spätpaläolithikum in südlichen Mitteleuropa:
        Naturhistorische Studien,* edited by W. Taute. Tübingen: Manuscript.
n.d. d Tierknochenfunde aus den prähistorischen Kulturschichten unter dem Fels lach
        Lautereck. In *Untersuchungen zum Mesolithikum und Spätpaläolithikum in südlichen
        Mitteleuropa: Naturhistorische Studien,* edited by W. Taute. Tübingen: Manuscript.
Boessneck, J., J. Jequier, and H. Stampfli
1963   Die Tierreste. In *Seeburg Burgäschisee-Süd* (Acta Bernensia II). Bern: Verlag Stampfli
        & Cie.
Bouchud, J.
1954   La Renne et la Probleme des Migrations. *L'Anthropologie* **58.**
Brinch-Petersen, E.
1973   A Survey of the Late Palaeolithic and Mesolithic of Denmark. In *The Mesolithic in
        Europe,* edited by S. K. Kozlowski. Warsaw: University of Warsaw Press.
Burckhardt, D., A. Kuster, and R. Schloeth
1961   Recherches Suisses sur les Ongules-Gibier. *La Terre et la Vie* **108**(1).

Burling, R.
  1962 Maximization Theories and the Study of Economic Anthropology. *American Anthropologist* **64**(4).

Busnita, T.
  1967 Die Ichthyofauna des Donauflusses. In *Limnologie der Donau,* edited by R. Liepolt. Stuttgart: Schweizerbart.

Butzer, K.
  1971 *Environment and Archeology* (2nd edition) Chicago: Aldine-Atherton.

Campbell, J. M.
  1968 Territoriality among Ancient Hunters: Interpretations from Ethnography and Nature. In *Anthropological Archeology in the Americas,* edited by B. Meggers. Washington: Anthropological Society of Washington.

Casteel, R. W.
  1972 Two Static Maximum Population-Density Models for Hunter—Gatherers: A First Approximation. *World Archeology* **4**(1).

Chang, K.
  1962 Typology of Settlement and Community Patterns in Some Circumpolar Societies. *Arctic Anthropology* **1**.

Churchman, C. W.
  1968 *The Systems Approach.* New York: Dell.

Clark, J. G. D.
  1954 *Excavations at Star Carr.* Cambridge: Cambridge University Press.
  1958 Blade and Trapeze Industries of the European Stone Age. *Proceedings of the Prehistoric Society* **24**.
  1972 Star Carr: A Case Study in Bioarchaeology. *Addison-Wesley Modular Publications* **10**.

Cook, S.
  1966 The Obsolute "Anti-Market Mentality": A Critique of the Substantive Approach to Economic Anthropology. *American Anthropologist* **68**(2).

Crowe, K. J.
  1969 A Cultural Geography of Northern Foxe Basin, N. W. T. Northern Science Research Group, Department of Indian Affairs and Northern Development Ottawa.

Dalton, G.
  1961 Economic Theory and Primitive Society. *American Anthropologist* **63**(1).

Damas, D.
  1968 The Diversity of Eskimo Societies. In *Man the Hunter,* edited by R. B. Lee and I. Devore. Chicago: Aldine.
  1969 Environment, History, and Central Eskimo Society. National Museum of Canada *Bulletin 230.*
  1972 The Copper Eskimo. In *Hunters and Gatherers Today,* edited by M. G. Bicchieri. New York: Holt.

Darling, F. F.
  1964 *A Herd of Red Deer.* New York: Anchor Books.

Degerbøl, M.
  1964 Some Remarks on Late- and Post-glacial Vertebrate Fauna and its Ecological Relations in Northern Europe. *Supplement to the Journal of Animal Ecology* **3**.

Denniston, R. H.
  1956 Ecology, Behavior and Population Dynamics of the Wyoming or Rocky Mountain Moose. *Zoologica* **41**(3).

Dillon, J. L., and E. O. Heady
  1960 Theories of Choice in Relation to Farmer Decisions. Iowa State University, Agricultural and Home Economics Experiment Station *Research Bulletin 485.*

Douglas, M.
  1966   Population Control in Primitive Groups. *British Journal of Sociology* **66**.
Draper, P.
  1973   Crowding among Hunter—Gatherers: The !Kung Bushmen. *Science* **182**: 301—303.
Drucker, P.
  1951   The Northern and Central Nootkan Tribes. U. S. Bureau of American Ethnology *Bulletin 144*.
Dunning, R. W.
  1959   *Social and Economic Change among the Northern Ojibwa* Toronto: University of Toronto Press.
Eddy, S., and T. Surber
  1947   *Northern Fishes* (3rd edition). Minneapolis: University of Minnesota Press.
Emlen, J. M.
  1966   The Role of Time and Energy in Food Preference. *American Naturalist* **100**.
Eggan, F.
  1968   In Discussions, Part II. In *Man the Hunter*, edited by R. B. Lee and I. Devore. Chicago: Aldine.
Feit, H.
  1973   The Ethno-Ecology of the Waswanipi Cree: or How Hunters Can Manage Their Resources. in *Cultural Ecology*, edited by B. Cox. Toronto: Carleton Library 65.
Firbas, F.
  1949   *Waldgeschichte Mitteleuropas.* Jena: Gustav Fischer.
Fisher, A. D.
  1973   The Cree of Canada: Some Ecological and Evolutionary Considerations. In *Cultural Ecology*, edited by B. Cox. Toronto: Carleton Library 65.
Fitzhugh, W. W.
  1972   Environmental Archeology and Cultural Systems in Hamilton Inlet, Labrador. *Smithsonian Contributions to Anthropology* **16**. Washington, D.C.
Flannery, K. V.
  1971   Archaeological Systems Theory and Early Mesoamerica. In *Man's Imprint from the Past*, edited by J. Deetz. Boston: Little, Brown.
Fleming, A.
  1972   The Genesis of Pastoralism in European Prehistory. *World Archeology* **4**(2).
Flint, R. F.
  1971   *Glacial and Quaternary Geology.* New York: John Wiley.
Freeman, L. G.
  1973   The Significance of Mammalian Faunas from Paleolithic Occupations in Cantabrian Spain. *American Antiquity* **38**.
Freund, G.
  1963   Die ältere und die mittlere Steinzeit in Bayern. *Jahresbericht der Bayrischen Bodendenkmalpflege* **4**.
Fundberichte aus Schwaben
  1965—1950   Stuttgart.
Ganssen, R.
  1957   *Bodengeographie.* Stuttgart: Koehler Verlag.
Garner, B. J.
  1967   Models of Urban Geography and Settlement Location. In *Models in Geography*, edited by R. J. Chorley and P. Haggett. London: Methuen.
Gersbach, E.
  1951   Das Mittelbadische Mesolithikum. *Badische Fundberichte* **19**.
Geyer, O. F. and M. P. Gwinner
  1968   *Geologie von Baden-Württemberg.* Stuttgart: Schweizerbart Verlag.

Göttlich, K.
1961 Vegetationsgeschichte. In *Der Federsee*, edited by W. Zimmermann. Stuttgart: Verlag des Schwäbischen Albvereins.
1965 Der Vorgeschichtliche Damm von Moosburg zum "Insele" im Seelenhofer Ried. *Jahreshefte des Vereins für vaterländische Naturkunde in Württemberg* **120**.
Gould, R. A.
1968 Living Archaeology: The Ngatatjara of Western Australia. *Southwestern Journal of Anthropology* **24** (2).
Grube, W.
1972 *Die Stadt und der Landkreis Ulm*. Stuttgart: Staatliche Archivverwaltung Baden-Württemberg.
Grzimek, B.
1970 *Enzyklopädie des Tierreiches*. Zurich: Heinemann Verlag.
Gubser, N. J.
1965 *The Nunamiut Eskimos: Hunters of Caribou*. New Haven: Yale University Press.
Gulder, A.
1953 Beiträge zur Kenntnis des Niederösterreichischen Mesolithikums. *Archaeologica Austriaca* **12**.
Gumpert, K.
1929 Der Tardenoisienmensch in der Fränkischen Schweiz als Höhlen- und Abrisbewohner. *Mannus* **21**.
1933 Eine Paläolithische und Mesolithisch Abri-Siedlung an der Steinbergwand bei Ensdorf in der Oberpfalz. *Mannus* **25**.
1938 Die Tardenoisienstation Hohlstein im Klumpertal BA Pegnitz. *Germania* **22**.
1942 Mittelsteinzeit. *Bayrische Vorgeschichtsblätter* **16**.
Haas, G.
1964 Fischsterben im Federsee während des strengen Winters 1962–3. *Jahreshefte des Vereins für vaterländische Naturkunde in Württemberg* **118/119**.
1965 Vorkommen und Ökologie des Birkhuhns in Baden-Württemberg. *Jahreshefte des Vereins für vaterländische Naturkunde in Württemberg* **120**.
Haber, A.
1961 Le Sanglier en Pologne. *La Terre et la Vie* **108** (1).
Hagen, A.
1972 Man and Nature: Reflections on Culture and Ecology. *Norwegian Archeological Review* **5** (1).
Haggett, P.
1965 *Locational Analysis in Human Geography*. London: Edward Arnold.
Hahn, J., H. Müller-Beck, and W. Taute
1973 *Eiszeithöhlen im Lonetal*. Stuttgart: Müller and Gräff.
Hallam, J. S., B. Edwards, B. Barnes, and A. Stuart
1973 The Remains of a Late Glacial Elk Associated with Barbed Points from High Furlong, near Blackpool, Lancashire. *Proceedings of the Prehistorical Society* **39**.
Hamilton, F. E. I.
1967 Models of Industrial Location. In *Models in Geography*, edited by R. J. Chorley and P. Huggett. London: Methuen.
Harvey D.
1969 *Explanation in Geography*. New York: St. Martin's Press.
Hawkes, E. W.
1916 The Labrador Eskimo. Canada, Department of Mines, Geological Survey *Memoir 91*, *No. 14*. Ottawa.

194

Hayden, B.
1972   Population Control among Hunter—Gatherers. *World Archeology* **4**(2).
Heck, L.
1935   *Der Deutsche Edelhirsch.* Hamburg: Paul Parey.
1950   *Schwarzwild: Lebensbild des Wildschweins.* Hamburg: Paul Parey.
Hegg, R.
1961   Analysen von Grosswildkot aus dem Schweizerischen Nationalpark zur Ermittlung der Nahrungszusammensetzung. *Revue Suisse de Zoologie* **68**(2).
Heizer, R. F.
1958   Aboriginal California and Great Basin Cartography. *University of California Archeology Survey Report 41.*
Helfer, H.
1949   Die Wirtschaftliche und kulturelle Bedeutung der Binnengewässer. *Die Binnengewässer* **XVII**.
Helm, J.
1961   The Lynx Point People. National Museum of Canada *Bulletin 176.*
1969a   Remarks on the Methodology of Band Composition Analysis. National Museum of Canada *Bulletin 228.*
1969b   Relationship Between Settlement Pattern and Community Pattern. National Museum of Canada *Bulletin 230.*
1972   The Dogrib Indians. In *Hunters and Gatherers Today,* edited by M. G. Bicchieri. New York: Holt.
Herskovits, M. J.
1952   *Economic Anthropology.* New York: Norton.
Holloway, C. W., and H. Jungius
1973   Reintroduction of Certain Mammal and Bird Species into the Gran Paradiso National Park. *Zoologischer Anzeiger* **191**(1/2).
Hölzinger, J.
1970   *Die Vögel Baden-Württembergs—eine Übersicht.* Stuttgart: Schweizerbart.
Honigmann, J. J.
1946   Ethnography and Acculturation of the Fort Nelson Slave. *Yale University Publications in Anthropology* **33**.
1961   *Foodways in a Muskeg Community.* Northern Coordination and Research Centre, Department of Northern Affairs and Natural Resources, Ottawa.
Horn, H. S.
1968   The Adaptive Significance of Colonial Behavior in the Brewer's Blackbird. *Ecology* **49**(4).
Huff, D. L.
1961   Ecological Characteristics of Consumer Behavior. *Regional Scientific Association, Papers and Proceedings* **7**.
Itani, J., and A. Suzili
1967   The Social Unit of Chimpanzees. *Primates* **8**(4).
Izawa, K.
1970   Unit Groups of Chimpanzees and their Nomadism in the Savanna-Woodland. *Primates* **11**(1).
Jackson, H. H. T.
1961   *Mammals of Wisconsin.* Madison: University of Wisconsin Press.
Jarman, M. R.
1972   A Territorial Model for Archaeology: A Behavioural and Geographical Approach. In *Models in Archaeology,* edited by D. L. Clarke. London: Methuen.
Kendeigh, S. C.
1961   *Animal Ecology.* Englewood Cliffs, New Jersey: Prentice Hall.

Kiefer, F.
1972   *Naturkunde des Bodensees.* Zurich: Heinemann.
Kleiber, H. and B. Nievergelt
1973   Biberfrasspuren im Uferwald der Nussbaumer Seen. *Revue Suisse de Zoologie* **80**(3).
Kley, A.
1938−1951   (Untitled Report). *Fundberichte aus Schwaben* **11**.
1952   (Untitled Report). *Fundberichte aus Schwaben* **12**.
Knight, R.
1965   A Re-examination of Hunting, Trapping, and Territoriality among the Northeastern
         Algonkian Indians. In *Man, Culture, and Animals,* edited by A. Leeds and A. J. Vayda.
         Washington: American Association for the Advancement of Science.
Kroeber, A. L.
1925   *Handbook of the Indians of California.* Washington: U. S. Government Printing Office.
1939   Cultural and Natural Areas of Native North America. *University of California Publications
         in American Archeology and Ethnology* **38**.
Kummer, H.
1971   Spacing Mechanisms in Social Behavior. In *Man and Beast,* edited by J. F. Eisenberg and
         W. S. Dillon. Washington: Smithsonian Institution Press.
Kurt, F.
1966   Feldbeobachtungen und Versuche über das Revierverhalten der Rehböcke. *Revue Suisse
         de Zoologie* **73**(3).
1968   *Das Sozialverhalten des Rehes: Eine Feldstudie.* Zurich: Conzett and Huber.
Kurten, B.
1968   *Pleistocene Mammals of Europe.* London: Weidenfeld and Nicolson.
Lais, R.
1929   Ein Werkplatz des Azilio-Tardenoisiens am Isteiner Klotz. *Badische Fundberichte* **2**.
Laughlin, W. S.
1968   Hunting: An Integrating Biobehavior System and Its Evolutionary Importance. In *Man
         the Hunter,* edited by R. B. Lee and I. DeVore. Chicago: Aldine.
Leacock, E.
1973   The Montagnais-Naskapi Band. In *Cultural Ecology,* edited by B. Cox. Toronto: Carleton
         Library 65.
LeClair, E. E., Jr.
1962   Economic Theory and Economic Anthropology. *American Anthropologist* **64**(6).
Lee, R. B.
1968   What Hunters Do for a Living, or, How to Make Out on Scarce Resources. In *Man
         the Hunter,* edited by R. B. Lee and I. DeVore. Chicago: Aldine.
1969   !Kung Bushman Subsistence: An Input−Output Analysis. National Museum of Canada
         Bulletin **230**.
1972   The !Kung Bushmen of Botswana. In *Hunters and Gatherers Today,* edited by M. G.
         Bicchieri. New York: Holt.
Lee, R. B. and I. DeVore (Eds.)
1968   *Man the Hunter.* Chicago: Aldine.
Lepiksaar, J.
n.d.   Die Fischreste aus den prähistorischen Kulturschichten unter dem Feldsdach Lautereck.
         In *Untersuchungen zum Mesolithikum und zum Spätpaläolithikum in südlichen Mitteleuropa:
         Naturhistorische Studien,* edited by W. Taute. Tübingen: Manuscript.
Lowe, V. P. W.
1961   A Discussion on the History, Present Status and Future Conservation of Red Deer in
         Scotland. *La Terre et la Vie* **108**(1).
1966   Observations on the Dispersal of Red Deer on Rhum. In *Play, Exploration and Territory
         in Mammals* (Symposia, Zoological Society of London 18).

Luce, R. D., and H. Raiffa
   1957   *Games and Decisions.* New York: Wiley.
MacArthur, R. H.
   1972   *Geographical Ecology.* New York: Harper and Row.
MacArthur, R. H., and E. R. Pianka
   1966   On Optimal Use of a Patchy Environment. *American Naturalist* **100**.
Marshall, L.
   1968   In "Discussions, Part II." In *Man the Hunter,* edited by R. B. Lee and I. DeVore. Chicago: Aldine.
Martinka, C. J.
   1969   Population Ecology of Summer Resident Elk in Jackson Hole, Wyoming. *Journal of Wildlife Management* **33**(3).
Mason, J. A.
   1946   Notes on the Indians of the Great Slave Lake Area. *Yale University Publications in Anthropology* **34**.
Mauser, P. F.
   1970   Die Jungpaläolithische Höhlenstation Petersfels im Hegau. *Badische Fundberichte, Sonderheft* **13**.
McCance, R. A., and E. M. Widdowson
   1947   *The Chemical Composition of Foods.* Brooklyn: Chemical Publishing.
Mellars, P.
   1970   Some Comments on the Notion of "Functional Variability" in Stone Tool Assemblages. *World Archeology* **2**(1).
Mills, D.
   1971   *Salmon and Trout: A Resource, Its Ecology, Conservation, and Management.* New York: Macmillan.
Milne, L., and M. Milne
   1958   *Paths across the Earth.* New York: Harper and Brothers.
Murdock, G. P.
   1969   Correlations of Exploitive and Settlement Patterns. National Museum of Canada *Bulletin 230.*
Murie, O. J.
   1951   *The Elk of North America.* Baltimore: Williams and Wilkins.
Naroll, R. S.
   1962   Floor Area and Settlement Population. *American Antiquity* **27**(4).
Nishida, T.
   1968   The Social Group of Wild Chimpanzees in the Mahali Mountains. *Primates* **9**(3).
Noe-Nygaard, N.
   1973   The Vig Bull. *Bulletin of the Geological Society of Denmark* **22**.
Nuber, A. H.
   1954   *Zur Schichtenfolge des kleingerätigen Mesolithikum in Württemberg und Hohenzollern.* Festschrift für Peter Goessler (Tübinger Beitrage zur Vor- und Frühgeschichte).
Oberg, K.
   1973   *The Social Economy of the Tlingit Indians.* Seattle: University of Washington Press.
Odum, E. P.
   1971   *Fundamentals of Ecology* (3rd edition). Philadelphia: Saunders.
Orr, R. T.
   1970   *Animals in Migration.* New York: Macmillan.
Osgood, C. B.
   1932   The Ethnography of the Great Bear Lake Indians. National Museum of Canada *Bulletin 70.*

1936 Contributions to the Ethnography of the Kutchin. *Yale University Publications in Anthropology* **14**.

Paine, R.
1973 Animals as Capital: Comparisons among Northern Nomadic Herders and Hunters. In *Cultural Ecology*, edited by B. Cox. Toronto: Carleton Library 65.

Paret, O.
1951 Die "Strassendämme" am Rand des Federseebeckens. *Germania* **29**.
1961 *Württemberg in Vor- und Frühgeschichtlicher Zeit.* Stuttgart: Verlag Müller und Gräff.

Peters, E.
1934 Das Mesolithikum der Oberen Donau. *Germania* **18**.
1935a Die Mesolithische Silex- und Knochenindustrie vom Rappenfels auf der Schwäbischen Alb. *Germania* **19**.
1935b Die Falkensteinhöhle bei Tiergarten. *Fundberichte aus Hohenzollern* **3**.
1941 Die Stuttgarter Gruppe der Mittelsteinzeitlichen Kulturen. *Veröffentlichungen des Archivs der Stadt Stuttgart* **7**.
1946 *Meine Tätigkeit im Dienst der Vorgeschichte Südwestdeutschlands.* Veringenstadt: Privatdruck.

Peterson, R. L.
1955 *North American Moose.* Toronto: University of Toronto Press.

Petersson, M.
1951 *Mikrolithen als Pfeilspitzen: ein Fund aus dem Lilla Loshult-Moor, Ksp. Loshult, Skane.* Meddelande fran Lunds Universities Historiska Museum.

Philipowicz, I.
1961 Das Rotwild de Ostkarpathen. *Zeitschrift für Jagdwissenschaft* **7**(1).

Pimlot, D. H.
1961 The Ecology and Management of Moose in North America. *La Terre et la Vie* **108** (2–3).

Polanyi, K.
1959 Anthropology and Economic Theory. In *Readings in Anthropology*, edited by M. H. Fried. New York: Crowell.

Prior, R.
1968 *The Roe Deer of Cranborne Chase.* London: Oxford University Press.

Rapoport, A.
1960 *Fights, Games and Debates.* Ann Arbor: University of Michigan Press.

Rappaport, R.
1969 Some Suggestions Concerning Concept and Method in Ecological Anthropology. National Museum of Canada *Bulletin 230*.

Reinerth, H.
1929 Das Federseemoor als Siedlungsland des Vorzeitmenschen. *Führer zur Urgeschichte* **9**.
1930 Ausgrabung eines Wohplatzes der Tardenois-Stufe im oberschwäbischen Federseemoore. *Nachrichtenblatt für deutsche Vorzeit* **6**.

Ricard, M.
1969 *The Mystery of Animal Migration.* New York: Hill and Wang.

Ricklefs, R. E.
1973 *Ecology.* Newton, Massachusetts: Chiron Press.

Rieth, A.
1938 Vorgeschichte der Schwäbischen Alb. *Mannus-Bücherei* **61**.

Roedelberger, F. A., and M. Phillips
1960 *The Wonderful World of Nature.* New York: Viking Press.

Rogers, E. S.
1962 The Round Lake Ojibwa. Royal Ontario Museum, Division of Art and Archeology, *Occasional Papers 5*.

1963   The Hunting Group—Hunting Territory Complex among the Mistassini Indians.
        National Museum of Canada *Bulletin 195.*
1969   Band Organization among the Indians of Eastern Subarctic Canada. National
        Museum of Canada *Bulletin 228.*
1972   The Mistassini Cree. In *Hunters and Gatherers Today,* edited by M. G. Bicchieri.
        New York: Holt.
Rostlund, E.
1952   Freshwater Fish and Fishing in Native North America. *University of California Publica-
        tions in Geography* **IX**.
Ruddell, R.
1973   Chiefs and Commoners: Nature's Balance and the Good Life among the Nootka. In
        Cultural Ecology, edited by B. Cox. Toronto: Carleton Library 65.
Saaty, T. L.
1972   Operations Research: Some Contributions to Mathematics. *Science* **178**.
Sahlins, M.
1968   Notes on the Original Affluent Society. In *Man the Hunter,* edited by R. B. Lee and I.
        DeVore. Chicago: Aldine.
1972   *Stone Age Economics.* Chicago: Aldine.
Sarasin, F.
1918   Die Steinzeitlichen Stationen des Birstales zwischen Basel und Delsberg. *Neue Denk-
        schrift des Schweizerischen Naturforschungsgesellschaft* **54**.
Schaller, G. B.
1972a   Predators of the Serengeti: Part I: The Social Carnivore. *Natural History* **81**(2).
1972b   Predators of the Serengeti: Part II: Are you Running with Me, Hominid? *Natural History*
        81(3).
Schindler, O.
1953   *Unsere Süsswasser Fische.* Stuttgart: Franckh'sche Verlag.
Schloeth, R.
1961   Einige Verhaltensweisen im Hirschrudel. *Revue Suisse de Zoologie* **68**(2).
Schloeth, R. and D. Burckhardt
1961   Die Wanderungen des Rotwildes im Gebiet des Schweizerischen Nationalparkes.
        Revue Suisse de Zoologie **68**(2).
Schmid, E.
1962   Der Isteiner Klotz in Ur- und Frühgeschichtlicher Zeit. In *Istein und der Isteiner Klotz,*
        edited by F. Schühn. Freiburg: Rombach.
1965   Altsteinzeit bis Hallstattzeit. In *Freiburg im Breisgau: Stadtkreis und Landkreis* **I/1**.
Schönweis, W.
1965a   Wachendorf-Süd, eine Freilandstation des Tardenoisien im Landkreis Fürth. *Bayrische
        Vorgeschichtsblätter* **30**(1/2).
1965b   Endpaläolithikum und Mesolithikum im Coburger Land. *Jahrbuch der Coburger Landes-
        stiftung.*
1967a   Mesolithische Stationen im Bereich von Veitsbronn. *Fürther Heimatblätter* **1**.
1967b   Funde aus dem Mesolithikum im Altdorfer Raum. *Jahrbuch der Historischen Verein
        für Mittelfranken* **84**.
1967c   Mittelsteinzeit in Franken. *Abhandlungen der Naturhistorischen Gesellschaft Nürnberg* **34**.
1968   Eine Frühmesolithische Silexgesellschaft von Hochstadt-Gruben, Landkreis Lichtenfels.
        Quartär **19**.
Schwerdtfeger, F.
1968   *Autökologie.* Hamburg: Paul Parey.
Sedlmeier, J.
1968   Der Abri Tschäpperfels. *Jahrbuch des Bernischen Historischen Museums* **47—8**.

Silberbauer, G. B.
  1972 The G/Wi Bushmen. In *Hunters and Gatherers Today*, edited by M. G. Bicchieri. New
         York: Holt.
Slobodin, R.
  1973 Variation and Continuity in Kutchin Society. In *Cultural Ecology*, edited by B. Cox.
         Toronto: Carleton Library 65.
Soergel, E.
  n.d.   Die Tierknochenfunde der Schuntershöhle bei Weilersteusslingen. In *Untersuchungen
         zum Mesolithikum und zum Spätpaläolithikum in südlichen Mitteleuropa*, edited by W.
         Taute. Tübingen: Manuscript.
Southern, H. N.
  1964   *The Handbook of British Mammals*. Oxford University Press.
Spector, W. S. (Ed.)
  1956   *Handbook of Biological Data*. Philadelphia: Saunders Company.
Sprecker, D.
  1969   Verlauf und Ausbreitung der Schweinepest in der Eifel in 1963 und 1964. *Zeitschrift
         für Jagdwissenschaft* **15**(4).
Stahl, D.
  1972   Möglichkeiten und Aussichten einer Wiedereinbürgerung des Luchses im westlichen
         Harz. *Zeitschrift für Jagdwissenschaft* **18**(2).
Steward, J. H.
  1959   The Concept and Method of Cultural Ecology. In *Readings in Anthropology*, edited by M.
         H. Fried. New York: Crowell.
  1969   Observations on Bands. National Museum of Canada *Bulletin 228*.
Ströbel, R.
  1959   Tardenoisspitze in einem Bovidenknochen von Schwenningen am Neckar. *Fundberichte
         aus Schwaben* **15**.
Sugiyama, Y.
  1968   Social Organization of Chimpanzees in the Budongo Forest, Uganda. *Primates* **9**(3).
  1969   Social Behavior of Chimpanzees in the Budongo Forest, Uganda. *Primates* **10**(3–4).
Suttles, W.
  1960   Affinal Ties, Subsistence and Prestige among the Coast Salish. *American Anthropologist*
         62.
  1968   Coping with Abundance: Subsistence on the Northwest Coast. In *Man the Hunter*, edited
         R. B. Lee and I. DeVore. Chicago: Aldine.
Suzuki, A.
  1969   An Ecological Study of Chimpanzees in a Savanna-Woodland. *Primates* **10**(2).
Szederjei, A.
  1962   Rotwildwanderungen. *Zeitschrift für Jagdwissenschaft* **8**(3).
Tanner, A.
  1973   The Significance of Hunting Territories Today. In *Cultural Ecology*, edited by B. Cox.
         Toronto: Carleton Library 65.
Taute, W.
  1967a Grabungen zur mittleren Steinzeit in Höhlen und unter Felsdächern der Schwäbischen
         Alb, 1961 bis 1965. *Fundberichte aus Schwaben* **18/1**.
  1967   Das Felsdach Lautereck: Eine Mesolithisch-Neolithisch Bronzezeitliche Stratigraphie
         an der Oberen Donau. *Palaeohistoria* **XII**.
  1972a *Funde aus der Steinzeit in der Jägerhaus-Höhle bei Bronnen. Fridingen—Stadt an der Oberen
         Donau*. Sigmaringen.
  1972b Die spätpaläolithisch-frühmesolithische Schichtenfolge im Zigeunerfels bei Sigmaringen
         (Vorbericht). *Archäologische Information* **1**.

1973 Neue Forschungen zur Chronologie von Spätpaläolithikum und Mesolithikum in Süddeutschland. In *Neue Paläolithische und Mesolithische Ausgrabungen in der Bundesrepublik Deutschland,* edited by H. Müller-Beck. Tübingen: Druckerei Tübinger Chronik.

n.d. a *Untersuchungen zum Mesolithikum und zum Spätpaläolithikum in südlichen Mitteleuropa: Chronologie.* Tübingen: Manuscript.

n.d. b *Untersuchungen zum Mesolithikum und zum Spätpaläolithikum in südlichen Mitteleuropa: Naturhistorische Studien.* Tübingen: Manuscript.

Teit, J. A.

1930 The Salishan Tribes of the Western Plateaus. U.S. Bureau of American Ethnology *Annual Report 45.*

Thomas, D. H.

1972 A Computer Simulation Model of Great Basin Shoshonean Subsistence and Settlement Patterns. In *Models in Archaeology,* edited by D. L. Clarke. London: Methuen.

1973 An Empirical Test of Steward's Model of Great Basin Settlement Patterns. *American Antiquity* **38.**

Thomson, D. F.

1939 The Seasonal Factor in Human Culture. *Proceedings of the Prehistorical Society* **10.**

Tindale, N. B.

1972 The Pitjandjara. In *Hunters and Gatherers Today,* edited by M. G. Bicchieri. New York: Holt.

Trigger, B.

1973 Settlement as an Aspect of Iroquoian Adaptation at the Time of Contact. In *Cultural Ecology,* edited by B. Cox. Toronto: Carleton Library 65.

Turnbull, C. M.

1965 The Mbuti Pygmies: An Ethnographic Survey. *Anthropological Papers,* American Museum of Natural History, **50**(3).

1968 The Importance of Flux in Two Hunting Societies. In *Man the Hunter,* edited by R. B. Lee and I. DeVore. Chicago: Aldine.

Turney-High, H. H.

1937 The Flathead Indians of Montana. *Memoirs of the American Anthropological Association* **48.**

Ueckermann, E., and G. Goepel

1973 Die Auswirkung der Massnahmen zur Wildstandsbewirtsschaftung beim Rotwild im Land Rheinland-Pfalz. *Zeitschrift für Jagdwissenschaft* **19**(1).

Ueckermann, E., and H. Scholz

1970 Ergebnisse zehnjähriger Arbeiten im Rehwildversuchsrevier Helden-Ahausen. *Zeitschrift für Jagdwissenschaft* **16**(4).

Van den Brink, F. H.

1957 Die Säugetiere Europas. Hamburg: Paul Parey.

Vogel, R.

1940 Die alluvialen Säugetiere Württembergs. *Jahresheft des Vereins für vaterländische Naturkunde in Württemberg* **96**(4).

Von Koenigswald, W.

1972 Der Faunenwandel an der Pleistozän-Holozän-Grenze in der steinzeitlichen Schichtenfolge vom Zigeunerfels bei Sigmaringen. *Archäologische Information* **1.**

Von Lehmann, E.

1960 Das Problem der Grössenabnahme beim Reh. Zeitschrift für *Jagdwissenschaft* **6**(2).

Von Raesfeld, F.

1899 *Das Rotwild.* Hamburg: Paul Parey.

1970 *Das Rehwild* (7th edition) Hamburg: Paul Parey.

Wagner, E.
1973 Das Mittelpaläolithikum der Grossen Grotte bei Blaubeuren. In *Neue Paläolithische und Mesolithische Ausgrabungen in der Bundesrepublik Deutschland,* edited by H. Müller-Beck. Tübingen: Druckerei Tübinger Chronik.

Wagner, G.
1961 Vom Werden des Federsees. In *Der Federsee,* edited by W. Zimmermann. Stuttgart: Verlag des Schwäbischen Albvereins.

Wall, E.
1961 Der Federsee von der Eiszeit bis zur Gegenwart. In *Der Federsee,* edited by W. Zimmermann. Stuttgart: Verlag des Schwäbischen Albvereins.

Wandeler, A., and W. Huber
1969 Gewichtswachstum und Jahreszeitliche Gewichtsschwankungen bei Reh und Gemse. *Revue Suisse de Zoologie* **76**(3).

Warren, E. R.
1927 *The Beaver.* Baltimore: Williams and Wilkins.

Watanabe, H.
1968 Subsistence and Ecology of Northern Food Gatherers with Special Reference to the Ainu. In *Man the Hunter,* edited by R. B. Lee and I. DeVore. Chicago: Aldine.

Waterbolk, H. T.
1968 Food Production in Prehistoric Europe. *Science* **162**.

Weinberg, D.
1973 Models of Southern Kwakiuti Social Organization. In *Cultural Ecology,* edited by B. Cox. Toronto: Carleton Library 65.

White, T. E.
1953 A Method of Calculating the Dietary Percentage of Various Food Animals Utilized by Aboriginal Peoples. *American Antiquity* **18**(4).

Williams, B. J.
1974 A Model of Band Society. *American Antiquity* **39**(4): Part 2.

Wilson, E. O.
1971 Competitive and Aggressive Behavior. In *Man and Beast,* edited by J. F. Eisenberg and W. S. Dillon. Washington: Smithsonian Institution Press.

Wobst, H. M.
1974 Boundary Conditions for Paleolithic Social Systems: A Simulation Approach. *American Antiquity* **39**.

Woodburn, J.
1968a An Introduction to Hadza Ecology. In *Man the Hunter,* edited by R. B. Lee and I. DeVore. Chicago: Aldine.
1968b Stability and Flexibility in Hadza Residential Groupings. In *Man the Hunter,* edited by R. B. Lee and I. DeVore. Chicago: Aldine.

Worsley, P.
1961 The Utilization of Natural Food Resources by an Australian Aboriginal Tribe. *Acta Ethnographica* **X**. Budapest.

Wyss, R.
1957 Eine Mesolithische Station bei Liesbergmühle. *Zeitschrift für Schweizerische Archäologie und Kunstgeschichte* **17**.
1973 Zum Problemkreis des Schweizerischen Mesolithikums. In *The Mesolithic in Europe,* edited by S. K. Kozlowski. Warsaw: University of Warsaw Press.

Yarnell, R. A.
1964 Aboriginal Relationships between Culture and Plant Life in the Upper Great Lakes Region. Museum of Anthropology, University of Michigan *Anthropological Papers* **23**.

Zettel, J.

1972 Nahrungsökologische Untersuchungen an Birkhühnern in den Schweizerischen Alpen. *Revue Suisse de Zoologie* **79**(3).

Zürn, H.

1958 *Eine Jungsteinzeitliche Siedlung bei Ehrenstein, Kr. Ulm.* Neue Ausgrabungen in Deutschland (Römisch-Germanisch Kommission des deutschen Archäologischen Instituts). Berlin: Verlag Gebrüder Mann.

Subject Index